# FOOD PROCESSOR BAKING MAGIC

*Also by Mary Moon Hemingway and Suzanne de Lima*

FOOD PROCESSOR MAGIC

# FOOD PROCESSOR BAKING MAGIC

by MARY MOON HEMINGWAY

and SUZANNE DE LIMA

*Illustrations by Sheila Camera*

HASTINGS HOUSE · PUBLISHERS
New York 10016

Second printing, December 1980

Copyright © 1978 by Mary Moon Hemingway and Suzanne de Lima

LIBRARY OF CONGRESS CATALOGING IN PUBLICATION DATA

ISBN: 0-8038-2321-6
LC: 78-72519

Published simultaneously in Canada by
Saunders of Toronto, Ltd., Don Mills, Ontario

*Printed in the United States of America*

# CONTENTS

—◆·◆—

INTRODUCTION   7

1—YEAST BREADS   17

2—QUICK BREADS   97

3—CAKES AND TORTES   109

4—COOKIES AND SMALL CAKES   133

5—DESSERT PUDDINGS   153

6—BASIC PASTRIES   161

7—PASTRY, PIES AND TARTS FOR ENTRÉE AND HORS D'OEUVRE   171

8—PASTRY, PIES AND TARTS FOR DESSERT   179

9—FILLINGS, FROSTINGS, SYRUPS AND SAUCES   197

INDEX   211

# INTRODUCTION

Food processors have captivated the hearts of cooks all over the country—chopping, grinding, slicing, puréeing, blending, kneading in countless kitchens, turning amateurs into chefs. Some are powered by direct drive, some belt. All of them have the same basic blades for mixing, slicing and grating or shredding. All of them can handle normal procedures but some do a better job than others with specific problems such as chopping meat and kneading heavy doughs. The instructions for each make will tell you what the machine can or cannot do, or whether it will take to hot liquids or yeast mixtures. "Let the buyer beware."

The Cuisinart™, *grande dame* of all processors, can handle any processor technique admirably. The Cuisinart™ also has additional blades for different types of grating, julienning and slicing, which are interchangeable with both of their direct drive machines. Their belt-driven smaller machine, the Omnichef, does a very good job with doughs and meats too, as well as the usual processing.

Some machines have pulsers to control the action, others use the top for on and off turns. Whatever machine you have, practice with it to gain the maximum control. Try out your machine with onions, apples, a few cubes of meat, bread slices, carrots, until you get the hang of each blade.

## The Machine

- Read the directions for your machine.
- Place the container on the base before placing the attachment on the shaft. Be sure the steel blade is in place before putting any ingredients in the bowl. Should the blade or disc seem reluctant to drop into the proper position, rotate it gently back and forth until it does. Do not force it.
- Processors have automatic cut-off devices to prevent overheating. Should your machine stop, turn off the switch or unplug it lest it start up later when you are not expecting it.
- For efficiency's sake process dry ingredients first—nuts, crumbs, cheese. Set them aside and proceed with the messier mixtures. It saves on washing up.
- Almost all the parts are dishwasher safe, but check. Hollow pushers may be put in the dishwasher but not the older solid ones which may warp.
- Keep your machine out in the open and use it for almost everything, bread to marmalade. It's a remarkable instrument.

## The Steel Blade

The steel crescent blade or knife does about 80 percent of most processing jobs—puréeing, blending, chopping, grinding, kneading. Tips to remember when using this workhorse blade:

- Time is of the essence. Food processors work so quickly you must learn to switch the motor on and off in a matter of seconds lest you overprocess.
- Do not be afraid to stop the machine and take the top off the bowl to see how you are doing. Coarse-chop with very quick on and off turns or switches. Run a very little longer for medium chop, still a bit more for fine or purées.
- Never crowd the bowl. Far better to do little batches at a time. It is so fast, that is no trouble.
- Always cut solid ingredients into manageable pieces before processing to give the blade a chance to grab hold. When grinding meats or hard cheeses it is better to drop the pieces into the bowl with the motor running, letting them fall, one batch at a time, through the tube onto the moving blades for more efficient processing.
- When possible, grind citrus rinds with a heavier ingredient such as sugar. Fresh herbs may also be chopped with other ingredients rather than separately.

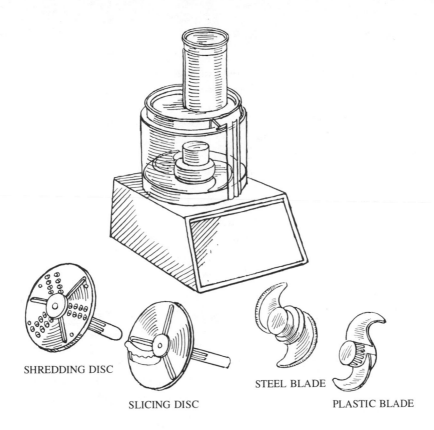

SHREDDING DISC

SLICING DISC

STEEL BLADE

PLASTIC BLADE

- Always scrape down the sides of the bowl from time to time with a rubber spatula. When using sugary mixtures or anything sticky you may have to wipe off the rim of the bowl and the inside of the lid from time to time if yours is a processor that is activated by turning the machine on and off by the lid.
- Before removing mixtures from the bowl, take the bowl from the spindle, place your ring finger in the bottom hole and grasp the rim of the bowl with your thumb. This makes a "handle" and will keep the knife from falling out and help you to pour.
- Be sure the inner hole of the blade is cleaned well. Food can get into it with later unpleasant results. A swab, jet of water or small bottle brush may be used.

## The Plastic Blade

The least used of processor attachments, the plastic blade is, however, excellent for chopping soft ingredients such as hard-cooked eggs, chicken livers, anything which the steel blade would turn to mush. It may also be used for soft pastry doughs and uncooked frostings as well as mayonnaise and creamy fillings.

- Do not use the plastic blade with a quantity of liquid ingredients. The machine will leak as this blade does not have as firm a seal around the spindle as the steel blade does.
- Cream of a whipping variety may be whipped with this blade but be sure the pusher-plunger is not in place as air must get into the bowl. As least one cup of cream must be used. You will have a creditable whipped cream but not as voluminous as cream beaten with rotary beaters.
- Egg whites may also be whipped but whip no fewer than three, preferably more. The pusher-tube should not be in place. They will not have the volume of eggs beaten in a more conventional way.

## The Slicing Disc

- Always use the pusher to process the food.
- Never take off the cover until the disc has stopped rotating.
- Be sure the tube is well packed or the material will skitter around.
- If you want neat slices, be sure the bottom of the material on top of the disc is cut flat to sit firmly against it.
- The more pressure on the pusher, the thicker the slices.
- It is easier with some foods—lemons, apple pieces, potatoes, cucumbers, etc.—to feed the material into the tube from the bottom of the tube. Hold the lid upside down and push the food in from the bottom, packing it firmly.
- For slicing meats, partially freeze the meats to give the blade something to work on.
- For long slices place the material across the tube, not up and down.

## The Shredding Disc

- The same rules hold for the shredding disc as for the slicing disc except you will probably almost always put the food in lengthwise. Standing it up vertically is apt to give you bits and pieces rather than nice shreds.
- To grate Cheddar-type cheeses with this disc a better result is achieved if you chill the cheese a bit to make it firmer. Do not grate hard cheese with this disc; instead use the steel blade.
- For grating chocolate, soften chocolate a little until it is somewhat malleable.

# A USEFUL INVENTORY OF UTENSILS
# FOR BREAD AND PASTRY MAKING
### (*Necessary and DeLuxe*)

Measuring spoons
Set of dry-measure cups
Set of liquid-measure cups
Good pastry brush
Yeast-meat thermometer
Kitchen towels for covering rising bread
A working surface—counter or board
Pastry cloth
Real rolling pin, big with ball bearings, or tapered
Knitted sock for a rolling pin
Bowls in which to raise bread
Pastry scraper
Rubber spatulas
Metal spatula for leveling flour measure and frosting cakes, etc.
Sifter
Loaf pans, varying sizes and proportions
Baking sheets
Jelly-roll pan
Muffin tins, varying sizes
Quiche pans (deep)
Flan pans or rings (shallow)
False-bottom cake pans, varying sizes
Cake pans, varying sizes
Pie pans, varying sizes
Springform pans, varying sizes
Tube pans, varying sizes
Bundt pan
Cake tester
Water sprayer bottle
Sharp, long knife
Serrated bread knife
Cooling racks
Whisk
Slotted spoon
Cookie or baking sheets
Cookie cutters
Pastry cutter
Brioche molds

**a** *banneton* (reed basket for raising and shaping round loaves)

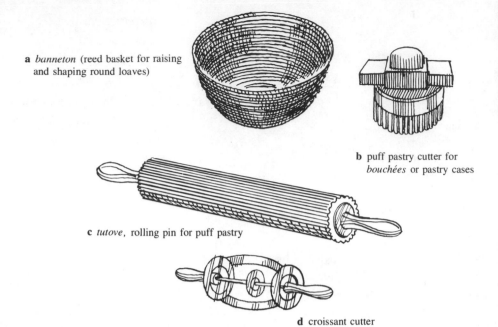

**b** puff pastry cutter for *bouchées* or pastry cases

**c** *tutove*, rolling pin for puff pastry

**d** croissant cutter

## DeLuxe Extras

*Banneton,* a reed basket from France for raising and shaping round loaves in the traditional manner

*Tutove,* a rolling pin specifically for rolling out puff-pastry

Croissant cutter

Puff-pastry cutters

*Pain de mie* pan, a pan with a cover for baking bread

French *baguette* pans

Ceramic baking tile

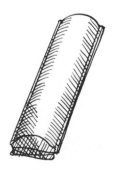

*PAIN DE MIE* PAN, OPEN,          CLOSED

## Converting to the Metric System

We have included metric measurements because the metric system will soon be in universal use. The transition from the U.S. Customary System to Metrics presents some problems to the American cook, who is used to measuring ingredients in volume measures—teaspoon, tablespoon, cup, etc. Metric measures are based on exact weights. Thus, when an American recipe calls for 1 cup of flour or 1 cup of milk, one must compensate for the different weights of milk and flour when converting to metric equivalents. Metric volume measures for liquids—liter (1) and deciliter (dl)—have exact weights also. Dry ingredients are usually measured in grams and kilograms, liquid ingredients in liters and deciliters.

The metric measures in the ingredient lists were determined by actually weighing, on a gram scale, standard items such as flour, salt, sugar, cornmeal, raisins, nuts, etc. No attempt has been made to convert to metrics such ingredients as 1 cup parsley sprigs or 1 cup crumbled cooked bacon. Conventional volume measures will continue to be used when the ingredient as prepared for the recipe has no specific weight.

The brief tables that follow should help you to make your own conversions. For more exact or scientific conversions, you will find help in U. S. government publications, available in most public libraries.

MASS AND WEIGHT

| 1 ounce | = 28.35 grams (abbr, g) |
|---|---|
| 1 pound | = 453.6 grams or .453 kilograms (abbr, kg) |
| 1 tablespoon (liquid) | = 14.3 grams |
| 1 tablespoon (dry) | = 9 grams (based on all-purpose flour) |
| 1 cup (liquid) | = 227 grams |
| 1 cup (dry) | = 144 grams (based on all-purpose flour) |

CAPACITY

| 1 ounce | = 29.57 milliliters (abbr, ml) |
|---|---|
| 1 cup (liquid) | = .237 liter (abbr, 1); for convenience we are calling this .24 liter |
| .42 cup (liquid) | = 1 deciliter (abbr, dl); for convenience we are calling ½ cup a deciliter and ¼ cup .5 deciliter; for more exact measuring, remember that ½ cup is a scant deciliter. |

PAN SIZES

In order to save space in the recipes, we are not listing there the metric dimensions of baking pans, but instead we are listing here the approximate metric sizes of the most commonly used pans.

```
loaf pans, 4½ x 2½ x 2½ inches = 11   x 6.4 x 6.4 cm
           7½ x 2½ x 2½ inches = 19   x 6.4 x 6.4 cm
           7⅜ x 3⅝ x 2¼ inches = 19   x 9   x 5.7 cm
           8½ x 4½ x 2½ inches = 21.6 x 11  x 6.4 cm
           9   x 5   x 3   inches = 23   x 13  x 7.6 cm
```

```
round pans, cake pans, pie pans or quiche dishes,
           8 inches in diameter = 20.3 cm
           9 inches in diameter = 23   cm
          10 inches in diameter = 25.4 cm
```

```
tube pans or springform pans,
           8 inches          = 20.3 cm
           9 inches          = 23   cm
          10 inches          = 25.4 cm
```

```
jelly-roll pan, 15 x 10 inches (or 15½ x 10½) =
                              38 x 25.4 cm
```

```
rectangular pans
          11¾ x 7½ x 1¾ inches = 30   x 19   x 4.5 cm
          11½ x 9   x 2   inches = 29   x 23   x 5   cm
          12   x 8   x 2   inches = 30.5 x 20.3 x 5   cm
          13   x 9   x 2   inches = 33   x 23   x 5   cm
```

If your pan is slightly larger than these, the cake layer will be thinner. To make your own conversions to metrics, use this conversion factor:
    1 inch = 2.54 centimeters (abbr, cm)

TEMPERATURES

Exact temperatures for baking are important for good results. In the case of yeast breads, temperatures for dissolving yeast and for raising dough are critical, since too high or too low a temperature will impede the action of the yeast.

To avoid studding the text with double sets of figures, we will list the critical temperatures for yeast breads in that chapter introduction.

Oven temperatures for baking will be given in conventional figures and metrics in the recipes. To make your own conversions, use this conversion factor:

to convert Fahrenheit (F.) to Celsius (C.), subtract 32 from the Fahrenheit figure, multiply by 5, then divide by 9.

A few recipes from *Food Processor Magic,* which are in the general domain of classical cookery, such as piecrust, basic cakes and cookies, have been included in this book. In some cases minor revisions have been made, either to make the recipe better or to make it easier for you to work with.

# 1

# YEAST BREADS

Any food processor that can handle yeast doughs makes bread baking a simple pleasure as it mixes and does most of the kneading as well, and does it very quickly. Although the capacity of most of the processor bowls is limited so that only one loaf can be made at a time, the whole process is so rapid that it is simple to repeat the recipe as often as necessary. The steel blade is always used.

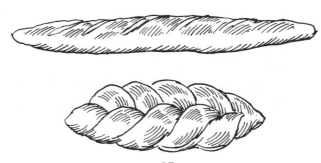

# INGREDIENTS

## Yeast

Don't be afraid of yeast. It is a living and growing plant that needs a sugar—brown or white, or maple, honey, molasses, etc.—as well as air and moisture to produce the gas that leavens the dough and gives bread aroma and taste. All the recipes in the book use active dry yeast which can be bought in individual, dated, airtight packages or in a jar. The jar of yeast should be refrigerated after opening and returned to room temperature before using. One package of dry yeast equals 1 tablespoon from the jar. Dry yeast should be dissolved in liquid at a temperature of 105° to 115°F. (40.5° to 46.1°C.). Compressed fresh yeast may be used interchangeably but it too must be dissolved before using and in a liquid at a temperature not to exceed 85° to 90°F. (29.4° to 32.2°C.). Unless refrigerated or CoolRise© methods are used, as for icebox rolls or refrigerator bread, yeast doughs must be kept warm from beginning to end. Warm the bowl in which the dough will rise by rinsing it out with warm water. Dough should be allowed to rise in a draft-free warm atmosphere of 80° to 85°F. (26.7° to 29.4°C.).

## Flours and Grains

*White Flour*—Unbleached white flour is good for making yeast breads since it has a greater amount of gluten. Hard wheat flour has the greatest amount of gluten but makes a coarser bread; it is not generally used as it is difficult to find. Most breads, no matter whether they are corn, whole wheat, rye, or other grain, usually have a proportion of white flour to give added gluten.

*Whole-Wheat Flour*—Whole-wheat flour, ground from the entire wheat berry, has less gluten and makes heavier breads. For greater volume it is usually mixed with some white flour.

*Graham Flour*—Graham flour is made from the entire wheat berry and is coarser than whole-wheat flour as the bran is left flaky, not powdered.

*Rye Flour*—Rye flour is ground from the entire rye kernel; it is one of the heaviest flours and makes a sticky dough.

*Specialty Flours*—Oatmeal, rice, barley, cornmeal, buckwheat, soy and bran, when added to unbleached white flour, provide delicious variations of taste and texture. Interesting breads can also be made with the addition of breakfast cereals, wheat germ and miller's bran.

## Liquids

Liquids must be used at the particular temperature called for in the recipe. Breads made with water and no fat have a crisper crust. Milk gives a smoother crust and softer bread. (Dried milk may be added for additional nutrition.) Sour milk or cream, cottage cheese, beer, juices—all manner of liquids may be used.

## Shortenings

Butter, margarine, oil, bacon fat, etc., help make a soft bread which will keep longer and stay fresher than those made without shortening. These shortenings also add flavor and nutrition. Margarine may be substituted for butter.

## Sweeteners

Brown and white sugars and honey help the yeast to grow and change the flavor of the bread, as do molasses and syrups.

## Other Additions

Salt brings out the flavor of the ingredients and arrests the overgrowth of yeast in the baking. Eggs add nutrition and color. Nuts, raisins and fruits slow the rising time, but add a great deal to special breads. They are always added just before the last rising. Flouring the nuts and fruits makes it easier to incorporate them into the dough.

## Baking Pans

Aim for a pan of the proper size for the amount of dough. The standard loaf pans, made of metal, glass or terracotta, are approximately 9 x 5 x 3 inches or 8½ x 4½ x 2½ inches (23 x 13 x 7.6 cm, or 21.6 x 11 x 6.4 cm). There are also smaller ones, 4½ x 2½ x 2½ inches (11 x 6.4 x 6.4 cm). The important thing to remember is that the pan should be two-thirds filled with dough to make a nicely shaped loaf. Bread may be baked in a round casserole, in a ring mold, in special French bread pans; or it may be shaped by hand into a loaf and placed on a baking sheet, quarry tiles or one of the patented ceramic baking plates. When using glass pans reduce the required baking temperature by 25°F. (about 5°C.).

# TECHNIQUES

## Proofing the Yeast

This old-fashioned term describes the method of dissolving the yeast and starting it to work. A teaspoon of sugar or other sweetener is mixed with the warm liquid at 105° to 115°F. (40.5° to 46.1°C.), the yeast is sprinkled on top, and it is stirred with a fork until dissolved. In 5 to 10 minutes the mixture should be bubbly and increase slightly in volume. Be sure to use a large-enough measuring cup or bowl to allow for the expansion of the yeast. Too hot a liquid will kill the yeast and too cool a liquid will not activate it so, when in doubt, use a bread-making, candy or meat thermometer. When yeast is used in a recipe that uses the Rapidmix© method, without being previously dissolved, it is added to the dry ingredients in the processor bowl and is proofed by the addition of the warm liquid. This liquid should be at a temperature of 120° to 130°F. (48.9° to 54.4°C.).

Most of the recipes in the book call for proofing the yeast first in order to be sure that the yeast is fresh. However, the Rapidmix© method may be used.

If in doubt about the freshness of the yeast, proof 1 teaspoon in ¼ cup water at 105° to 115°F. (40.5° to 46.1°C.), mixed with ½ teaspoon of sugar. If it does not become bubbly and the volume has not increased in 10 minutes, the yeast is not good.

When doubling a recipe increase the amount of yeast only 1½ times, but remember the rising will be slower. When halving a recipe, never use less than 1 package or 1 tablespoon of yeast (7 g).

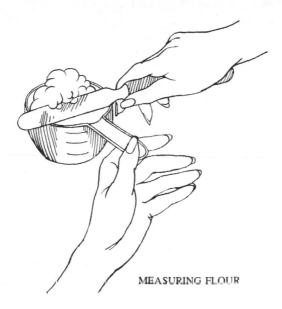

MEASURING FLOUR

## Measuring the Flour

Flour is not sifted unless specified in the recipe. Fill a dry measuring cup to overflowing and level it with a knife or spatula. Do not pack down the flour.

## Instructions for Making the Bread

Each recipe will give specific instructions for the particular type of bread being made. As a general rule, when making a single loaf of yeast bread, the yeast is set to proof, then the dry ingredients, and shortening if used, are put in the processor bowl fitted with the steel blade, and are blended together with quick on and off turns, until the mixture resembles cornmeal. The proofed yeast is added and incorporated with 2 or 3 quick turns. With the motor running the liquid is poured, a little at a time, through the tube until a ball of dough forms, giving the liquid time to incorporate completely with the dry ingredients. Depending on conditions—humidity, temperature and type of flour—the specified amount of liquid is not always needed. However, should the dough not form a ball, dribble in a little more warm liquid until it does. For a 2-loaf recipe the specific method will be spelled out. Doughs vary. Some should be sticky, some stiff, some satiny, some soft.

Knead the dough by allowing it to spin for approximately 1 minute. If it is a very sticky dough, the machine may slow down. In this event, carefully remove the dough, unless otherwise specified, to a floured surface, kneading in a little more flour by hand until the dough reaches the consistency called for in the recipe.

If the dough forces up the lid of the processor, stopping the machine, readjust the lid and hold it down by keeping your hand on the feed tube while the machine is running. Whenever you remove dough from the machine, you may want to flour your hands to make it easier to handle the dough. Be careful of the steel blade!

Turn the dough out on a lightly floured surface and knead it for 2 or 3 minutes. Should the dough seem stickier than called for in the recipe, knead in a little more flour by hand until the dough is elastic. To test if it has been sufficiently kneaded, poke a finger into the dough. If the indentation springs back the dough is ready. Shape dough into a ball and place it in a warm, greased bowl, rolling it over so that it becomes completely coated with the shortening used to grease the bowl. This keeps the surface from drying out. Cover the bowl with a towel.

## First Rising

Place the bowl in a draft-free warm spot (80° to 85°F. or 26.7° to 29.4°C.) and let the dough rise until it has doubled in bulk. If you have a gas stove with a pilot light the temperature of the oven should be just about right. If you have an electric oven, preheat at the lowest setting for 1 minute and turn oven off. Wait 5 minutes, then place the dough in the oven. Any cozy draft-free spot may be used.

Rising time varies with the humidity and temperature and the quality of the flour. Most yeast doughs require 2 risings, one before shaping. For the first rising, dough is doubled in bulk and this generally takes from 1 to 2 hours. Successive risings may not require as long a time. Soft doughs take less time than heavier doughs. The dough will be ready when 2 fingers pressed into it lightly will leave an indentation that does not spring back.

When the whole baking process must be delayed, the rising may be held back by refrigerating the dough, either right after it is mixed or after the first rising and shaping. It must be well greased and loosely covered with plastic wrap. Refrigerated dough may need more time to rise. However, overnight rising in a refrigerator is one method of handling some doughs.

## Punching Down

When the dough has doubled in bulk at the first rising, punch the dough down with your fist and pull the edges to the middle, forming a ball. Place the dough on a lightly floured surface. Cover and let rest for 10 minutes. The dough is then ready to be shaped and placed in the pan or on the surface on which it is to be baked.

KNEADING

COVERING DOUGH FOR FIRST RISING

ESTING DOUGH AFTER FIRST RISING

PUNCHING DOWN DOUGH AFTER FIRST RISING

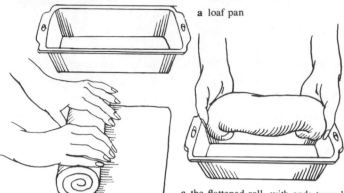

**a** loaf pan

**c** the flattened roll, with ends turned under and seam side down, ready to be placed in the greased pan

**b** rolling up the dough, jelly-roll fashion

## Shaping

When a rectangle of dough is called for, pat the dough into a rough rectangle before rolling out.

When using a loaf pan it is easier to make a neat loaf by rolling the dough into a rectangle with a rolling pin. Starting with the short end, roll up the dough, jelly-roll fashion, pinching the ends with each turn. Flatten each end of the roll and tuck it under. Place in a greased pan, seam side down. The easiest way to grease pans is to brush them with melted shortening, using a pastry brush.

Bread may be shaped into free-standing rounds, loaves, ovals or rectangles.

## Second Rising

The test for the second rising, to see if the dough is ready to be baked, is the same as that for the first rising. However, at this stage make an indentation with 2 fingers on the side of the loaf so as not to mar its appearance. If the bread is to be glazed at this point, brush the glaze on carefully so that the dough does not collapse. A good-quality pastry brush, made of feathers or a small, flat artist's brush, is needed for the gentle glazing.

## Finish for Crusts

*Soft Golden Crusts*—Brush with melted butter, margarine or cream before baking, or brush with melted butter right after baking and then cover with a towel for 10 minutes.

*Shiny Crisp Crusts*—Brush with egg white mixed with 1 tablespoon of water and a pinch of salt.

*Very Crisp Crusts*—Spray the dough with water three times, the first time as you put the dough in the preheated oven, the second and third times at 5-minute intervals while the bread is baking.

*Shiny Dark Crusts*—Brush with egg yolk mixed with 1 tablespoon of water and a pinch of salt. Coffee may be brushed on dark breads to give a deep color.

*Seeded Crusts*—Brush with egg white mixed with 1 tablespoon of water and sprinkle with seeds.

## Baking

Preheat the oven to the temperature specified in the recipe. You can tell when the bread is done by rapping the top and bottom and listening for a hollow sound. When baking more than 1 loaf at a time, allow 2 inches of space between the pans for heat circulation. When baking 4 loaves stagger the pans on 2 shelves. When making free-form bread on a cookie or baking sheet use the center rack of the oven. If using a ceramic baking sheet, follow the manufacturer's instructions. Should the bread seem to be browning too quickly, cover with foil.

## Last Step

Always remove bread from pans immediately after taking them from the oven, and cool loaves on a rack in a draft-free place.

## Storing

Because of the lack of preservatives, homemade breads may not keep as well as store-bought products. Breads without shortening (French-type) have an even more fragile life-span and should be eaten immediately or frozen. Cool breads, wrap in plastic or foil, and keep in the refrigerator or bread box. If bread is frozen, use quickly after thawing. Frozen bread is thawed at room temperature or heated in a preheated 350°F. (176.7°C.) oven for 20 to 25 minutes.

## BASIC WHITE BREAD

Read the introduction
for yeast bread.

Makes 1 large loaf
or 2 small loaves.

This is an excellent daily bread, simple to make as it is so quick. Keep repeating the recipe until you have made enough dough for as many loaves as you need.

*1 tsp. sugar*
*¼ cup warm water or milk (.5 dl) (105° to 115°F.)*
*1 pkg. or 1 Tbsp. active dry yeast (7 g)*
*3 cups unbleached flour (450 g)*
*1 tsp. salt*
*1 Tbsp. butter (15 g)*
*2 Tbsp. sugar or honey (25 or 40 g)*
*¾ cup warm water or milk (1.5 dl)*

Mix 1 teaspoon sugar in ¼ cup warm water or milk in a 1-cup measure. Sprinkle the yeast on the water and stir lightly with a fork until dissolved. Let work for 5 to 10 minutes, or until bubbly.

In the processor bowl fitted with the steel blade, put the flour, salt, butter, and sugar or honey. Blend together with on and off quick turns until the mixture resembles cornmeal. Pour the proofed yeast into the dry ingredients and blend with 2 or 3 quick turns. With the machine running, pour the ¾ cup warm water or milk, little by little, through the tube until a ball of dough forms, giving the liquid time to incorporate completely with the dry ingredients. (Depending on conditions—

humidity, temperature and type of flour, the specified amount of liquid is not always needed. However, should the dough not form a ball, dribble in a little more warm water until it does.)

Knead the dough by allowing it to spin for about 1 minute. If the dough forces up the lid of the processor and stops the machine, readjust the lid and hold your hand over the feed tube while the machine is running. Turn the dough out onto a lightly floured surface and knead by hand for 2 or 3 minutes. It may be necessary to knead in a little more flour (no more than ¼ cup at a time) to make the dough moderately stiff and elastic. Shape the dough into a ball and place it in a greased warm bowl, turning it around to grease the entire surface of the dough. Cover with a towel and let dough rise in a warm draft-free place (80° to 85°F.) until doubled in bulk, which will take 1 to 2 hours.

Punch the dough down with your fist and pull the edges to the middle. Place the dough on a lightly floured surface. Cover and let rest for 10 minutes. Shape into 1 large loaf and place in a greased loaf pan (8½ x 4½ x 2½ inches), or shape into 2 small loaves and place in 2 loaf pans (7⅜ x 3⅝ x 2¼ inches). Cover and let rise again in a warm draft-free place until doubled in bulk, about 1 hour.

Carefully brush the dough with milk or 1 egg white beaten with 1 tablespoon water, or melted butter. Bake in a preheated 375°F. (190.6°C.) oven for 40 to 50 minutes, or until the loaf sounds hollow when tapped. Remove bread from the pan and cool on a rack.

TEMPERATURES FOR YEAST

dissolving dry yeast, 105° to 115°F. = 40.5° to 46.1°C.
dissolving fresh yeast, 85° to 90°F. = 29.4° to 32.2°C.
raising yeast doughs, 80° to 85°F. = 26.7° to 29.4°C.
liquid for Rapidmix© method, 120° to 130°F. = 48.9° to 54.4°C.

## ADDITIONS TO BASIC WHITE BREAD

*Raisins or Currants*—Flour 1½ cups raisins or currants (150 g). Before the last rising pat the floured raisins or currants on top of the punched-down flattened dough and knead a few minutes to distribute the fruit. A nice addition to the bread, after it is baked, is to frost the loaf with Confectioners' Icing (see Index).

*Nutmeats (pecans, walnuts, almonds or a mixture)*—Knead 1½ cups floured chopped nuts (180 g) into the dough after the first rising and before shaping it into loaves. Slash the tops and brush with melted butter. Sprinkle with cinnamon and sugar if desired.

*Cracked Wheat*—Use ¼ cup molasses (80 g) instead of the sugar and 1 cup cracked-wheat flour for 1 cup of the white flour in the basic recipe. Glaze the shaped loaves with 1 egg white mixed with 1 tablespoon water, and dust with more cracked wheat.

*Onion*—Blend 1 cup canned French fried onions with the flour before the addition of the liquids.

*Sour Milk and Herbs*—In place of the milk or water, substitute 1 cup sour milk. Chop 1 cup fresh parsley sprigs in the machine and add 1 to 2 teaspoons dried herbs (orégano, basil, chives, thyme), or use small mixed bunches of fresh herbs. Add herbs before adding the liquid.

## VARIATIONS ON BASIC WHITE BREAD
### Baked in a Flat Pan

These variations make good luncheon dishes or may be cut into bite-size pieces for hors d'oeuvre.

Follow the basic recipe. At the second rising grease a jelly-roll pan (15½ x 10½ inches) or an ovenproof dish (13 x 9 x 2 inches). Roll out the dough into a rectangle and press it into the pan. Brush with melted butter, then spread with one of the toppings below. Let rise until doubled in bulk. Bake in a preheated 375°F. oven for 15 to 20 minutes. Cut into squares or strips. May be reheated.

*Bacon-Cheese*—In the processor bowl fitted with the steel blade, process ½ pound cut-up Cheddar cheese (250 g) until grated. Add ⅓ cup milk (1 dl), ½ teaspoon salt and 1 egg, and continue processing until the mixture is of a spreading consistency. Spread the mixture on top of the dough. Sprinkle with 1 cup crumbled bacon. (2 tablespoons of bacon fat may be substituted for the butter in the original recipe.)

*Niçoise*—Use ¼ pound Parmesan cheese (125 g), about ½ cup after grating, 7½ ounces pitted black olives (210 g), 1.5-ounce tube of anchovy paste, 3 tablespoons butter (45 g), 1-pound, 15-ounce jar or can of thick tomato sauce (.9 l). Grate the cheese with the steel blade; set cheese aside. Slice the olives with the slicing disc; set aside. With the steel blade process anchovy paste with butter and spread thinly over the dough. Top with the tomato sauce. Cover with a layer of olives and dust with Parmesan cheese. Cover and let rise. Bake following directions for white bread baked in a flat pan.

*Onion*—Use 4 medium-size onions, peeled and cut up, 2 tablespoons butter (30 g), 2 eggs, ⅓ cup milk (1 dl), salt and pepper to taste, 2 teaspoons poppy or caraway seeds. Chop onions coarsely with the steel blade. Squeeze dry and sauté in the butter. In the processor bowl fitted with the steel blade, blend eggs, milk and salt and pepper. Stir in the cooked onions and spread the mixture over the top of the dough. Sprinkle with poppy or caraway seeds. Bake following directions for white bread baked in a flat pan.

*Pizza*—Substitute 2 tablespoons oil (30 g) for the butter and use water in the basic recipe for white bread. Stretch and pat the dough into a pizza pan. Let rise for 30 minutes. Fill to taste. Bake at 400°F. (204.4°C.) for 20 minutes, or until the edges are golden.

### Monkey Bread

Before second rising form dough into balls about the size of Ping-Pong balls. Dip each one into melted butter. Place at random in a loaf pan, filling the pan well. Drizzle with more melted butter. Bake following directions for basic white bread. Serve warm and break off individual pieces.

### Roll-Ups

Many interesting variations can be made by rolling up the dough with additional ingredients. After the first rising, punch down the dough, turn out onto a lightly floured surface, and allow to rest for 10 minutes. Then roll out to a rectangle 12 x 8 inches and ¼ inch thick. Brush the entire surface with beaten egg or melted butter. Spread filling on the dough, leaving a 1-inch border all around. Roll up the dough as you would a jelly roll, beginning at the narrow end. To insure a firm shape, roll tightly; with each turn pinch the length of the roll to the bottom layer and pinch the ends. Tuck the ends under and pinch along the seam. Place the roll, seam side down, in a greased loaf pan 9 x 5 x 3 inches. Cover and let rise in a draft-free warm place for about 1 hour. Bake in a preheated 375°F. (190.6°C.) oven for 40 to 50 minutes, as for regular white bread.

ROLL-UPS

## Fillings for Roll-Ups

*Cinnamon, Sugar and White Raisins*—Brush dough with melted butter. Pat 1½ cups (150 g) plumped raisins on the dough. Sprinkle ¼ cup sugar (50 g) mixed with 1 teaspoon ground cinnamon over the raisins.

*Marmalade-Nut*—Brush dough with melted butter. Spread dough with a thin layer of marmalade. Chop 1 cup shelled nuts (120 g)—walnuts, pecans, toasted almonds—fine with the steel blade. Sprinkle nuts over marmalade and pat down with the back of a spoon.

*Green Goddess*—Brush dough with beaten egg. In the processor bowl fitted with the steel blade, put 1 cup parsley, 3 cut-up scallions, including the green part, 1 cup watercress, 2 tablespoons fresh dill (optional) or any combination of fresh greens, and finely chop. Cook the mixture in 2 tablespoons butter (30 g) until wilted. Cool. Mix in 1 beaten egg.

*Duxelles*—Brush dough with beaten egg. Spread the dough with 2 cups duxelles (sautéed chopped mushrooms and shallots).

# WHOLE-WHEAT BREAD

Read the introduction
for yeast bread.

Makes 1 loaf.

This is a delicious full-bodied bread, good plain or toasted.

*1 tsp. sugar*
*¼ cup warm water (.5 dl)*
   *(105° to 115°F.)*
*1 pkg. or 1 Tbsp. active*
   *dry yeast (7 g)*
*2 cups whole-wheat flour*
   *(300 g)*
*1 cup unbleached flour*
   *(150 g)*
*½ Tbsp. salt*
*3 Tbsp. honey or molasses*
   *(60 g)*
*2 Tbsp. butter (30 g)*
*½ cup warm milk (1 dl)*
*½ cup warm water (1 dl)*

Mix 1 teaspoon sugar and ¼ cup warm water in a 1-cup measure. Sprinkle the yeast on the water and stir lightly with a fork until dissolved. Let work for 5 to 10 minutes, or until bubbly.

In the processor bowl fitted with the steel blade, put the flours, salt, honey or molasses and the butter. Blend together with on and off quick turns until the mixture resembles cornmeal. Pour the proofed yeast into the dry ingredients and blend with 2 or 3 quick turns. With the machine running, pour the mixed warm milk and water slowly through the tube until a ball of dough forms, giving the liquid time to incorporate completely with the dry ingredients. (Depending on conditions—humidity, temperature and type of flour, the specified amount of liquid is not always needed. However, should the dough not form a ball, dribble in a little warm water until it does.)

Knead the dough by allowing it to spin for 1 minute. If the dough forces up the lid of the processor and stops the machine, readjust the lid and hold your hand over the feed tube while the machine is running. Turn the dough out onto a lightly floured surface and knead by hand for 2 or 3 minutes. It may be necessary to knead in a little more flour (no more than ¼ cup at a time) to make the dough moderately stiff and elastic. Shape dough into a ball and place it in a greased warm bowl, turning it around to grease the entire surface of the dough. Cover with a towel and let dough rise in a warm draft-free place (80° to 85°F.) until doubled in bulk, 1 to 2 hours.

Punch the dough down with your fist and pull the edges to the middle. Place the dough on a lightly floured surface. Cover and let rest for 10 minutes. Shape as desired. Cover and let rise again in a warm place until doubled in bulk, about 1 hour.

Brush the dough with milk and bake in a preheated 375°F. (190.6°C.) oven for 40 to 60 minutes, or until the loaf sounds hollow when it is tapped. Remove bread from the pan and cool on a rack.

## VARIATIONS ON WHOLE-WHEAT BREAD

*Wheat Germ*—Add ½ cup wheat germ (70 g) to each batch of dough. Substitute brown sugar for molasses or honey; use ¼ cup (50 g) per loaf.

*Cheese Wheat*—Substitute ¼ cup sugar (50 g) for molasses or honey. Shred ¼ pound Swiss cheese (125 g) with the shredding disc. Mix shredded cheese in with the milk and the water and heat until warm. The cheese may not melt. Combine with dissolved yeast and proceed as in the basic recipe.

*Maple*—Substitute 6 tablespoons maple sugar (75 g) or ¼ cup maple syrup (80 g) for molasses or honey.

*Apple Nut*—Coarsely chop 2 unpeeled cored and seeded cooking apples with the steel blade. Leave in the bowl and continue with the recipe. Before the final rising knead in 1 cup (120 g) floured chopped walnuts. Shape; sprinkle loaf with sugar or a cinnamon and sugar mixture.

## TWO-TONE BREADS

Use recipe for 1 loaf Basic White Bread and 1 loaf Whole-Wheat Bread.

SPIRAL LOAF

After the first rising and after dough has been punched down and allowed to rest, divide both white dough and whole-wheat dough into halves. Roll out a white section and a whole-wheat section into rectangles 12 x 8 inches. Place one on top of the other. Tightly roll up in jelly-roll fashion, beginning at the shorter side, pinching the length of the roll to the bottom layer and pinching the

TWO-TONE BREAD

ends with each turn. Shape into a loaf. Let rise in a greased pan (9 x 5 x 3 inches) until doubled in bulk. Bake in a preheated 375°F. (190.6°C.) oven for 45 to 50 minutes. Repeat with the remaining dough. Remove from pans and cool on a rack.

DARK AND WHITE BRAID

After first rising and after dough has been punched down and allowed to rest, divide 1 recipe of each dough into thirds, and shape each third into a ball. Form each ball into a long rope by rolling the dough back and forth and pressing outward. Each rope should be about 15 inches (38 cm) long. On a greased baking sheet line up 2 dark ropes and 1 white rope 1 inch part, alternating the colors. Braid loosely, beginning in the middle and working toward the ends. Pinch ends and tuck under. On another baking sheet repeat the braiding with 2 white ropes and 1 dark rope. Glaze both braids with 1 egg yolk beaten with 1 tablespoon water and a pinch of salt. Let rise until doubled in bulk. Bake in a preheated 375°F. (190.6C.) oven for 25 to 30 minutes.

## RYE BREAD

Read the introduction
for yeast bread.

Makes 2 small loaves
or 1 large loaf.

¼ *cup molasses (80 g)*
¼ *cup warm water (.5 dl)*
  *(105° to 115°F.)*
*1 pkg. or 1 Tbsp. active dry*
  *yeast (7 g)*
*1½ cups rye flour (225 g)*
*1 ½ cups unbleached flour*
  *(225 g)*
*1 tsp. salt*
*1 Tbsp. butter (15 g)*
*2 tsp. caraway seeds*
  *(optional)*
*1 cup warm water (.24 l)*
*1 egg yolk, for glaze*

Mix the molasses with ¼ cup warm water in a 1-cup measure. Sprinkle the yeast on the water and stir lightly with a fork until dissolved. Let work for 5 to 10 minutes, or until bubbly.

In the processor bowl fitted with the steel blade, put the flours, salt, butter and caraway seeds. Blend together with on and off quick turns until the mixture resembles cornmeal. Pour in the yeast mixture and blend with 2 or 3 quick turns. With the machine running, pour the warm water slowly through the tube until a ball of dough forms, giving the liquid time to incorporate completely with the dry ingredients. (Depending on conditions—humidity, temperature and type of flour, the specified amount of liquid is not always needed. However, should the dough not form a ball, dribble in a little more warm water until it does.)

Knead the dough by allowing it to spin for about 1 minute. If the dough forces up the lid of the processor and stops the machine, readjust the lid and hold your hand over the feed tube while the machine is running. Turn the dough out on a lightly floured surface and knead by hand for 2 or 3 minutes, adding just enough more white flour, if necessary, to make an elastic dough. Shape dough into a ball and place it in a greased warm bowl, turning it around to grease the entire surface of the dough. Cover loosely with a towel and let dough rise in a warm draft-free place (80° to 85°F.) until doubled in bulk, 1 to 2 hours.

Punch the dough down with your fist and pull the edges to the middle. Place the dough on a lightly floured surface. Cover and let rest for 10 minutes. Shape into 2 small free-form loaves or 1 big one. Slash the tops 2 or 3 times with the processor steel blade to make ¼-inch gashes. Place on a greased cookie sheet. Cover with a towel and let rise in a warm place until doubled in bulk, about 1 hour. Glaze with egg yolk, beaten with 1 tablespoon water and a pinch of salt. Bake in a preheated 375°F. (190.6°C.) oven for 1 hour, or until the loaf sounds hollow when tapped. Remove bread from the cookie sheet and cool on a rack.

TEMPERATURES FOR YEAST

dissolving dry yeast, 105° to 115°F. = 40.5° to 46.1°C.
dissolving fresh yeast, 85° to 90°F. = 29.4° to 32.2°C.
raising yeast doughs, 80° to 85°F. = 26.7° to 29.4°C.
liquid for Rapidmix© method, 120° to 130°F. = 48.9° to 54.4°C.

# SOUR-CREAM RYE

Read the introduction
for yeast bread.

Makes 2 loaves.

A light fine-textured bread

*1 tsp. granulated sugar*
*½ cup warm water (1 dl)*
*(105° to 115°F.)*
*2 pkg. or 2 Tbsp. active*
*dry yeast (14 g)*
*3 ½ cups unbleached flour*
*(525 g)*
*2 ½ cups rye flour (375 g)*
*1 Tbsp. caraway seeds*
*(10 g)*
*1 Tbsp. salt (17 g)*
*½ cup brown sugar*
*(100 g)*
*4 Tbsp. butter (60 g)*
*2 cups sour cream*
*(500 g) , lukewarm*

Mix 1 teaspoon sugar and ½ cup warm water in a 1-cup measure. Sprinkle the yeast on the water and stir lightly with a fork until dissolved. Let work for 5 to 10 minutes, or until bubbly.

Mix both flours with the caraway seeds in a large bowl, stirring to combine. In the processor bowl fitted with the steel blade, put 3 cups of the flour mixture, ½ tablespoon salt, ¼ cup brown sugar and 2 tablespoons butter. Blend together with on and off quick turns until the mixture resembles cornmeal. Combine the yeast mixture with the sour cream. Stir very well and divide into 2 portions. Pour 1 portion of the yeast and sour-cream mixture into the processor bowl. Let it run and give the mixture a chance to form a ball. It may take longer than usual. Should the dough not form a ball, dribble in more warm water until the ball forms, but be sure to give the liquid a chance to work before adding more. The dough will be rather sticky.

Knead the dough by allowing it to spin for about 1 minute. Turn the dough out onto a lightly floured surface and knead by hand for 2 or 3 minutes, adding just enough flour (no more than ¼ cup at a time) to make a soft and elastic dough. Shape dough into a ball and place it in a greased warm bowl, turning it around to grease the entire surface of the dough. Cover loosely with a towel.

Repeat the process with remaining ingredients. Let both batches rise in a warm draft-free place (80° to 85°F.) until doubled in bulk, 1 to 2 hours.

Punch the dough down with your fist and pull

the edges to the middle. Place the dough on a lightly floured surface. Cover and let rest for 10 minutes. Shape into loaves. This bread is attractive when baked in a 2-humped loaf (2 small balls of dough placed side by side in a greased loaf pan, 9 x 5 x 3 inches). Cover and let rise again in a warm place until doubled in bulk, about 1 hour. Bake in a preheated 375°F. (190.6°C.) oven for 40 to 50 minutes, or until the loaves sound hollow when tapped. Remove loaves from pans and let cool on a rack.

## PUMPERNICKEL BREAD I

Read the introduction for yeast bread.

Makes 1 loaf.

*1 tsp. sugar*
*2 tsp. instant coffee powder*
*¼ cup warm water (.5 dl) (105° to 115°F.)*
*2 pkg. or 2 Tbsp. active dry yeast (14 g)*
*1 cup pumpernickel flour (150 g)*
*1 cup medium rye or whole-wheat flour (150 g)*
*1 cup white flour (150 g)*
*3 Tbsp. molasses (60 g)*
*1 Tbsp. salt (17 g)*
*2 Tbsp. butter (30 g)*
*1 cup warm water (.24 l)*
*1 egg white, for glaze*
*caraway seeds (optional)*

Mix 1 teaspoon sugar, the instant coffee powder and ¼ cup warm water in a 1-cup measure. Sprinkle the yeast on the water and stir lightly with a fork until dissolved. Let work for 5 to 10 minutes, or until bubbly.

In the processor bowl fitted with the steel blade, put pumpernickel, rye and white flours, molasses, salt and butter. Blend together with on and off quick turns until the mixture resembles cornmeal. Pour the proofed yeast into the dry ingredients and blend with 2 or 3 quick turns. With the machine running, pour 1 cup warm water slowly through the tube until a ball of dough forms, giving the liquid time to incorporate completely with the dry ingredients. (Depending on conditions—humidity, temperature and type of flour, the specified amount of liquid is not always needed. However, should the dough not form a ball, dribble in a little more warm water until it does.)

Knead the dough by allowing it to spin for about 1 minute. If the dough forces up the lid of the processor and stops the machine, readjust the

lid and hold your hand over the feed tube while the machine is running. The dough will be sticky. With floured hands turn the dough out onto a lightly floured surface. Knead the dough by hand for 2 or 3 minutes. It may be necessary to knead in a little more flour (no more than ¼ cup at a time) to make the dough fairly stiff. Shape dough into a ball and place it in a greased warm bowl, turning it around to grease the entire surface of the dough. Cover loosely with a towel and let dough rise in a warm draft-free place (80° to 85°F.) until doubled in bulk, 1 to 2 hours.

Punch the dough down with your fist and pull the edges to the middle. Place the dough on a lightly floured surface. Cover and let rest for 10 minutes. Shape into 1 or 2 round or oval loaves. Place on a greased baking sheet. Slash the tops 3 times with the processor steel blade to make ¼-inch gashes or crosses. Cover and let rise again in a warm place until doubled in bulk, about 1 hour. Glaze with the egg white mixed with 1 tablespoon water. Sprinkle with caraway seeds. Bake in a preheated 375°F. (190.6°C.) oven for 45 to 60 minutes, or until the loaf sounds hollow when tapped. Remove from pans and cool on a rack.

# PUMPERNICKEL BREAD II

Read the introduction
for yeast bread.

Makes 2 small loaves.

This bread is darker in color than the first pumpernickel bread. When formed into long thin loaves, this may be cut into party-size rounds. Admirable with smoked fish or cream cheese and caviar.

*1 tsp. sugar*
*¼ cup warm water (.5 dl)*
*(105° to 115°F.)*
*1 pkg. or 1 Tbsp. active*
*dry yeast (7 g)*
*¾ cup pumpernickel or*
*dark rye flour (110 g)*
*2 cups unbleached flour*
*(300 g)*
*½ Tbsp. sugar*
*2 tsp. salt*
*¼ cup salad oil (48 g)*
*1 oz. unsweetened*
*chocolate (28.4 g),*
*melted*
*1 Tbsp. vinegar (15 g)*
*¾ to 1½ cups ice water*
*1 egg white, for glaze*
*coarse salt*

Mix 1 teaspoon sugar and ¼ cup warm water in a 1-cup measure. Sprinkle the yeast on the water and stir lightly with a fork until dissolved. Let work for 5 to 10 minutes, or until bubbly.

In the processor bowl fitted with the steel blade, put all the ingredients except proofed yeast, ice water, egg white and coarse salt. Blend all together with on and off quick turns. Pour in the yeast and blend quickly. With the machine running pour the ice water slowly through the tube until a ball of dough forms, giving the liquid time to incorporate completely with the dry ingredients.

Knead the dough by allowing it to spin for about 1 minute. If the dough forces up the lid of the processor and stops the machine, readjust the lid and hold your hand over the feed tube while the machine is running. Turn the dough out onto a lightly floured surface and knead by hand for 2 or 3 minutes, until dough is smooth and elastic. Shape into narrow loaves. Place on a greased baking sheet and let rise for 30 minutes. Glaze with the egg white, mixed with 1 tablespoon water. Sprinkle with coarse salt. Bake in a preheated 350°F. (176.7°C.) oven for 35 minutes, or until the loaf sounds hollow when tapped. Remove from baking sheet and let cool.

TEMPERATURES FOR YEAST

dissolving dry yeast, 105° to 115°F. = 40.5° to 46.1°C.
dissolving fresh yeast, 85° to 90°F. = 29.4° to 32.2°C.
raising yeast doughs, 80° to 85°F. = 26.7° to 29.4°C.
liquid for Rapidmix© method, 120° to 130°F. = 48.9° to 54.4°C.

# LIMPA BREAD

Read the introduction
for yeast bread.

Makes 2 loaves.

A traditional Swedish treat

*¼ cup corn syrup (80 g)*
*12 oz. warm beer (1.5 dl)*
*(105° to 115°F.)*
*2 pkg. or 2 Tbsp. active*
*dry yeast (14 g)*
*4 Tbsp. candied orange*
*peel (50 g)*
*2 cups rye flour (300 g)*
*3 cups unbleached flour*
*(450 g)*
*3 Tbsp. butter (45 g)*
*1 Tbsp. whole fennel*
*seeds or aniseeds*
*(10 g), pounded*
*2 tsp. salt*
*1 egg yolk, for glaze*

Mix corn syrup and warm beer in a 4-cup measure. Sprinkle the yeast on the beer and stir lightly with a fork until dissolved. Let work for 5 to 10 minutes, or until bubbly.

In the processor bowl fitted with the steel blade, place 2 tablespoons of the candied orange peel, 1 cup rye flour, 1½ cups unbleached flour, 1½ tablespoons butter, ½ tablespoon pounded fennel seeds or aniseeds and 1 teaspoon salt. Blend all together with on and off quick turns until the mixture resembles cornmeal. Stir the yeast mixture well and divide it into 2 portions. With the machine running, pour 1 portion of yeast mixture through the tube until a ball of dough forms, giving the liquid time to incorporate completely with the dry ingredients. If the machine slows down because of the stickiness of the dough, add ¼ cup flour at a time until the machine returns to normal.

Knead the dough by allowing it to spin for about 1 minute. If the dough forces up the lid of the processor and stops the machine, readjust the lid and hold your hand over the feed tube while the machine is running. The dough will be sticky. Turn the dough out onto a lightly floured surface and knead by hand for 2 or 3 minutes, adding a little more flour, until the dough is firm and glossy. Shape dough into a ball and place in a greased warm bowl, turning it around to grease the entire surface of the dough. Cover loosely with a towel.

Repeat the process with remaining ingredients. Let both batches rise in a warm draft-free place (80° to 85°F.) until doubled in bulk, which will take 1 to 2 hours.

Punch the dough down several times with

your fist and pull the edges to the middle. Place the dough on a lightly floured surface. Cover and let rest for 10 minutes. Shape into free-form loaves, and place them on a greased baking sheet. Slash the tops with the processor steel blade. Cover and let rest again in a warm place until doubled in bulk, about 1 hour. Glaze with the egg yolk mixed with 1 tablespoon water. Bake in a preheated 375°F. (190.6°C.) oven for 1 hour, or until loaves sound hollow when tapped. Remove from baking sheet and let cool.

# BREAKFAST CEREAL BREADS

Many familiar breakfast cereals can be incorporated into bread dough for crunchy texture; these breads are good toasted or plain.

## MAYPO BREAD

Read the introduction
for yeast bread.

Makes 1 loaf.

*1 tsp. sugar*
*¼ cup warm water (.5 dl)*
*(105° to 115°F.)*
*1 pkg. or 1 Tbsp. active*
*dry yeast (7 g)*
*½ cup Maypo*
*1 cup whole-wheat flour*
*(150 g)*
*1½ cups unbleached flour*
*(225 g)*
*¼ cup brown sugar (50 g)*
*4 Tbsp. butter (60 g)*
*2 Tbsp. dried milk (whole*
*or nonfat)*
*1 tsp. salt*
*¼ cup wheat germ (35 g)*
*¾ to 1½ cups warm water*

Mix 1 teaspoon sugar with ¼ cup warm water in a 1-cup measure. Sprinkle the yeast on the liquid and stir lightly with a fork until dissolved. Let work for 5 to 10 minutes, or until bubbly.

In the processor bowl fitted with the steel blade, put the Maypo, the flours, brown sugar, butter, dried milk, salt and wheat germ. Blend together with on and off quick turns until the mixture resembles cornmeal. Pour the proofed yeast into the dry ingredients and blend with 2 or 3 on and off quick turns. With the machine running, pour just enough warm water through the tube to form a ball of dough, giving the liquid time to incorporate completely with the dry ingredients.

Knead the dough by allowing it to spin for about 1 minute. If the dough forces up the lid of the processor and stops the machine, readjust the lid and hold your hand over the feed tube while the machine is running. Turn the dough out onto a lightly floured surface and knead by hand for 2 or 3 minutes. The stiff dough should be elastic. Shape into a ball and place in a greased warm bowl, turning it around to grease the entire surface of the dough. Cover with a towel and let rise in a warm draft-free place (80° to 85°F.) until doubled in bulk, which will take 1 to 2 hours.

Punch the dough down with your fist and pull the edges to the middle. Place the dough on a lightly floured surface. Cover and let rest for 10 minutes. Shape dough into a free-form loaf and place on a greased baking sheet, or put in a loaf pan. Cover and let rise again in a warm place until doubled in bulk, about 1 hour. Bake in a preheated 375°F. (190.6°C.) oven for 40 to 50 minutes, or until loaf sounds hollow when tapped. Remove from the pan and cool on a rack.

## MALTEX BREAD

Read the introduction for yeast bread.

Makes 1 loaf.

*1 tsp. honey*
*½ cup warm water (1 dl)*
  *(105° to 115°F.)*
*1 pkg. or 1 Tbsp. active*
  *dry yeast (7 g)*
*½ cup Maltex*
*1 cup boiling water (.24 l)*
*2 Tbsp. butter (30 g)*
*1 tsp. salt*
*2 Tbsp. honey (40 g)*
*3 cups unbleached flour*
  *(450 g)*

Mix 1 teaspoon honey with ½ cup warm water in a 1-cup measure. Sprinkle the yeast on the water and stir lightly with a fork until dissolved. Let work for 5 to 10 minutes, or until bubbly.

Stir the Maltex into the boiling water and add butter, salt and honey. Let cool to lukewarm and stir in the proofed yeast.

Put the flour in the processor bowl fitted with the steel blade. With the machine running, spoon the Maltex mixture through the tube and process until a ball forms. Should the dough not form a ball, dribble in a little more warm water until it does.

Knead the dough by allowing it to spin for about 1 minute. If the dough forces up the lid of the processor and stops the machine, readjust the

lid and hold your hand over the feed tube while the machine is running. Turn the dough out onto a lightly floured surface and knead by hand for 2 or 3 minutes, adding a little more flour, if necessary, to make a stiff but elastic dough. Shape dough into a ball and place in a greased warm bowl, turning it around to grease the entire surface of the dough. Cover loosely with a towel and let rise in a warm draft-free place (80° to 85°F.) until doubled in bulk, which will take 1 to 2 hours.

Punch the dough down with your fist and pull the edges to the middle. Place the dough on a lightly floured surface. Cover and let rest for 10 minutes. Shape into a loaf and put in a greased loaf pan, or shape into a round loaf and place in a greased 1½-quart casserole. Cover and let rise again in a warm place until doubled in bulk, about 1 hour.

Bake in a preheated 375°F. (190.6°C.) oven for 40 to 50 minutes, or until loaf sounds hollow when tapped. Remove from the pan and cool on a rack.

## GRANOLA BREAD

Read the introduction for yeast bread.

Makes 1 loaf.

*1 tsp. honey*
*½ cup warm water (1 dl)*
  *(105° to 115°F.)*
*1 pkg. or 1 Tbsp. active*
  *dry yeast (7 g)*
*3 cups unbleached flour*
  *(450 g)*
*1 cup Granola*
*½ cup honey (160 g)*
*2 Tbsp. butter (30 g)*
*1 tsp. salt*
*1 egg*
*½ cup warm milk (1 dl)*

Mix 1 teaspoon honey with ½ cup warm water in a 1-cup measure. Sprinkle the yeast on the liquid and stir lightly with a fork until dissolved. Let work for 5 to 10 minutes, or until bubbly.

In the processor bowl fitted with the steel blade, blend the flour, Granola, honey, butter and salt together with on and off quick turns until the mixture resembles cornmeal. Add the egg and blend quickly. Pour the proofed yeast into the dry ingredients and blend with 2 or 3 on and off quick turns. With the machine running, pour the warm milk slowly through the tube until a ball of dough forms. (Depending on conditions—humidity, temperature and type of flour—the specified amount of liquid is not always needed. However, should the dough not form a ball, dribble in a little more warm water until it does.)

Knead the dough by allowing it to spin for about 1 minute. If the dough forces up the lid of the processor and stops the machine, readjust the lid and hold your hand over the feed tube while the machine is running. Turn the dough out onto a lightly floured surface and knead by hand for 2 or 3 minutes. It may be necessary to knead in a little more flour (no more than ¼ cup at a time) to make the dough firm and elastic. Shape dough into a ball and place in a greased warm bowl, turning it around to grease the entire surface of the dough. Cover loosely with a towel and let dough rise in a warm draft-free place (80° to 85°F.) until doubled in bulk, 1 to 2 hours.

Punch the dough down with your fist and pull the edges to the middle. Place the dough on a lightly floured surface. Cover and let rest for 10 minutes. Shape dough into a loaf and place on a greased baking sheet or in a greased loaf pan. Cover and let rise again in a warm draft-free place until doubled in bulk, about 1 hour. Bake in a preheated 350°F. (176.7°C.) oven for 40 to 45 minutes, or until loaf sounds hollow when tapped. Remove from the pan and cool on a rack.

TEMPERATURES FOR YEAST

dissolving dry yeast, 105° to 115°F. = 40.5° to 46.1°C.
dissolving fresh yeast, 85° to 90°F. = 29.4° to 32.2°C.
raising yeast doughs, 80° to 85°F. = 26.7° to 29.4°C.
liquid for Rapidmix© method, 120° to 130°F. = 48.9° to 54.4°C.

# THREE-GRAIN BREAD

Read the introduction
for yeast bread.

Makes 1 loaf.

*1 tsp. sugar*
*¼ cup warm water (.5 dl)*
  *(105° to 115°F.)*
*1 pkg. or 1 Tbsp. active*
  *dry yeast (7 g)*
*1½ cups unbleached flour*
  *(225 g)*
*½ cup bran flour (60 g)*
*1 cup rye flour (150 g)*
*2 Tbsp. butter (30 g)*
*2 Tbsp. honey (40 g)*
*2 Tbsp. molasses (40 g)*
*1 tsp. salt*
*1 cup warm milk (.24 l)*
*1 egg white, for glaze*

Mix 1 teaspoon sugar with ¼ cup warm water in a 1-cup measure. Sprinkle the yeast on top of the water and stir lightly with a fork until dissolved. Let work for 5 to 10 minutes, or until bubbly.

In the processor bowl fitted with the steel blade, put the flours, butter, honey, molasses and salt. Blend together with on and off quick turns until the mixture resembles cornmeal. Pour the proofed yeast into the dry ingredients and blend with 2 or 3 quick turns. With the machine running, pour the milk slowly through the tube until a ball of dough forms, giving the liquid time to incorporate completely with the dry ingredients. (Depending on conditions—humidity, temperature and type of flour—the specified amount of liquid is not always needed. However, should the dough not form a ball, dribble in a little more warm water until it does.)

Knead the dough by allowing it to spin for about 1 minute. If the dough forces up the lid of the processor and stops the machine, readjust the lid and hold your hand over the feed tube while the machine is running. Turn the dough out onto a lightly floured surface and knead by hand for 2 or 3 minutes. It may be necessary to knead in a little more flour (no more than ¼ cup at a time) to make the dough moderately stiff and elastic. Shape dough into a ball and place in a greased warm bowl, turning it around to grease the entire surface of the dough. Cover loosely with a towel and let dough rise in a warm place (80° to 85°F.) until doubled in bulk, which will take 1 to 2 hours.

Punch the dough down with your fist and pull the edges to the middle. Place the dough on a lightly floured surface. Cover and let rest for 10 minutes. Shape into a loaf and put into a greased loaf pan. Or form into a fat oval and slash the top 3 times with the processor steel blade. Place on a greased baking sheet. Cover and let rise again in a warm place until doubled in bulk, about 1 hour. Glaze with the egg white beaten with 1 tablespoon water. Bake in a preheated 375°F. (190.6°C.) oven for 50 to 60 minutes, or until the loaf sounds hollow when tapped. Remove from pan or baking sheet and cool on a rack.

## ANADAMA BREAD

Read the introduction for yeast bread.

Makes 2 loaves.

*1 tsp. sugar*
*½ cup warm water (1 dl)*
*(105° to 115°F.)*
*2 pkg. or 2 Tbsp. active*
*dry yeast (14 g)*
*½ cup cornmeal (90 g)*
*2 cups boiling water*
*(.48 1)*
*½ cup dark molasses*
*(160 g)*
*4 cups unbleached flour*
*(600 g)*
*2 cups whole graham*
*flour (300 g) (whole*
*wheat may be used)*
*1 Tbsp. salt (17 g)*
*4 Tbsp. butter (60 g)*

Mix 1 teaspoon sugar and ½ cup warm water in a 1-cup measure. Sprinkle the yeast on the water and stir lightly with a fork until dissolved. Let work for 5 to 10 minutes, or until bubbly.

Pour the cornmeal into the boiling water, stirring constantly. Add molasses and bring again to a boil. Remove from heat and cool to 105° to 115°F. Stir the proofed yeast into the cornmeal mixture and put into a 4-cup measure.

In the processor bowl fitted with the steel blade, put 2 cups unbleached flour and 1 cup graham flour, ½ tablespoon salt and 2 tablespoons butter. Blend all together with on and off quick turns. Stir the yeast-molasses mixture well and divide into 2 portions. Again stir yeast mixture vigorously. With the machine running pour 1 portion of yeast mixture slowly through the tube until a ball of dough forms, giving the liquid time to incorporate completely with the dry ingredients. (Depending on conditions—humidity, temperature and type of flour—the specified amount of liquid is not always needed.)

Knead the dough by allowing it to spin for about 1 minute. If the dough forces up the lid of the processor and stops the machine, readjust the

lid and hold your hand over the feed tube while the machine is running. The dough will be sticky. Turn the dough out onto a lightly floured surface and knead by hand for 2 or 3 minutes, adding just enough flour (no more than ¼ cup at a time) to make a soft and elastic dough. Shape dough into a ball and place it in a greased warm bowl, turning it around to grease the entire surface of the dough. Cover loosely with a towel.

Repeat the process with remaining ingredients. Let both batches rise in a warm draft-free place (80° to 85°F.) until doubled in bulk, 1½ to 2 hours.

Punch the dough down with your fist and pull the edges to the middle. Place the dough on a lightly floured surface. Cover and let rest for 10 minutes. Shape into loaves and place in 2 greased loaf pans (8½ x 4½ x 2½ inches), or form into round loaves and place in greased 8-inch cake pans. Cover and let rise again in a warm place until doubled in bulk, about 1 hour. Bake in a preheated 375°F. (190.6°C.) oven for 35 to 40 minutes, or until loaves are well browned and sound hollow when tapped. Remove from pans and cool on a rack.

BREAD PANS

4½ x 2½ x 2½ inches = 11 x 6.4 x 6.4 cm
7½ x 2½ x 2½ inches = 19 x 6.4 x 6.4 cm
9 x 5 x 3 inches = 23 x 13 x 7.6 cm

# HONEY OATMEAL BREAD

Read the introduction
for yeast bread.

Makes 2 loaves.

*2 cups boiling water
 (.48 l)
1 cup quick-cooking
 rolled oats (45 g)
1 tsp. sugar
½ cup warm water (1 dl)
 (105° to 115°F.)
2 pkg. or 2 Tbsp. active
 dry yeast (14 g)
½ cup honey (160 g)
6 cups unbleached flour
 (900 g)
1 Tbsp. salt (17 g)
2 Tbsp. butter (30 g)
butter or milk for topping*

Pour the boiling water over the oats. Stir and set aside for 30 minutes. Mix 1 teaspoon sugar and ½ cup warm water in a 2-cup measure. Sprinkle the yeast on top of the water and stir lightly with a fork until yeast is dissolved. Let work for 5 to 10 minutes, or until bubbly. Add honey and yeast mixture to oatmeal, mixing thoroughly.

In the processor bowl fitted with the steel blade, put 3 cups flour, ½ tablespoon salt and 1 tablespoon butter. Blend all together with on and off quick turns. Stir the yeast-honey-oatmeal mixture and divide into 2 portions. Again stir the mixture vigorously. With the machine running pour 1 portion of yeast mixture slowly through the tube until a ball forms, giving the liquid time to incorporate completely with the dry ingredients. Should a ball of dough not form, dribble in a little more warm water until it does.

Knead the dough by allowing it to spin for about 1 minute. If the dough forces up the lid of the processor and stops the machine, readjust the lid and hold your hand over the feed tube while the machine is running. The dough will be sticky. Turn the dough out onto a lightly floured surface and knead by hand for 2 or 3 minutes, adding just enough flour (no more than ¼ cup at a time) to make a fairly firm and elastic dough. Shape dough into a ball and place it in a greased warm bowl, turning it around to grease the entire surface of the dough. Cover loosely with a towel.

Repeat the process with remaining ingredients. Let both batches rise in a warm draft-free place (80° to 85°F.) until doubled in bulk, 1 to 2 hours.

Punch the dough down with your fist and

pull the edges to the middle. Place the dough on a lightly floured surface. Cover and let rest for 10 minutes. Shape into 2 loaves and place in greased loaf pans (8½ x 4½ x 2½ inches). Cover and let rise until doubled in bulk, about 1 hour.

Carefully brush the dough with butter or milk. Bake in a preheated 375°F. (190.6°C.) oven for about 1 hour, or until the loaves sound hollow when tapped. Remove from pans and cool on a rack.

## WHEAT GERM BREAD

Read the introduction for yeast bread.

Makes 1 loaf.

*1 tsp. brown sugar*
*½ cup warm water (1 dl)*
  *(105° to 115°F.)*
*1 pkg. or 1 Tbsp. active*
  *dry yeast (7 g)*
*3 cups unbleached flour*
  *(450 g)*
*¼ cup brown sugar (50 g)*
*½ cup wheat germ (70 g)*
*2 Tbsp. butter (30 g)*
*2 tsp. salt*
*2 Tbsp. dried milk (10 g)*
  *(whole or nonfat)*
*1 cup warm water (.24 l)*

Mix 1 teaspoon brown sugar with ½ cup warm water in a 1-cup measure. Sprinkle the yeast on the liquid and stir lightly with a fork until dissolved. Let work for 5 to 10 minutes, or until bubbly.

In the processor bowl fitted with the steel blade, put the flour, brown sugar, wheat germ, butter, salt and dried milk. Blend together with on and off quick turns until the mixture resembles cornmeal. Pour the proofed yeast into the dry ingredients and blend with 2 or 3 on and off quick turns. With the machine running pour the warm water slowly through the tube until a ball of dough forms, giving the liquid time to incorporate completely with the dry ingredients. (Depending on conditions—humidity, temperature and type of flour—the specified amount of liquid is not always needed. However, should the dough not form a ball, dribble in a little more warm water until it does.)

Knead the dough by allowing it to spin for about 1 minute. If the dough forces up the lid of the machine, readjust the lid and hold your hand over the feed tube while the machine is running.

Turn the dough out onto a lightly floured surface and knead by hand for 2 or 3 minutes to make the dough fairly stiff but elastic. Shape dough into a ball and place in a greased warm bowl, turning it around to grease the entire surface of the dough. Cover loosely with a towel and let rise in a warm draft-free place (80° to 85°F.) until doubled in bulk, 1 to 2 hours.

Punch the dough down with your fist and pull the edges to the middle. Place the dough on a lightly floured surface. Cover and let rest for 10 minutes. Shape into a loaf and place on a greased baking sheet or in a greased loaf pan. Cover and let rise again in a warm place until doubled in bulk. Bake in a preheated 350°F. (176.7°C.) oven for 40 to 45 minutes, or until loaf sounds hollow when tapped. Remove from the pan and cool on a rack.

## CORNMEAL BREAD
### (Rapidmix© Method)

Read the introduction for yeast bread.

Makes 1 loaf.

*3 cups unbleached flour (450 g)*
*½ cup cornmeal (90 g)*
*1 tsp. salt*
*¼ cup brown sugar (50 g)*
*6 Tbsp. butter (90 g)*
*1 egg*
*1 pkg. or 1 Tbsp. active dry yeast (7 g)*
*1 cup buttermilk (250 g), warm (120° to 130°F.)*

In the processor bowl fitted with the steel blade, put the flour, cornmeal, salt, brown sugar, butter, egg and dry yeast. Blend all together with on and off quick turns. With the machine running add the warm buttermilk slowly through the tube, until a ball forms. Knead the dough by letting it spin for about 1 minute. The dough will be soft and sticky. With floured hands turn the dough out on a floured surface and knead by hand for 2 or 3 minutes, adding a little more flour (no more than ¼ cup at a time) to make a soft dough. Shape dough into a ball and place in a greased warm bowl, turning the ball around to grease the entire surface of the dough. Cover loosely with a towel and let rise in a warm draft-free place (80° to 85°F.) until doubled in bulk, 1 to 2 hours.

Punch the dough down and pull the edges to the middle. Place in a greased loaf pan. Cover and let rise again in a warm draft-free place until doubled in bulk, about 1 hour. Bake in a preheated 375°F. (190.6°C.) oven for about 1 hour, or until loaf sounds hollow when tapped.

## POTATO BREAD

Read the introduction for yeast bread.

Makes 2 large loaves.

An excellent hearty bread for sandwiches

*3 medium-size potatoes (about 1 lb., .45 kg), peeled*
*2 Tbsp. sugar (25 g)*
*½ cup warm water (1 dl) (105° to 115°F.)*
*½ cup warm milk (1 dl) (105° to 115°F.)*
*½ cup warm potato water (1 dl) (105° to 115°F.)*
*2 pkg. or 2 Tbsp. active dry yeast (14 g)*
*6 cups unbleached flour (900 g)*
*2 tsp. salt*
*4 Tbsp. butter (60 g)*

Cook the potatoes. Drain, but save cooking water. Shred the potatoes with the shredding disc (there should be 1½ cups after shredding) and set aside.

Combine the sugar, warm water, milk and ½ cup potato cooking water. Sprinkle the yeast on the liquid and stir lightly with a fork until dissolved. Let work for 5 to 10 minutes, or until bubbly.

In the processor bowl fitted with the steel blade, put ¾ cup shredded potatoes, 3 cups flour, 1 teaspoon salt and 2 tablespoons butter. Process with on and off quick turns until the mixture is well blended.

Stir the yeast mixture vigorously and divide it into 2 portions. With the machine running, pour just enough of 1 portion of the yeast liquid through the tube to form a ball, but be sure to give the liquid a chance to work before adding more. (All of the liquid may not be needed. However, should the dough not form a ball, dribble in a little more warm water until it does.)

Knead the dough by allowing it to spin for about 1 minute. If the dough forces up the lid of the processor and stops the machine, readjust the lid and hold your hand over the feed tube while the machine is running. Turn the dough out onto a lightly floured surface and knead by hand for 2 or 3 minutes, adding a little flour if needed to make an elastic dough. Shape dough into a ball and place in a greased warm bowl, turning it around to grease the entire surface of the dough. Cover with a towel.

Repeat the process with remaining ingredients. Let both batches rise in a warm draft-free place (80° to 85°F.) until doubled in bulk, about 1 hour.

Punch the dough down with your fist and pull the edges to the middle. Place the dough on a lightly floured surface. Cover and let rest for 10 minutes. Shape into 2 loaves and place in greased pans (8½ x 4½ x 2½ inches), or form into round loaves and place on a greased baking sheet. Cover and let rise again in a warm place until doubled in bulk, about 1 hour. Dust with flour.

Bake in a preheated 375°F. (190.6°C.) oven for 40 to 45 minutes, or until loaves sound hollow when tapped. Remove from the pans and cool on a rack.

## CHEESE BREAD

Read the introduction
for yeast bread.

Makes 1 loaf.

*1 tsp. sugar*
*¼ cup warm water (.5 dl)*
*(105° to 115°F.)*
*1 pkg. or 1 Tbsp. active dry yeast (7 g)*
*2 oz. Parmesan cheese (56 g)*
*¼ lb. Cheddar cheese (125 g)*
*3 cups unbleached flour (450 g)*
*½ Tbsp. salt*
*½ cup warm milk (1 dl)*
*¼ cup warm water (1 dl)*
*1 egg yolk, for glaze*

Mix 1 teaspoon sugar with ¼ cup warm water in a 1-cup measure. Sprinkle the yeast on top of the water and stir lightly with a fork until dissolved. Let work for 5 to 10 minutes, or until bubbly.

Grate Parmesan cheese with the steel blade; set aside. Shred Cheddar cheese with the shredding disc; set aside.

In the processor bowl fitted with the steel blade, blend the Cheddar cheese, the flour and salt together with on and off quick turns. Pour the proofed yeast into the dry ingredients and blend with 2 or 3 quick turns. With the machine running, pour the warm milk and water slowly through the tube until a ball of dough forms, giving the liquid time to incorporate completely with the dry ingredients. (Depending on conditions—humidity, temperature and type of flour—the specified amount of liquid is not always needed. However, should the dough not form a ball, dribble in a little more water until it does.)

Knead the dough by allowing it to spin for about 1 minute. If the dough forces up the lid of the processor and stops the machine, readjust the lid and hold your hand over the feed tube while the machine is running. Turn the dough out onto a lightly floured surface and knead by hand for 2 or 3 minutes. It may be necessary to knead in a little more flour (no more than ¼ cup at a time) to make the dough firm and elastic. Shape dough into a ball and place in a greased warm bowl, turning it around to grease the entire surface of the dough. Cover with a towel and let rise in a warm draft-free place (80° to 85°F.) until doubled in bulk, 1 to 2 hours.

Punch the dough down with your fist and pull the edges to the middle. Place the dough on a lightly floured surface. Cover and let rest for 10 minutes. Shape dough into a loaf and put in a greased loaf pan. Cover and let rise again in a warm place until doubled in bulk, about 1 hour. Glaze with the egg yolk mixed with 1 tablespoon water and a pinch of salt. Dust with grated Parmesan cheese. Bake in a preheated 350°F. (176.7°C.) oven for 35 to 40 minutes, or until loaf is well browned and sounds hollow when tapped. Remove from pan and cool on a rack.

## BASIC TOASTING BREAD

Read the introduction
for yeast bread.

Makes 1 round loaf.

This porous bread is best when toasted; it is very good for grilled sandwiches and special for French toast.

*½ tsp. sugar*
*¼ cup warm water (.5 dl)*
  *(105° to 115°F.)*
*1 pkg. or 1 Tbsp. active*
  *dry yeast (7 g)*
*2½ to 3 cups unbleached*
  *flour (375 to 450 g)*
*1 tsp. salt*
*1 Tbsp. sugar (13 g)*
*1¼ cups warm water*
  *(.30 l)*
*cornmeal*

Mix ½ teaspoon sugar with ¼ cup warm water in a 1-cup measure. Sprinkle the yeast on the water and stir lightly with a fork until dissolved. Let work for 5 to 10 minutes, or until bubbly.

In the processor bowl fitted with the steel blade, put 2½ cups flour, the salt and sugar. Blend with on and off quick turns. Pour the proofed yeast into the dry ingredients and blend with 2 or 3 quick turns. With the machine running, pour the warm water slowly through the tube until a ball of dough forms, giving the liquid time to incorporate completely with the dry ingredients. The dough will be sticky.

Knead the dough by allowing it to spin for about 1 minute. Should the dough force up the lid of the processor and stop the machine, readjust the lid and hold your hand over the feed tube while the machine is running. Turn the dough out onto a lightly floured surface and knead by hand for 2 or 3 minutes, adding a little more flour (no more than ¼ cup at a time) to make a soft dough. Shape dough into a ball and place in a greased warm bowl, turning the ball around to grease the entire surface of the dough. Cover loosely with a towel and let rise in a warm draft-free place (80° to 85°F.) until doubled in bulk, 1 to 2 hours.

Punch the dough down with your fist and pull the edges to the middle. Place the dough on a lightly floured surface. Cover and let rest for 10 minutes. Shape into a round loaf and place in a buttered 1- to 1½-quart casserole that has been sprinkled with cornmeal. Brush the bread with melted butter and sprinkle more cornmeal on top. Cover and let rise in a warm place until almost doubled, 1 to 1½ hours. Bake in a preheated 400°F. (204.4°C.) oven for 40 to 45 minutes. Remove from casserole and cool on a rack.

## VARIATIONS ON BASIC TOASTING BREAD

Subtle or strong flavors may be incorporated with the basic ingredients, depending on the accompaniments and occasion.

*Garlic*—Use 2 teaspoons garlic, finely chopped with 1 tablespoon butter (15 g), and add to the flour. Terrific for steak sandwiches.

*Beefy Bread*—Add 1 tablespoon Bovril with the flour. Serve this bread hot and buttered. Great with cold meats.

*Saffron Bread*—Dissolve 1 teaspoon crushed saffron and 1 teaspoon sugar in 2 tablespoons milk, and add to the flour. A tea delicacy, toasted and served with jam.

*Cardamom Bread*—Add 2 teaspoons crushed cardamom and 1 teaspoon ground cinnamon to the flour. Fitting fare for a coffee gathering.

## MEDITERRANEAN BREAD I (ITALIAN-TYPE)

Read the introduction                                    Makes 2 to 4 loaves.
for yeast bread.

This recipe makes lovely crusty bread in the Mediterranean mode. It can be shaped into free-form round loaves, horseshoes, long loaves, long narrow *baguettes* or hard rolls.

There are many ways of baking French-type bread, and they can be used for either recipe. One method is to place a pan of boiling water on the lowest shelf of a preheated 400°F. (204.4°C.) oven in order to create steam for a good crust. Another method is to spray the bread with water the moment it is put into a preheated 400°F. (204.4°C.) oven and then repeat the spraying 3 more times at 5-minute intervals. A third method is to use quarry tiles or a patented ceramic baking plate; either is placed in a cold oven, on the lowest shelf, and heated to 400°F. (204.4°C.) The free-form bread is placed directly on the hot tiles or baking plate and sprayed with water. French-type bread may be baked free-form on a baking sheet or in French bread pans or dark steel *baguette* pans. Cornmeal is usually dusted on the baking surface.

*1 tsp. sugar*
*2 cups water (.48 l) (105°*
  *to 115°F.)*
*1 pkg. or 1 Tbsp. active*
  *dry yeast (7 g)*
*7 cups unbleached flour*
  *(1.05 kg)*
*1 Tbsp. salt (17 g)*
*1 egg white (optional)*

Mix 1 teaspoon sugar and the warm water in a 4-cup measure. Sprinkle the yeast on top of the water and stir lightly with a fork until dissolved. Let work for 5 to 10 minutes, or until bubbly.

In the processor bowl fitted with the steel blade, put 3 cups flour and ½ tablespoon salt. Stir the yeast mixture vigorously and divide into 2 portions. With the machine running pour 1 portion of the liquid slowly through the tube until a ball of dough forms, giving the liquid time to incorporate completely with the dry ingredients. (Depending on conditions—humidity, temperature and type of flour—the specified amount of liquid is not always needed. However, should the dough not form a ball dribble in a little more warm water until it does.)

Knead the dough by allowing it to spin for about 1 minute. If the dough forces up the lid of the processor and stops the machine, readjust the lid and hold your hand over the feed tube while the machine is running. Turn the dough out on a lightly floured surface and knead by hand for 2 or 3 minutes. It may be necessary to add additional flour (no more than ¼ cup at a time) to make the dough soft and elastic. Shape dough into a ball and place in a greased warm bowl, turning the ball around to grease the entire surface of the dough. Cover loosely with a towel.

Repeat the process with remaining ingredients. Let both batches rise in a warm draft-free place (80° to 85°F.) until doubled in bulk, 1 to 2 hours.

Punch the dough down with your fist and pull the edges to the middle. Cut the dough into the number of loaves desired and let rest for 10 minutes. Shape the loaves and slash the tops with the processor steel blade. Cover and let rise again in a warm place until doubled in bulk, about 1 hour. Glaze with the egg white mixed with 1 tablespoon water for a shiny crust, or spray with water for a crisp crust.

Bake in a preheated 400°F. oven for 35 to 40 minutes, using one of the methods described in the introduction to the recipe.

Another method for baking the bread is to place it in a cold oven and then bake it at 400°F. (204.4°C.) for 40 to 45 minutes for large loaves, or until brown and hollow-sounding when tapped. Small loaves will take less time—30 to 35 minutes—and rolls will take about 20 minutes. Remove from the pans and cool on a rack.

MEDITERRANEAN BREAD

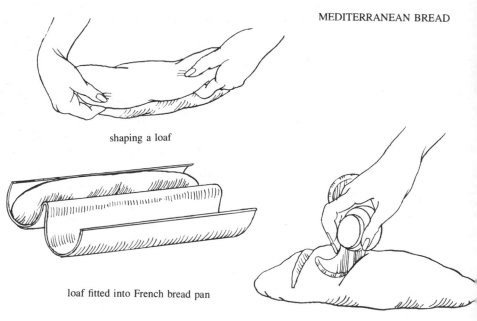

shaping a loaf

loaf fitted into French bread pan

slashing the top with the steel blade

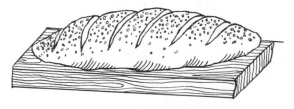

the finished loaf

# MEDITERRANEAN BREAD II (FRENCH-TYPE)

Read the introduction
for yeast bread and
the introduction for
Mediterranean Bread I.

Makes 3 loaves.

This is a slow-rising bread and more porous than the first type. There
is no sugar in this bread.

*1 pkg. or 1 Tbsp. active*
*dry yeast (7 g)*
*¼ cup warm water (.5 dl)*
*(100° to 105°F.)*
*3½ cups unbleached flour*
*(525 g)*
*2 tsp. salt*
*1¼ cups water (.30 l),*
*warm (85°F.)*

Dissolve the yeast in ¼ cup warm water, stirring
well with a fork.

In the processor bowl fitted with the steel
blade, blend the flour and salt with 2 or 3 quick on
and off turns. Add the dissolved yeast and 1¼
cups warm water to the dry ingredients and blend
until a ball of dough forms. The dough will be
sticky. Let the dough rest in the bowl for 5 minutes.

Knead the dough by allowing it to spin for 30
seconds. Scrape the dough out onto a floured surface. Knead by hand for 2 or 3 minutes. Do not
add any more flour than is absolutely necessary to
make the dough soft and elastic. Form dough into a
ball and place in a lightly greased large warm
bowl; brush top of dough lightly with melted butter. Cover loosely with a towel. Let dough rise in a
warm draft-free place (80° to 85°F.) until it is
*tripled* in bulk, which will take 3 to 5 hours.

Lightly punch the dough down and turn out
onto a floured surface. The dough will be spongy.
Gingerly knead dough for 30 seconds. Return
dough to the bowl. Brush a little more melted butter on top. Cover and let rise until almost tripled,
1½ to 2 hours. Divide the dough into thirds. Cover
and let rest for 10 minutes. Pat each portion into an
oval. Fold the dough lengthwise and seal the edges
of the dough together. Roll back and forth to make
dough long enough to fit on a baking sheet or into
French bread pans, leaving a 2-inch space on each

end. Slash the tops of the loaves with the steel blade of the processor. Cover and allow to double in bulk, about 1½ hours.

Preheat oven to 450°F. (232°C.). Put the loaves in the oven and immediately spray them with water. Repeat the spraying 3 more times at 5-minute intervals. Bake for 25 minutes, or until loaves sound hollow when tapped. Remove from pans and cool on a rack. This bread should be eaten the same day, or frozen.

FRENCH BREAD PANS FOR *BAGUETTES* (LONG THIN LOAVES)

## COTTAGE-CHEESE HERB BREAD

Read the introduction
for yeast bread.

Makes 1 loaf.

An interesting casserole bread to accompany stews or hearty salads

*1 tsp. sugar*
*¼ cup warm water (.5 dl)*
  *(105° to 115°F.)*
*1 pkg. or 1 Tbsp. active*
  *dry yeast (7 g)*
*2½ to 3 cups unbleached*
  *flour (375 to 450 g)*
*2 Tbsp. butter (30 g)*
*1 egg*
*1 Tbsp. salt (17 g)*
*1 tsp. baking soda, mixed*
  *in 2 Tbsp. water*
*1 cup parsley sprigs*
*1 Tbsp. fresh or freeze-*
  *dried chives*
*1 tsp. onion powder*

Mix 1 teaspoon sugar and ¼ cup warm water in a 1-cup measure. Sprinkle the yeast on the water and stir lightly with a fork until dissolved. Let work for 5 to 10 minutes, or until bubbly.

In the processor bowl fitted with the steel blade, put 2½ cups flour and all remaining ingredients except cottage cheese and sesame seeds. (The fresh herbs do not need to be processed beforehand.) Blend all together with on and off quick turns. Add the yeast mixture and blend with 2 or 3 quick turns. Add the warmed cottage cheese and process until a ball of dough forms. If the dough does not form a ball, and if it is very sticky and slows down the machine, stop the machine and add ¼ cup flour. Process again and continue to add ¼ cup flour until the dough forms a ball.

*1 cup cottage cheese,*
  *(226 g), lukewarm*
*sesame seeds*
*melted butter, for topping*

Knead the dough by allowing it to spin for about 1 minute. If the dough forces up the lid of the processor and stops the machine, readjust the lid and hold your hand over the feed tube while the machine is running. Turn the dough out onto a floured surface and knead by hand for 2 or 3 minutes. It may be necessary to knead in a little more flour (no more than ¼ cup at a time) to make the dough soft and elastic. Shape dough into a ball and place in a greased warm bowl, turning the ball around to grease the entire surface of the dough. Cover loosely with a towel and let rise in a warm draft-free place (80° to 85°F.) until doubled in bulk, from 1 to 2 hours.

Punch the dough down with your fist and pull the edges to the middle. Place the dough on a lightly floured surface. Cover and let rest for 10 minutes. Put the dough into a buttered 1½- to 2-quart casserole which has been sprinkled with sesame seeds. Cover and let rise again in a warm place until doubled in bulk, about 1 hour.

Brush the top of the dough with melted butter and sprinkle with more sesame seeds. Bake in a preheated 350°F. (176.7°C.) oven for 40 minutes, or until the loaf sounds hollow when it is tapped. Remove from the casserole and cool on a rack.

## VARIATIONS ON COTTAGE-CHEESE HERB BREAD

In place of the herbs a choice of the following ingredients may be incorporated into the bread:

- 2 teaspoons curry powder and a 1-inch piece of peeled fresh gingerroot, grated, or 1 teaspoon ground ginger.
- 2 tablespoons dried onion and 2 teaspoons caraway seeds or celery seeds.
- 2 tablespoons bacon fat in place of the butter plus 1 cup crumbled cooked bacon.

Use any combination of fresh or dried herbs and dust the top of the bread with grated Parmesan cheese.

# TALL BREAD MADE IN A COFFEE CAN I

Read the introduction
for yeast bread.

Makes 2 loaves.

This pop-up bread with a mushroomlike shape (when the dough blows its lid) is a delicious light bread which cuts admirably into neat circular slices. It may be made with an interesting combination of flavors—grated orange, grated lemon, nuts, grated cheese—as long as the basic recipe is followed.

It has the advantage of only a single rising. The dough is stickier than regular kneaded bread and because of its stickiness it may stop the machine. If it does, don't worry; just scoop it out and bake according to directions.

*1 tsp. sugar*
*½ cup warm water (1 dl)*
*(105° to 115°F.)*
*1 pkg. or 1 Tbsp. active*
*dry yeast (7 g)*
*2 tsp. ground mace or*
*ginger*
*2 tsp. celery seeds*
*1 tsp. dried tarragon*
*13 oz. evaporated milk*
*(.37 l)*
*4 cups unbleached flour*
*(525 g)*
*2 Tbsp. sugar (25 g)*
*2 tsp. salt*
*2 Tbsp. vegetable oil*
*(24 g)*
*½ cup cornmeal (90 g)*

Mix 1 teaspoon sugar and ½ cup warm water in a 1-cup measure. Sprinkle the yeast on the water and stir lightly with a fork until dissolved. Let work for 5 to 10 minutes. When bubbly stir in the spice and herbs, and add to the evaporated milk.

In the processor bowl fitted with the steel blade, put 2 cups flour, 1 tablespoon sugar, 1 teaspoon salt, 1 tablespoon oil and ¼ cup cornmeal. Blend together by turning the machine on and off 3 times.

Stir the yeast mixture again and divide into 2 portions. With the machine running pour 1 portion of the liquid slowly through the tube and blend quickly. This will produce a sticky dough which may slow down the machine. Should this happen stop the machine and spoon the dough into a well-greased 1-pound coffee can and cover with its well-greased plastic lid.

Repeat the process with remaining ingredients. Let both batches rise in a warm draft-free place (80° to 85°F.) until the lids pop up, 1 to 1½ hours. Remove the lids. Bake in a preheated 350°F. (176.7°C.) oven for 50 to 60 minutes. Brush the tops with melted butter and let the loaves cool in the can for 20 minutes. Remove loaves from the cans and let them continue to cool on a rack.

# TALL BREAD MADE IN A COFFEE CAN II

Read the introduction
for yeast bread.

Makes 2 loaves.

To this basic recipe you may add ¼ cup grated Parmesan or Cheddar cheese; or ½ cup chopped nuts and ½ cup raisins; or ¼ cup grated citrus rinds.

*½ tsp. sugar*

*½ cup warm water (1 dl)*
*(105° to 115°F.)*

*½ cup warm milk (1 dl)*
*(105° to 115°F.)*

*1 pkg. or 1 Tbsp. active*
*dry yeast (7 g)*

*3 cups flour (450 g)*

*1 tsp. salt*

*½ cup oil (96 g)*

*2 eggs*

*melted butter, for topping*

Mix ½ teaspoon sugar and ½ cup water and ½ cup milk in a 2-cup measure. Sprinkle the yeast on the water and stir lightly with a fork until dissolved. Let work for 5 to 10 minutes, or until bubbly.

In the processor bowl fitted with the steel blade, put the flour, salt, oil and eggs. Blend together well with on and off quick turns. With the machine running, pour the yeast mixture slowly through the tube and blend quickly. The dough will be sticky and may slow down the machine. Should this happen stop processing. Divide the dough into halves and spoon into 2 well-greased 1-pound coffee cans; cover with their well-greased plastic lids. Let rise in a warm draft-free place (80° to 85°F.) until the dough is ¼ inch from the top of the can, 1 to 1½ hours.

Bake in a preheated 350°F. (176.7°C.) oven for 50 to 60 minutes. Brush the tops with melted butter and let the loaves cool in the can for 20 minutes. Remove loaves from the cans and continue to cool on a rack.

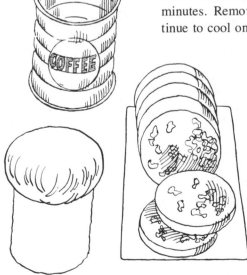

# PIE PAN BREAD

Read the introduction
for yeast bread.

Makes 1 pan of bread.

An out-of-the ordinary bread that is cut into wedges for serving. It needs only one rising and and may be treated to a number of flavorings, additions or toppings—herbs, chopped tongue, sautéed onions. Invent!

*2 oz. Parmesan cheese (57 g)*

*1 tsp. sugar*

*¼ cup warm water (.5 dl) (105° to 115° F.)*

*1 pkg. or 1 Tbsp. active dry yeast (7 g)*

*1½ cups unbleached flour (225 g)*

*1 tsp. minced fresh orégano, or ½ tsp. dried*

*1 tsp. minced fresh basil, or ½ tsp. dried*

*1 Tbsp. sugar (13 g)*

*1 tsp. salt*

*5 Tbsp. butter (75 g), cut up*

*1 egg*

*¼ cup dry vermouth (.5 dl)*

*butter for topping*

Grate the cheese with the steel blade and leave it in the bowl; there should be ½ cup after grating. Mix 1 teaspoon sugar and ¼ cup warm water in a 1-cup measure. Sprinkle the yeast on top of the water and stir lightly with a fork until dissolved. Let work for 5 to 10 minutes, or until bubbly.

Add to the processor bowl the flour, herbs, sugar, salt and butter. Blend together with on and off turns until the mixture resembles cornmeal. Blend in the egg. Add the proofed yeast and the vermouth and mix thoroughly. A ball will not form. Spoon into a greased 8- or 9-inch pie plate. Cover and let rise in a warm draft-free place (80° to 85°F.) until doubled in bulk, about 40 minutes. Dot with butter. Bake in a preheated 375°F. (196.6°C.) oven for 20 to 25 minutes. Cut into wedges and serve.

## CASSEROLE BATTER BREAD

Read the introduction
for yeast bread.

Makes 1 loaf.

This is a different, more porous bread. It is generally baked in a casserole, an 8-inch-square pan, or an 8-inch tube pan.

*1½ Tbsp. sugar (19 g)*
*½ cup warm water (1 dl)*
*  (105° to 115°F.)*
*1 pkg. or 1 Tbsp. active*
*  dry yeast (7 g)*
*2½ cups unbleached flour*
*  (375 g), sifted*
*½ tsp. salt*
*1 Tbsp. butter (15 g)*
*½ cup warm milk (1 dl)*

Mix 1½ tablespoons sugar with ½ cup warm water in a 1-cup measure. Sprinkle the yeast on the water and stir lightly with a fork until dissolved. Let work for 5 to 10 minutes, or until bubbly.

In the processor bowl fitted with the steel blade, blend the flour, salt and butter together with on and off quick turns until the mixture resembles cornmeal. Pour the proofed yeast into the dry ingredients and blend with 2 or 3 quick turns. With the machine running, pour the milk slowly through the tube until well mixed. It does not usually form a ball. Should the machine slow down, immediately remove the dough to a greased bowl. Cover and let rise until doubled in bulk, 40 to 60 minutes. Stir down and put in a greased 1½-quart casserole or greased tube pan or ring mold. Cover and let rise again in a warm place until doubled in bulk, about 1 hour.

Bake in a preheated 375°F. (190.6°C.) oven for about 1 hour. Test the bread for doneness by rapping the top and listening for a hollow sound. Remove from casserole or pans and cool on a rack.

# PITA BREAD

Read the introduction
for yeast bread.

Makes 16 pitas.

This Mideastern pocket bread may be filled with all manner of goodies—tuna, falafal and tahini, vegetables and cheese; or they can be split, buttered, and toasted in the oven to make "crackers."

½ tsp. sugar
¼ cup warm water (.5 dl)
  (105° to 115°F.)
1 pkg. or 1 Tbsp. active
  dry yeast (7 g)
3 cups unbleached flour
  (450 g)
½ Tbsp. salt
2 Tbsp. oil (24 g)
1 cup warm water (.24 l)

Mix ½ teaspoon sugar with ¼ cup warm water in a 1-cup measure. Sprinkle the yeast on the liquid and stir lightly with a fork until dissolved. Let work for 5 to 10 minutes, or until bubbly.

In the processor bowl fitted with the steel blade, blend the flour, salt and oil together with on and off quick turns until the mixture resembles cornmeal. Pour the proofed yeast into the dry ingredients and blend with on and off quick turns. With the machine running, pour the warm water slowly through the tube until a ball of dough forms, giving the liquid time to incorporate completely with the dry ingredients. (Depending on conditions—humidity, temperature and type of flour—the specified amount of liquid is not always needed. However, should the dough not form a ball, dribble in a little more warm water until it does.)

Knead the dough by allowing it to spin for about 1 minute. If the dough forces up the lid of the processor and stops the machine, readjust the lid and hold your hand over the feed tube while the machine is running.

Turn the dough out onto a lightly floured surface. If necessary, knead in a little more flour (no more than ¼ cup at a time) to make the dough soft, smooth and elastic. Shape dough into a ball and place in a greased warm bowl, turning it around to grease the entire surface of the dough. Cover with a towel and let the dough rise in a warm draft-free place (80° to 85°F.) until doubled in bulk, 1 to 2 hours.

Punch the dough down with your fist and pull the edges to the middle. Place the dough on a lightly floured surface. Cover and let rest for 10 minutes. Form dough into a 16-inch roll. Cut into 1-inch pieces and form each piece into a ball. With a rolling pin flatten each ball into a circle ¼ inch thick. Place on a floured surface and let rest uncovered for 30 minutes.

Place the oven rack on the lowest position and cover with aluminum foil. Preheat oven to 550°F. (267.7°C.) and put the circles, four at a time, on the rack; bake for 4 to 5 minutes, or until they have puffed. To brown the tops place under a hot broiler for 1 minute until brown. Watch carefully as they brown very rapidly. Immediately remove the pitas from the oven and cover with a cloth to keep them moist. Store in plastic bags at once to keep them soft. (If they are left unwrapped, they become hard very quickly.) They may be frozen.

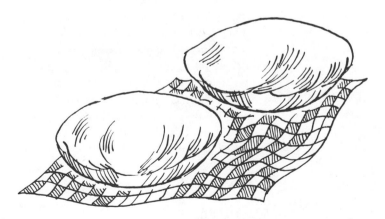

PITA BREAD

# WATER ROLLS

Read the introduction
for yeast bread.

Makes 18 rolls.

These rolls are great with soup and salad.

*1 Tbsp. sugar (13 g)*
*1 cup warm water (.24 l)*
  *(105° to 115°F.)*
*1 pkg. or 1 Tbsp. active*
  *dry yeast (7 g)*
*3½ cups unbleached flour*
  *(525 g), sifted*
*1 tsp. salt*
*2 Tbsp. butter (30 g)*
*2 egg whites, slightly*
  *beaten*
*1 egg yolk, for glaze*

Mix 1 tablespoon sugar in the warm water. Sprinkle the yeast on the water and stir lightly with a fork until dissolved. Let work for 5 to 10 minutes, or until bubbly.

In the processor bowl fitted with the steel blade, blend the flour, salt and butter with on and off quick turns. Pour the proofed yeast into the dry ingredients and blend with 2 or 3 quick turns. With the machine running, add the slightly beaten egg whites through the tube until a ball of dough forms, giving the egg whites time to incorporate completely with the dry ingredients. Should the dough not form a ball, dribble in a little warm water until it does.

Knead the dough by allowing it to spin for about 1 minute. If the dough forces up the lid of the processor and stops the machine, readjust the lid and hold your hand over the feed tube while the machine is running. Turn the dough out onto a lightly floured surface and knead by hand for 2 or 3 minutes. It may be necessary to knead in a little more flour to make a soft and elastic dough. Shape dough into a ball and place in a greased warm bowl, turning the ball around to grease the entire surface of the dough. Cover loosely with a towel and let rise in a warm draft-free place (80° to 85°F.) until doubled in bulk, about 1 hour.

Punch the dough down with your fist and pull

the edges to the middle. Place the dough on a lightly floured surface. Cover and let rest for 10 minutes. Form into round or pillow rolls and place 2 inches apart on a greased baking sheet. Cover and let rise again until doubled in bulk. Glaze with the egg yolk, mixed with 1 tablespoon water and a pinch of salt. Place a large shallow pan of boiling water on the bottom rack of the oven. Preheat oven to 450°F. (232°C.) and bake rolls on a rack above the water for 12 to 15 minutes. Cool rolls on a rack.

## BREAD STICKS

Read the introduction for yeast bread.

Makes about 30 bread sticks.

*1 tsp. sugar*
*¼ cup warm water (.5 dl)*
  *(105° to 115°F.)*
*1 pkg. or 1 Tbsp. active*
  *dry yeast (7 g)*
*3½ cups unbleached flour*
  *(525 g)*
*2 Tbsp. sugar (25 g)*
*1 tsp. salt*
*1 cup milk (.24 l)*
*4 Tbsp. butter (60 g)*
*1 egg white, stiffly beaten*
*1 egg yolk, for glaze*
*2 Tbsp. milk (28.3 g)*

Mix 1 teaspoon sugar and ¼ cup warm water in a 1-cup measure. Sprinkle the yeast on the water and stir lightly with a fork until dissolved. Let work for 5 to 10 minutes, or until bubbly.

In the processor bowl fitted with the steel blade, blend the flour, sugar and salt together with on and off quick turns. Pour the proofed yeast into the dry ingredients and blend with 2 or 3 quick turns. Scald 1 cup milk with the butter and cool to lukewarm. Add to the processor bowl along with the beaten egg white, and process until a ball of dough forms.

Knead the dough by allowing it to spin for about 1 minute. Turn the dough out onto a lightly floured surface and knead by hand for 2 or 3 minutes. The dough should be soft and smooth. Shape dough into a ball and place in a greased warm bowl, turning the ball around to grease the entire surface of the dough. Cover loosely with a towel and let rise in a warm draft-free place (80° to 85°F.) until doubled in bulk, about 2 hours.

Punch the dough down with your fist and pull the edges to the middle. Place the dough on a lightly floured surface. Cover and let rest for 10 minutes. Pinch off enough of the dough to make balls of Ping-Pong size, and roll and stretch each one into a cylinder about 6 inches long. Put the sticks on a greased baking sheet, leaving space between them. Glaze with egg yolk, mixed with 2 tablespoons milk. At this point bread sticks may be sprinkled with coarse salt or toasted sesame seeds. Let them rise again for 1½ hours. Put them in a preheated 425°F. (218.3°C.) oven for 10 minutes. Reduce heat to 350°F. (176.7°C.) and bake for 5 minutes more. Test one of the sticks; if it is not crisp all the way through, continue to bake. Cool on a rack.

## PRETZELS

Read the introduction
for yeast bread.

Makes 10 soft pretzels.

½ tsp. sugar
¼ cup warm water (.5 dl)
   (105° to 115°F.)
1 pkg. or 1 Tbsp. active
   dry yeast (7 g)
3½ cups unbleached flour
   (525 g)
½ Tbsp. salt
1 cup warm water
1 egg, for glaze
1 Tbsp. milk
coarse salt
caraway seeds
   (optional)

Mix ½ teaspoon sugar and ¼ cup warm water in a 1-cup measure. Sprinkle the yeast on the water and stir lightly with a fork until dissolved. Let work for 5 to 10 minutes, or until bubbly.

In the processor bowl fitted with the steel blade, blend the flour and salt together with quick on and off turns. Pour the proofed yeast into the flour and blend with 2 or 3 quick turns. With the motor running, pour the warm water through the tube until a ball of dough forms.

Knead the dough by allowing it to spin for about 1 minute. Turn the dough out onto a lightly floured surface and knead by hand for 2 or 3 minutes. The dough should be smooth and elastic. Shape dough into a ball and put in a greased warm bowl, turning the ball around to grease the entire surface of the dough. Cover loosely with a towel and let rise in a warm draft-free place (80° to 85°F.) until the dough is almost doubled in bulk, 50 to 60 minutes.

Turn the dough out onto a lightly floured surface and divide into 10 portions. Roll each portion into a rope about 12 inches long and ½ inch thick. Twist into pretzels and place on a greased baking sheet. Glaze pretzels with the egg mixed with 1 tablespoon milk. Sprinkle with coarse salt, and with caraway seeds if you like. Cover and let rise again in a warm place until doubled in bulk, about 1 hour. Bake in a preheated 475°F. (246.1°C.) for 12 to 15 minutes. Remove pretzels from the baking sheet and cool on a rack. They should be eaten soon after baking, or should be stored in a tightly covered container.

## ENGLISH MUFFINS

Read the introduction
for yeast bread.

Makes about 12 muffins.

*1 tsp. sugar*
*¼ cup warm water (.5 dl)*
  *(105° to 115°F.)*
*1 pkg. or 1 Tbsp. active*
  *dry yeast (7 g)*
*4 cups flour, sifted before*
  *measuring (600 g)*
*3 Tbsp. butter (45 g)*
*2 Tbsp. sugar (25 g)*
*½ Tbsp. salt*
*1 egg*
*1 cup warm milk (.24 l)*
*cornmeal*

Mix 1 teaspoon sugar and ¼ cup warm water in a 1-cup measure. Sprinkle the yeast on the water and stir lightly with a fork until dissolved. Let work for 5 to 10 minutes, or until bubbly.

In the processor bowl fitted with the steel blade, put 3½ cups flour, the butter, sugar, salt and egg. Blend with on and off quick turns. Pour the proofed yeast into the dry ingredients and blend with 2 or 3 quick turns. With the machine running, pour the warm milk slowly through the tube until a ball of dough forms, giving the liquid time to incorporate completely with the dry ingredients. (Depending on conditions—humidity, temperature and type of flour—the specified amount of liquid is not always needed. Should the dough not form a ball, dribble in a little more water until it does.)

Knead the dough by allowing it to spin for about 1 minute. If the dough forces up the lid of the processor and stops the machine, readjust the lid and hold your hand over the feed tube while the machine is running. Turn the dough out onto a lightly floured surface and knead by hand for 2 or 3 minutes, incorporating the remaining ½ cup flour to make a soft workable dough. Shape dough into a ball and put in a greased warm bowl, turning the ball around to grease the entire surface of the dough. Cover loosely with a towel and let rise in a warm draft-free place (80° to 85°F.) until doubled in bulk, about 1 hour.

Roll dough out on a floured surface to a sheet ¼ inch thick. Cut into 4-inch circles, and sprinkle tops with cornmeal. Cover and let rise on the floured surface until doubled in bulk. Heat an ungreased griddle to medium heat, sprinkle with cornmeal, and bake the muffins slowly for about 10 minutes on each side. Let cool. When ready to serve, split with a fork and toast.

## WHOLE-WHEAT ENGLISH MUFFINS

Read the introduction for yeast bread.

Makes about 12 muffins.

*1 tsp. sugar*
*¼ cup warm water (.5 dl)*
  *(105° to 115°F.)*
*1 pkg. or 1 Tbsp. active*
  *dry yeast (7 g)*
*2 cups whole-wheat flour*
  *(300 g)*
*2 cups unbleached flour*
  *(300 g)*
*3 Tbsp. butter (45 g)*
*1 Tbsp. sugar (13 g)*
*½ Tbsp. salt*
*1 cup warm milk (.24 l)*
*cornmeal*

Mix 1 teaspoon sugar with ¼ cup warm water in a 1-cup measure. Sprinkle the yeast on the water and stir lightly with a fork until dissolved. Let work for 5 to 10 minutes, or until bubbly.

In the processor bowl fitted with the steel blade, put 2 cups whole-wheat flour and 1½ cups unbleached flour, the butter, sugar and salt. Blend together with on and off quick turns until the mixture resembles cornmeal. Pour the proofed yeast into the dry ingredients and blend with on and off quick turns. With the motor running, slowly add the warm milk through the tube until a ball of dough forms, giving the liquid time to incorporate completely with the dry ingredients. (Depending on conditions—humidity, temperature and type of flour—the specified amount of liquid is not always needed. Should the dough not form a ball, dribble in a little more warm water until it does.)

Knead the dough by allowing it to spin for about 1 minute. Turn the dough out onto a lightly floured surface and knead by hand for 2 or 3 minutes, incorporating remaining ½ cup unbleached flour, if necessary, to make a soft workable dough. Shape dough into a ball and put in a greased warm bowl, turning the ball around to grease the entire surface of the dough. Cover loosely with a towel and let rise in a warm draft-free place (80° to 85°F.) until doubled in bulk, about 1 hour.

Roll dough out on a floured surface to a sheet ½ inch thick. Cut into 4-inch circles, and sprinkle tops with cornmeal. Cover and let rise on the floured surface until doubled in bulk. Heat an ungreased griddle to medium heat, sprinkle with cornmeal, and bake the muffins slowly for about 10 minutes on each side. Let cool. When ready to serve, split with a fork and toast.

## BAGELS
### (Rapidmix© Method)

Read the introduction for yeast bread.

Makes 12 bagels.

*4 cups flour (600 g), sifted*
*4 Tbsp. sugar (50 g)*
*1 tsp. salt*
*2 pkg. or 2 Tbsp. active*
  *dry yeast (14 g)*
*3 Tbsp. oil (36 g)*
*1 egg*
*1 cup warm water (.24 l)*
  *(120° to 130°F.)*
*2 Tbsp. sugar (25 g), for*
  *simmering*
*1 egg yolk, for glaze*

In the processor bowl fitted with the steel blade, put the flour, 4 tablespoons sugar, the salt and dry yeast. Blend with a quick on and off turn. Add oil and egg and blend with quick on and off turns. With the machine running add the warm water through the tube, and process until the dough forms a ball.

Knead the dough by allowing it to spin for about 1 minute. If the dough forces up the lid of the processor and stops the machine, readjust the lid and hold your hand over the feed tube while the machine is running. Turn the dough out onto a lightly floured surface and knead by hand for 2 or 3 minutes, or until the dough is smooth and elastic. The dough should be stiff. Shape it into a ball,

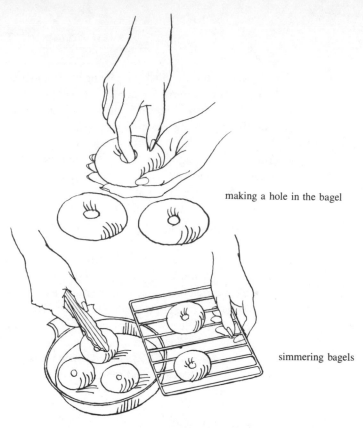

making a hole in the bagel

simmering bagels

place it in an *ungreased* bowl, and let it rise in a warm place for 20 minutes. (It should not double in bulk.)

Punch the dough down with your fist and pull the edges to the middle. Place the dough on a lightly floured surface, divide into 12 pieces, and shape into balls. Punch a hole in the center of each ball with your finger. Gently stretch the dough to make the hole the size of a quarter. Cover and let rise for 20 minutes.

Put a gallon of water and 2 tablespoons sugar into a large pot; bring to a boil and reduce heat to simmering. Gently simmer 4 bagels at a time for 7 minutes, turning them once. Drain them on a towel. Glaze bagels with the egg yolk, mixed with 1 tablespoon water. Bake on an *ungreased* baking sheet in a preheated 375°F. (190.6°C.) oven for 30 minutes.

# BRIOCHE

Read the introduction
for yeast bread.

Makes about 10 brioches.

*½ tsp. sugar*
*¼ cup warm water (.5 dl)*
  *(105° to 115°F.)*
*1 pkg. or 1 Tbsp. active*
  *dry yeast (7 g)*
*2⅓ cups flour (350 g)*
*⅓ cup sugar (70 g)*
*⅜ lb. cold butter (170 g)*
  *(1½ sticks)*, cut up
*3 eggs*
*1 egg yolk, for glaze*
*2 Tbsp. water (28.3 g)*

Mix ½ teaspoon sugar in ¼ cup warm water in a 1-cup measure. Sprinkle the yeast on the water and stir lightly with a fork until dissolved. Let work for 5 to 10 minutes, or until bubbly. In the processor bowl fitted with the steel blade, put the flour, ⅓ cup sugar and cold cut-up butter, and blend with on and off quick turns until the mixture resembles cornmeal. Add the proofed yeast and blend with 3 on and off quick turns. Put in the 3 whole eggs, and let the machine run for about 1 minute; if the motor stops consider the dough ready. Remove the spongy dough and drop it into a bowl. Cover with plastic wrap, then with a towel, and let rise in a warm place (80° to 85°F.). When dough is tripled in bulk, punch down and let rise again, covered, in the refrigerator for 6 hours or overnight.

Form two thirds of the dough into balls to fit *brioche* tins or muffin pans. Cut a deep cross in the center of each ball. With remaining dough, form small pear-shaped knobs; fit the pointed ends of the little knobs into the crosses, tamping them firmly in place. Let *brioches* rise uncovered in a warm spot until doubled in bulk. Glaze with the egg yolk beaten with 2 tablespoons water.

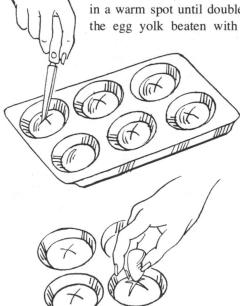

Bake in a preheated 375°F. (190.6°C.) oven for 25 minutes, or until nicely browned. If *brioches* brown too rapidly, cover the tops loosely with foil. The whole batch of dough can be baked in a ring mold if you prefer.

## BRIOCHE CRUST

*Brioche* wrapping is excellent for *coulibiac*, for sausage rolls, for some *croûtes*, for all manner of fillings.

Follow directions for Brioche. When the dough is removed from the refrigerator, immediately place it between 2 sheets of wax paper and roll out ¼ inch thick in the shape desired for filling. After filling, paint with an egg glaze, made with 1 egg yolk beaten with 2 tablespoons milk or cream, before baking.

## SOFT ROLLS

Read the introduction for yeast bread.

Makes 30 to 36 rolls.

This classical soft roll dough may be formed into cloverleaf, round, fantan, or Parker House rolls.

*1 tsp. sugar or honey*
*¼ cup warm water (.5 dl)*
*(105° to 115°F.)*
*1 pkg. or 1 Tbsp. active*
*dry yeast (7 g)*
*½ cup warm milk (1 dl)*
*3 Tbsp. butter (45 g)*
*4½ to 5 cups unbleached*
*flour (675 to 750 g)*
*3 Tbsp. sugar (38 g)*
*1 tsp. salt*
*3 eggs*
*melted butter, for topping*

Mix 1 teaspoon sugar or honey with ¼ cup warm water in a 1-cup measure. Sprinkle the yeast on the water and stir lightly with a fork until dissolved. Let work for 5 to 10 minutes, or until bubbly.

Scald the milk with the butter and cool to lukewarm.

In the processor bowl fitted with the steel blade, blend 3½ cups flour, the sugar and salt together with an on and off quick turn. Pour the proofed yeast into the dry ingredients and blend with on and off quick turns. Add the eggs, one at a time, turning the machine on and off after each addition. With the machine running, add the lukewarm milk and butter mixture. When the machine slows down, add ¼ cup flour and blend in. Repeat until 1 cup of additional flour has been incorporated, 4½ cups in all. Remove the sticky dough to a lightly floured surface and knead by hand until the dough is soft and elastic, adding an extra ½ cup flour if necessary. Gently shape into a ball and place it in a greased bowl. This dough is too soft to turn around in the bowl, therefore brush it with melted butter. Let dough rise in a warm place until doubled in bulk, about 1½ hours.

Punch the dough down with your fist and pull the edges to the middle. Place the dough on a lightly floured surface. Cover and let rest for 10 minutes. Shape as desired and place rolls on a greased baking sheet. Cover and let rise until doubled in bulk, about 40 minutes.

Brush rolls with melted butter and bake in a preheated 375°F. (190.6°C.) oven for 15 to 20 minutes. Remove from baking sheet and cool.

*Parker House Rolls*—Divide dough into halves. Roll out ¼ inch thick. Cut into rounds with a floured 2½-inch round cutter. Brush rounds with melted butter. Flour a dull knife and make an off-center crease in each round. Place small half over large half, press edges together, and press along crease. Place on a greased baking sheet. Let rolls rise, then bake according to directions.

*Cloverleaf Rolls*—Cut off small pieces of dough and shape into 1-inch balls. Place 3 balls in each greased muffin cup, smooth side up. Brush with melted butter. Let rolls rise, then bake according to directions.

*Fantans*—Cut dough into halves and roll out each half into a rectangle 9 x 12 inches and ¼ inch thick. Brush with melted butter. Cut each half into 3 strips 1½ inches wide. Stack the strips one on top of the other and even the ends with a sharp knife. Cut the stack with a string or sharp knife into 1½-inch lengths. Place pieces, cut side down, in greased muffin tins. Let rolls rise, then bake according to directions. No additional butter is needed when serving fantans.

*Crescents*—Divide the dough into thirds. Roll each portion into 3 circles each about 9 inches in diameter. Brush circles with melted butter and cut them into triangles. Roll up triangles from the base to the tip, shape into crescents, and place tip down on a greased baking sheet. Let rolls rise, then bake according to directions.

*Tulip Rolls*—Cut off pieces of dough and shape into 2¼-inch balls. Place in greased muffin tins, smooth side up. With floured scissors snip 2 deep cuts crosswise, making 4 points. Let rolls rise, and bake according to directions.

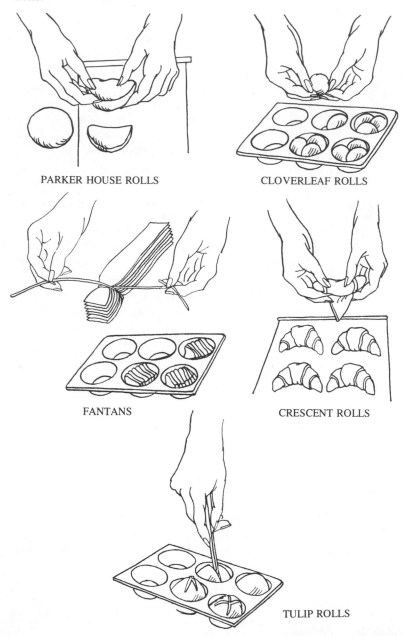

PARKER HOUSE ROLLS

CLOVERLEAF ROLLS

FANTANS

CRESCENT ROLLS

TULIP ROLLS

# BASIC SWEET DOUGH

Read the introduction
for yeast bread.

Makes 1 loaf or ring,
or about 16 buns.

This is a basic sweet dough which can be used in many ways. The dough can be made into rolls, buns, braids, coffee cakes, stollen, etc., filled or plain. They are often frosted with confectioners' icing or streusel topping.

*½ tsp. sugar*
*¼ cup warm water (.5 dl)*
  *(105° to 115°F.)*
*1 pkg. or 1 Tbsp. active*
  *dry yeast (7 g)*
*3 cups unbleached flour*
  *(450 g)*
*¼ cup sugar (50 g)*
*4 Tbsp. butter (60 g)*
*1 tsp. salt*
*1 egg*
*¾ cup warm milk (1.5 dl)*

Mix ½ teaspoon sugar with ¼ cup warm water in a 1-cup measure. Sprinkle the yeast on the water and stir lightly with a fork until dissolved. Let work for 5 to 10 minutes, or until bubbly.

In the processor bowl fitted with the steel blade, put the flour, ¼ cup sugar, the butter and salt. Blend together with on and off quick turns until the mixture resembles cornmeal. Add the egg and turn on and off 2 or 3 times. Pour the proofed yeast into the dry ingredients and blend with 2 or 3 quick on and off turns. With the machine running, pour the warm milk, little by little, through the tube until a ball of dough forms, giving the liquid time to incorporate completely with the dry ingredients. (Depending on conditions—humidity, temperature and type of flour—the specified amount of liquid is not always needed.) Should the motor slow down because the dough is too sticky, add ¼ cup flour at a time until the machine runs normally.

Knead the dough by allowing it to spin for about 1 minute. If the dough forces up the lid of the processor and stops the machine, readjust the lid and hold your hand over the feed tube while the machine is running. Turn the dough out onto a lightly floured surface and knead by hand for 2 or 3 minutes. If the dough seems too sticky, sprinkle more flour on top (no more than ¼ cup at a time), and knead by hand until the dough is smooth and elastic. Shape dough into a ball and place in a warm greased bowl, turning the ball around to grease the entire surface of the dough. Cover with a towel and let rise in a warm draft-free place (80° to 85°F.) until doubled in bulk, from 45 to 60 minutes.

Punch the dough down with your fist and pull the edges to the middle. Place the dough on a lightly floured surface. Cover and let rest for 10 minutes. Shape as desired. Cover and let rise again in a warm place until doubled in bulk, about 1 hour. Bake in a preheated 375°F. (190.6°C.) oven for the length of time given in the recipe for the variation you are using. (See variations that follow.)

## VARIATIONS ON BASIC SWEET DOUGH

Many coffee cakes are made with this dough. They may be frosted with Confectioners' Icing, or topped with Streusel or Honey Nut toppings (see Index). Shape dough after punching down and resting.

*Fruited Sweet Loaf*—Roll out the dough into a rectangle about 12 x 9 inches (30.5 x 23 cm). Brush with melted butter and scatter with 1 cup chopped candied citron (200 g) and 1 cup white raisins (100 g), plumped. Starting at the short end tightly roll up the dough jelly-roll fashion, pinching the ends at each turn. Flatten the ends and tuck under. Place seam side down in a greased loaf pan (8½ x 4½ x 2½ inches). Cover and let rise until doubled in bulk. Glaze with milk. Bake in a preheated 350°F. (176.7°C.) oven for 35 minutes, or until the loaf sounds hollow when thumped. Finish with Confectioners' Icing.

*Cinnamon Roll-Up*—Combine ½ cup light brown sugar (100 g) and 1 teaspoon ground cinnamon. Roll out the dough into a rectangle 9 x 12 inches (23 x 30.5 cm). Brush the dough with melted butter. Sprinkle the cinnamon-sugar mixture over the dough, leaving a 1-inch margin, and roll up and bake as for the Fruited Sweet Loaf. Frost with Confectioners' Icing.

*Citrus Loaf*—In the processor bowl fitted with the steel blade, grate the rind of ½ orange and 1 lemon. Leave in the bowl and proceed with the basic sweet dough recipe.

*Coffee Ring*—After the dough has risen for the first time, punch down and roll out into a rectangle 12 x 16 inches (30.5 x 40.6 cm). Brush with melted butter and spread with ¾ cup finely chopped nuts (100 g) and ¾ cup white raisins (75 g), plumped. Combine ½ cup sugar (100 g) and ½ tablespoon

COFFEE RING

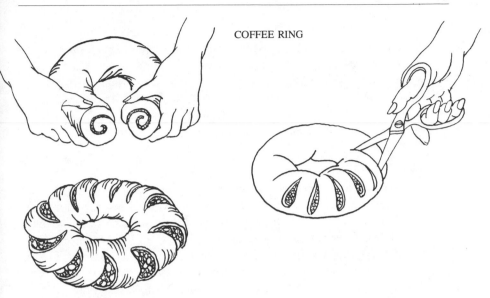

ground cinnamon, and sprinkle it over the filling. Roll up jelly-roll fashion, beginning at the long side, pinching ends at each turn. Form into a ring. Pinch edges to seal. With scissors snip the ring two thirds of the way through, every inch, twisting each section on its side. Cover and let rise in a warm place until doubled in bulk. Bake on a greased baking sheet in a preheated 350°F. (176.7°C.) oven for 25 to 30 minutes. Glaze with Confectioners' Icing while still warm.

*Pinwheels*—The same procedure may be used as for the Coffee Ring (preceding recipe), but instead of making a ring cut the rolled dough into pinwheels 1 inch thick. Cut the dough by placing a long piece of heavy thread or string under the rolled dough where the cut is to be made. Pull up the thread or the string, crisscross over the top of the dough, and pull quickly. This keeps the filling and dough together. Place the pinwheels in greased round or square baking pans and allow to rise until doubled in bulk. Brush with egg glaze and sprinkle with brown sugar. Bake in a preheated 350°F. (176.7°C.) oven for 15 to 20 minutes.

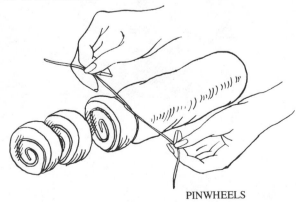

PINWHEELS

*Sticky Buns*—Make pinwheels (preceding recipe), and bake them in a greased baking pan (13 x 9 x 2 inches) which has been spread with a mixture of 1 cup dark brown sugar (200 g), ½ cup melted butter (120 g) and 2 tablespoons corn syrup (40 g). Place the pinwheels, cut side down, ½ inch apart. Cover and let rise until doubled in bulk. Bake in a preheated 375°F. (190.6°C.) oven for 25 to 30 minutes. Let buns stand in the pan for 10 minutes, then invert. Serve warm.

*Kolache*—For these filled buns from Czechoslovakia, any number of fillings may be used—fruits, nuts, jams, preserves. Experiment!

To the dry ingredients in the recipe add ½ teaspoon grated mace. After the first rising punch the dough down and let it rest for 10 minutes. One shape may be made by forming the dough into small balls about ¾ inch in diameter. Place on a greased baking sheet 2 inches apart. Cover and let rise until doubled in bulk. Flatten each ball and make an indentation in the center. Fill with your choice of filling. Bake in a preheated 400°F. (204.4°C.) oven for 12 to 15 minutes. Suggested fillings: Prune: partially cooked prunes, mixed with ¼ cup sugar (50 g) and ½ teaspoon ground cinnamon, chopped in the processor fitted with the steel blade. Honey Nut: 1½ cups nuts (180 g), coarsely chopped in the processor fitted with the steel blade, mixed with ¼ cup warm honey (80 g). Pocket and turnover shapes are also traditional for this dough.

KOLACHE

KULICH

*Saffron*—Add ½ teaspoon ground saffron, dissolved in 1 tablespoon brandy (14 g), to the liquid; or pound ½ teaspoon whole saffron with the sugar in the recipe. Saffron bread looks particularly good when braided and brushed with an egg-yolk glaze.

*Cardamom*—Add 1 teaspoon ground cardamom to the dry ingredients in the recipe.

*Bubble Loaf*—Sweet dough is appealing when baked in "bubbles." Pinch off enough of the dough to make balls of Ping-Pong size. Roll each ball in melted butter and sprinkle with sugar and cinnamon. Pile at random in a greased loaf pan or ring mold.

*Kulich*—A Russian holiday bread. After the first rising, knead into the dough ½ cup white raisins (50 g), plumped and floured, and ½ cup chopped blanched almonds (60 g). Divide the dough into halves and put in 2 greased 1-pound coffee cans, filling them not more than half full. Cover and let rise until doubled. Place cans on a baking sheet and bake in a preheated 375°F. (190.6°C.) oven for 30 to 40 minutes. Remove from cans and cool on a rack. Ice with Confectioners' Icing (see Index).

# SOUR-CREAM SWEET DOUGH

Read the introduction
for yeast bread.

Makes 1 ring or
about 18 buns.

A light base for sweet buns and tea rings

*1 tsp. sugar*
*½ cup warm water (1 dl)*
  *(105° to 115°F.)*
*1 pkg. or 1 Tbsp. active*
  *dry yeast (7 g)*
*3½ cups unbleached flour*
  *(525 g)*
*½ cup sugar (100 g)*
*1 tsp. salt*
*1 tsp. baking soda mixed*
  *with 2 Tbsp. water*
*2 Tbsp. butter (30 g)*
*1 egg*
*1 cup sour cream (250 g),*
  *lukewarm*

Mix 1 teaspoon sugar and ½ cup warm water in a 1-cup measure. Sprinkle the yeast on the water and stir lightly with a fork until dissolved. Let work for 5 to 10 minutes, or until bubbly.

In the processor bowl fitted with the steel blade, put the flour, ½ cup sugar, the salt, baking soda mixture and butter. Blend together with on and off quick turns until the mixture resembles cornmeal. Add the egg and turn on and off 2 or 3 times. Pour the proofed yeast into the dry ingredients and blend with 2 or 3 quick turns. Add the sour cream and process until a ball of dough forms. Should the motor slow down because the dough is too sticky, add ¼ cup flour at a time until the machine runs normally.

Knead the dough by allowing it to spin for about 1 minute. If the dough forces up the lid of the processor and stops the machine, readjust the lid and hold your hand over the feed tube while the machine is running. Turn the dough out onto a lightly floured surface and knead by hand for 2 or 3 minutes. If the dough seems too sticky, sprinkle more flour on top, a little at a time, and knead by hand until the dough is smooth. It will be a soft dough. Shape dough into a ball and place in a warm greased bowl, turning the ball around to grease the entire surface of the dough. Cover with a towel and let rise in a warm draft-free place (80° to 85°F.) until doubled in bulk, from 45 to 60 minutes.

Punch the dough down with your fist and pull the edges to the middle. Place the dough on a lightly floured surface. Let rest for 10 minutes. Shape as desired. Cover and let rise again in a warm place until doubled in bulk, about 1 hour.

Bake in a preheated 375°F. (190.6°C.) oven for the length of time given in the recipes for the variation you are using. (See variations on Basic Sweet Dough.)

## PORTUGUESE SWEET BREAD

Read the introduction for yeast bread.

Makes 1 round loaf.

A well-known delight for those who have ever been to Martha's Vineyard, Cape Cod, around Rhode Island, or in New Bedford, Massachusetts—wherever the Portuguese have settled in New England.

*1 tsp. sugar*
*¼ cup warm milk (.5 dl)*
  *(105° to 115°F.)*
*¼ cup warm water (.5 dl)*
  *(105° to 115°F.)*
*1 pkg. or 1 Tbsp. active*
  *dry yeast (7 g)*
*4 cups unbleached*
  *flour (600 g)*
*1 tsp. salt*
*⅓ cup sugar (75 g)*
*3 Tbsp. butter (45 g)*
*4 eggs*
*1 egg yolk, for glaze*

Mix 1 teaspoon sugar, ¼ cup milk and ¼ cup water in a 1-cup measure. Sprinkle the yeast on the liquid and stir lightly with a fork until dissolved. Let work for 5 to 10 minutes, or until bubbly.

In the processor bowl fitted with the steel blade, put 3½ cups flour, the salt, ⅓ cup sugar and the butter. Blend together with on and off quick turns until the mixture resembles cornmeal. Add the proofed yeast to the dry ingredients and blend with 2 or 3 on and off quick turns. Add the eggs, one at a time, processing after each addition. Add another ½ cup flour and blend quickly. The dough will be sticky. Turn out onto a lightly floured surface. Add ¼ cup flour, or as much as is needed to make a workable dough.

Knead the dough by hand for 2 or 3 minutes, until the dough is soft and elastic. Gently shape dough into a ball and place in a greased bowl; brush with butter. Let dough rise until doubled in bulk, about 1½ hours.

Punch down with your fist. Form into a round loaf and place in a well-buttered 1½-quart casserole, a Charlotte mold, or a 9-inch tube pan. Let double in bulk, 30 to 40 minutes. Brush with egg yolk glaze. Bake in a preheated 350°F. (176.7°C.) oven for 40 to 45 minutes, or until the loaf sounds hollow when tapped. Cool on a rack and store covered with plastic wrap.

# SWEDISH CARDAMOM COFFEE BREAD

Read the introduction
for yeast bread.

Makes 1 loaf.

*1 tsp. sugar*
*¼ cup warm milk (.5 dl)*
  *(105° to 115°F.)*
*1 pkg. or 1 Tbsp. active*
  *dry yeast (7 g)*
*3½ cups unbleached flour*
  *(525 g)*
*½ cup sugar (100 g)*
*¼ tsp. salt*
*1 tsp. ground cardamom*
*1 egg*
*1 cup milk (.24 l)*
*¼ lb. butter (1 stick or*
  *120 g)*
*1 egg white, for glaze*
*sugar, for topping*
*chopped almonds, for*
  *topping*

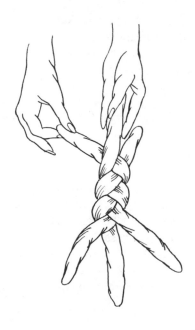

Mix 1 teaspoon sugar with ¼ cup warm milk in a 1-cup measure. Sprinkle the yeast on the milk and stir lightly with a fork until dissolved. Let work for 5 to 10 minutes, or until bubbly.

In the processor bowl fitted with the steel blade, put the flour, ½ cup sugar, the salt and cardamom. Blend with quick on and off turns. Add the egg and blend again with 2 or 3 on and off quick turns. Add the proofed yeast and quickly blend in.

Scald 1 cup milk with the butter and cool to lukewarm. With the machine running, slowly add the butter-milk mixture through the tube until a ball forms, giving the liquid time to incorporate completely with the dry ingredients. (Depending on conditions—humidity, temperature and type of flour—the specified amount of liquid is not always needed. However, should the dough not form a ball, dribble in a little more warm water until it does.)

Knead the dough by allowing it to spin for about 1 minute. If the dough forces up the lid of the processor and stops the machine, readjust the lid and hold your hand over the feed tube while the machine is running. Turn the dough out onto a lightly floured surface and knead by hand for 2 or 3 minutes. The dough will be sticky. It may be necessary to knead in a little more flour (no more than ¼ cup at a time) to make the dough smooth and elastic. Let rise until doubled in bulk, which may take from 2 hours to overnight.

Punch the dough down with your fist and pull the edges to the middle. Cover and let rest for 10 minutes.

The typical shape is a braided bread. Divide the dough into thirds and shape into balls. With both hands form the balls into long ropes by rolling the dough back and forth and pressing outward. Lay the 3 ropes 1 inch apart on a greased baking sheet. Braid loosely, beginning in the middle and working toward the ends. Cover loosely with a towel and let rise until doubled in bulk, about 1 hour. Brush with egg white mixed with 1 tablespoon water. Sprinkle with sugar and chopped almonds. Bake in a preheated 375°F. (190.6°C.) oven for 20 to 25 minutes. Remove from baking sheet and cool.

## EASTER BREAD

Read the introduction for yeast bread.

Makes 1 wreath.

In Italy it is traditional to eat the eggs with the bread on Easter.

*1 tsp. sugar*
*¼ cup warm water (.5 dl)*
  *(105° to 115°F.)*
*1 pkg. or 1 Tbsp. active*
  *dry yeast (7 g)*
*3 cups flour (450 g)*
*¼ cup sugar (50 g)*
*2 Tbsp. butter (30 g)*
*1 tsp. salt*
*2 eggs*
*1 cup warm milk (.24 l)*
*½ cup white raisins (50 g)*
*½ cup candied citron*
  *(100 g)*
*½ tsp. whole aniseeds*
*1 egg white, for glaze*
*6 raw eggs in the shell*
*Confectioners' Icing (see*
  *Index)*
*sprinkles or sugar for*
  *topping*

Mix 1 teaspoon sugar with ¼ cup warm water in a 1-cup measure. Sprinkle the yeast on the liquid and stir lightly with a fork until dissolved. Let work for 5 to 10 minutes, or until bubbly.

In the processor bowl fitted with the steel blade, put the flour, ¼ cup sugar, the butter and salt. Blend together with on and off quick turns until the mixture resembles cornmeal. Pour the proofed yeast into the dry ingredients and blend with on and off quick turns. Add the eggs, one at a time, turning the machine on and off after each addition. With the machine running, slowly add 1 cup milk through the tube until a ball of dough forms, giving the liquid time to incorporate completely with the dry ingredients. (Depending on conditions—humidity, temperature and type of flour—the specified amount of liquid is not always needed.)

Knead the dough by allowing it to spin for 1 minute. Turn the dough out on a lightly floured surface and knead it by hand for 2 or 3 minutes, adding more flour if necessary to make a soft dough. Shape dough into a ball and place in a warm greased bowl, rolling the ball around to grease the entire surface of the dough. Cover the bowl loosely with a towel and place in a warm draft-free spot (80° to 85°F.). Let the dough rise until doubled in bulk, 1 to 2 hours.

Punch the dough down and pull the edges to the middle. Place the dough on a lightly floured surface, and knead in the raisins, citron and aniseeds. Cover dough and let it rest for 10 minutes. Cut dough into halves. Form each half into a 24-inch rope. Twist the ropes and form into a wreath, pinching the ends together. Put on a greased baking sheet and glaze with the egg white mixed with 1 tablespoon water. Press the raw eggs, pointed ends down, into the dough, spacing them evenly around the wreath. They cook with the bread. Let the dough rise for 45 minutes. Bake in a preheated 350°F. (176.7°C.) oven for 30 minutes, or until golden. Cool on a wire rack. Frost with confectioners' icing and decorate with colored sprinkles or colored sugar.

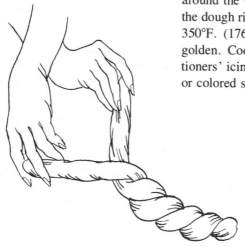

EASTER BREAD

# SAVARIN

Read the introduction
for yeast bread.

Makes 1 cake.

This is the big version of *baba au rhum*. The dough can be baked in
small molds for the traditional babas.

*1 tsp. sugar*
*¼ cup warm water (.5 dl)*
*(105° to 115°F.)*
*1 pkg. or 1 Tbsp. active*
*dry yeast (7 g)*
*¼ cup milk (.5 dl)*
*4 Tbsp. butter (60 g)*
*rind of 1 lemon*
*¼ cup sugar (50 g)*
*1¾ cups unbleached flour*
*(250 g)*
*2 egg yolks*

Mix 1 teaspoon sugar with ¼ cup warm water in a
1-cup measure. Sprinkle the yeast on the water and
stir lightly with a fork until dissolved. Let work for
5 to 10 minutes, or until bubbly. Scald the milk
with the butter and let cool to 105°F.

In the processor bowl fitted with the steel
blade, process the lemon rind and ¼ cup sugar
until lemon rind is finely chopped. Leave it in the
bowl and add the flour. Blend with quick on and
off turns. Add the proofed yeast and process
briefly. Add the egg yolks, one at a time, turning
the machine on and off after each addition. With
the machine running, slowly add the milk and butter mixture through the tube and blend for 10 seconds. This will be a sticky batter. Should the machine slow down, stop processing at once and
spoon the batter into a lightly greased and
floured bowl. Cover and let rise until batter is
doubled in bulk, 45 minutes to 1 hour.

Stir down and fill into a buttered Savarin pan
or 9-inch tube pan. Let dough rise until it almost
reaches the top of the pan, 30 to 40 minutes.
Bake in a preheated 375°F. (190.6°C.) oven for
40 to 50 minutes, or until a cake tester comes out
clean. Leave the cake in the pan and pierce several times with a skewer. Pour the syrup over it.
Let the cake soak in the pan for several hours.
Just before serving sprinkle with more rum or
brandy or Grand Marnier. Remove Savarin to a
serving platter and spoon any remaining syrup
over it. The center may be filled with fruits and/or
whipped cream.

SYRUP
*¾ cup water (1.5 dl)*
*1¾ cups sugar (350 g)*
*¼ cup dark rum, brandy*
*or Grand Marnier (.5*
*dl)*

Boil the water and sugar for 10 minutes, or until
syrupy, then add the rum or liqueur.

# ORANGE KUCHEN

Read the introduction
for yeast bread.

Makes 1 cake.

*1 tsp. sugar*
*¼ cup warm water (.5 dl)*
   *(105° to 115° F.)*
*1 pkg. or 1 Tbsp. active*
   *dry yeast (7 g)*
*rind of 1 orange, cut into*
   *strips*
*1 cup sugar (200 g)*
*¼ lb. butter (1 stick)*
   *(120 g)*
*3 cups unbleached flour*
   *(450 g)*
*½ tsp. grated nutmeg*
*4 eggs*
*¾ cup warm water*
   *(1.5 dl)*
*Orange Syrup (see Index)*

Mix 1 teaspoon sugar with ¼ cup warm water in a 1-cup measure. Sprinkle the yeast on the water and stir lightly with a fork until dissolved. Let work for 5 to 10 minutes, or until bubbly.

In the processor bowl fitted with the steel blade, process the strips of orange rind and 1 cup sugar for 30 seconds. Add the butter and blend until creamy. Add the flour and nutmeg and blend with on and off quick turns. Put in the eggs, one at a time, blending after each addition. Add the proofed yeast and blend in with 2 or 3 on and off quick turns. With the motor running, slowly add ¾ cup warm water through the tube until a ball of dough forms, giving the liquid time to incorporate completely with the dry ingredients. The dough will be sticky. Place dough in a greased bundt pan and let rise until the dough reaches the top of the pan, about 1 hour.

Bake in a preheated 350°F. (176.7°C.) oven for 45 to 60 minutes, or until the crust is golden. Remove from the pan and cool on a rack. Pierce the cake in several places and pour orange syrup over it. Repeat pouring to saturate the cake.

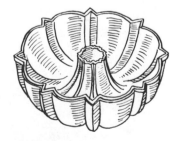

# SALLY LUNN

Read the introduction
for yeast bread.

Makes 1 large loaf.

This is a delicious light batter bread, elegant for tea, marvelous
toasted. Like angel-food cake, the bread is better if pulled apart with
2 forks.

*1 tsp. sugar*
*¼ cup warm water (.5 dl)*
*(105° to 115°F.)*
*1 pkg. or 1 Tbsp. active*
*dry yeast (7 g)*
*½ cup milk (1 dl)*
*4 Tbsp. butter (60 g)*
*1 tsp. salt*
*rind of 1½ lemons, cut*
*into strips*
*¼ cup sugar (50 g)*
*3½ cups unbleached flour*
*(525 g)*
*½ tsp. grated mace*
*3 eggs*

Mix 1 teaspoon sugar with ¼ cup warm water in a
1-cup measure. Sprinkle the yeast on the water and
stir lightly with a fork until dissolved. Let work for
5 to 10 minutes, or until bubbly.

Scald the milk with the butter and salt and
cool to lukewarm.

In the processor bowl fitted with the steel
blade, process the strips of lemon rind and ¼ cup
sugar until rind is finely chopped. Leave it in the
bowl and add 3½ cups of flour, the mace and the
proofed yeast; process briefly. Add the eggs, one
at a time, blending after each addition. With the
machine running, pour the milk-butter mixture
slowly through the tube and blend for 10 seconds.
This will be a sticky batter. Should the machine
slow down stop the processing and spoon the batter
into a greased bowl. Cover and let rise until doubled in bulk, about 1 hour. Stir down and put
dough in a greased and floured 10-inch tube pan or
bundt pan. Let dough rise until it reaches the top of
the pan. Bake in a preheated 350°F. (176.7°C.)
oven for 45 minutes. Remove from pan and cool
on a rack.

# HOT CROSS BUNS
## (Rapidmix© Method)

Read the introduction
for yeast bread.

Makes about 16 buns.

*3 medium-size potatoes*
*(about 1 lb. or .45 kg),*
*peeled*
*rind of 2 lemons*
*½ cup sugar (100 g)*
*5 cups unbleached flour*
*(750 g)*
*2 tsp. salt*
*2 pkg. or 2 Tbsp. active*
*dry yeast (14 g)*
*½ cup milk ( 1 dl)*
*½ cup potato*
*cooking water (1 dl)*
*¼ lb. butter (1 stick)*
*(120 g)*
*4 eggs*
*1 cup raisins (100 g)*
*1 egg, for glaze*
*Confectioner's Icing (see*
*Index)*

Cook the potatoes. Drain, but save the water. Shred the potatoes with the shredding disc and set aside. (There should be about 1 cup after shredding.)

In the processor bowl fitted with the steel blade, process the rind of 1 lemon and ¼ cup sugar until rind is finely chopped. Add 2½ cups of the flour, 1 teaspoon salt and 1 package or 1 tablespoon dry yeast. Blend well with quick on and off turns.

Heat the milk, ½ cup potato cooking water and the butter together to 120° to 130°F. (48.8° to 54.4°C.).Divide liquid into 2 portions. With the motor running pour 1 portion of the liquid through the tube. (Be sure the liquid is at the proper temperature.) Process quickly. Add ½ cup of the shredded potatoes and blend again. Add 2 eggs and let machine run until dough forms a ball. The dough will be very soft.

Knead the dough by allowing it to spin for about 1 minute. If the dough forces up the lid of the processor and stops the machine, readjust the lid and hold your hand over the feed tube while the machine is running. Turn the dough out onto a lightly floured surface and knead by hand for 2 or 3 minutes, adding a little flour to make a soft and elastic dough. Shape dough into a ball and place in a warm greased bowl, turning the ball around to grease the entire surface of the dough. Cover loosely with a towel.

Repeat the process with remaining ingredients, bringing remaining butter, milk and potato water to the proper temperature (120° to 130° F. or 48.8° to 54.4°C.). Let both batches rise in a warm draft-free place (80° to 85°F.) until doubled in bulk, about 1 hour.

Punch the dough down with your fist and pull the edges to the middle. Place the dough on a lightly floured surface and let rest for 10 minutes. Flour the raisins and knead them into the dough. Shape dough into buns. Place buns in greased 8-inch cake pans or greased 9-inch-square pans or on a greased baking sheet. Cover and let rise again until doubled in bulk, about 1 hour. Glaze with the egg yolk mixed with 1 tablespoon water. Bake in a preheated 375°F. (190.6°C.) oven for 25 minutes, or until browned. Remove from the pan and cool on a rack. Frost with confectioners' icing, making a cross on each bun.

## CROISSANTS

Makes about 12 medium-size croissants.

¾ lb. butter (3 sticks) (360 g)
pinch of sugar
¼ cup warm water (.5 dl) (105° to 115°F.)
2 pkg. or 2 Tbsp. active dry yeast (14 g)
3½ cups unbleached flour (525 g)
2 tbsp. butter (30 g)
½ tsp. salt
1 tsp. sugar
1½ cups milk (.36 l)
1 egg yolk, for glaze

To handle the butter easily, slice it with the slicing disc in the bowl of the processor. Place the little squares on a sheet of floured wax paper. Cover with another sheet of wax paper and gently roll or pat into an 8-inch square about ¼ inch thick. Chill.

Mix the pinch of sugar with the ¼ cup warm water in a 1-cup measure. Sprinkle the yeast on the water and let it dissolve. In the processor bowl fitted with the steel blade, put the flour, 2 tablespoons butter, the salt and 1 teaspoon sugar. Blend with 2 or 3 quick on and off turns until the mixture looks like cornmeal. Pour in the yeast mixture and blend with an on and off quick turn. With the motor running, slowly pour in the milk until a ball of dough forms. (You may not need all of it.) *Do not knead anymore!* Place the dough on a lightly floured surface. Cover and let rest for 10 minutes, then wrap and chill for 30 minutes.

Roll out the dough into a long rectangle, 3 times its width. Remove wax paper from chilled butter square, and divide the butter square into halves. Place 1 portion of the butter in the middle of the dough. Fold one third of the dough over the butter. Place the rest of the butter on top of this and cover by folding over the other third of the dough. Pinch the edges of the dough together.

Beginning at the short end parallel to the table and facing towards you, and using firm but not heavy strokes, roll the dough out into a rectangle 20 x 12 inches (50.8 x 30.5 cm). Fold each end to the center and fold again to make a book. Chill. This is a *turn*. Repeat 2 more times—folding, chilling, rolling—until you have made 3 turns. Carefully wrap the dough and chill overnight.

The next day roll out the dough and fold again twice more, making 2 more turns or 5 in all. Chill the dough for 1 hour.

Divide the dough into halves, leaving half in the refrigerator. Roll one half into a rectangle ⅛ inch thick and cut into 6-inch squares. Cut each square into 2 triangles. Starting with the base of the triangle (the longest side), roll loosely to form a cylinder and shape into crescents. Place crescents on a damp baking sheet. Make a tent over the croissants with towels supported by jars or bottles. Let dough rise in a warm place until doubled in bulk. Preheat oven to 425°F. (218.3°C.). Brush croissants with the 1 egg yolk beaten lightly with 1 teaspoon milk or cream. *Do not let the egg glaze drip on the sheet!* Bake for 15 to 20 minutes. Repeat with remaining dough.

Baked and cooled croissants may be sealed in airtight bags and frozen.

CROISSANTS

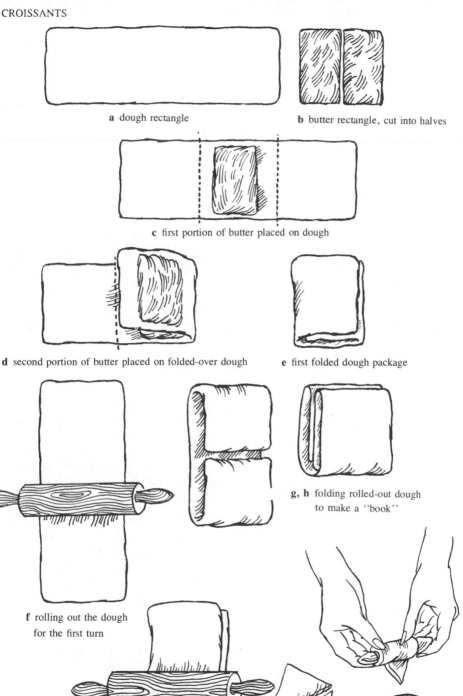

**a** dough rectangle

**b** butter rectangle, cut into halves

**c** first portion of butter placed on dough

**d** second portion of butter placed on folded-over dough

**e** first folded dough package

**g, h** folding rolled-out dough to make a "book"

**f** rolling out the dough for the first turn

**i** rolling out the "book" for another turn

**j** cutting the completed dough into triangles

**k** shaping the croissants

# DANISH PASTRY

Makes about 12 pastries.

¾ lb. butter (3 sticks)
  (360 g), cut up
⅓ cup flour (50 g)
pinch of sugar
1¼ cups milk (.30 l) (105°
  to 115°F.)
2 pkg. or 2 Tbsp. active
  dry yeast (14 g)
3½ cups flour (525 g)
¼ cup sugar (50 g)
1 egg
1 egg yolk, for glaze
Confectioners' Icing (see
  Index)

In the processor bowl fitted with the steel blade, blend the cut-up butter and ⅓ cup flour. Remove from bowl and spread on a sheet of wax paper. Top with another sheet of wax paper. Pat or roll into a rectangle 12 x 6 inches. Chill thoroughly.

Mix the pinch of sugar with the lukewarm milk. Spinkle yeast on the milk and let it dissolve. In the processor bowl fitted with the steel blade, blend 3½ cups flour and ¼ cup sugar with on and off quick turns. Add the egg and blend quickly. With the motor running, slowly add the yeast-milk mixture through the tube until a ball of dough forms. *Do not knead!* Place the dough on a lightly floured surface. It may be necessary to add a little more flour to make a soft and smooth dough. Cover and let rest for 10 minutes.

Roll out the dough into a 14-inch square (36 cm sq.). Peel wax paper from the chilled butter rectangle and place butter on the lower half of the dough. Fold the top half over the butter and pinch the edges together. With firm but not heavy strokes, roll the dough into a rectangle 20 x 12 inches (50.8 x 30.5 cm), starting at the short end. Fold the ends of the dough to meet in the middle, then fold together like a book. This is a *turn*. Chill for 20 minutes. Roll out again to a rectangle 20 x 12 inches (50.8 x 30.5 cm), always starting with the open short end parallel to the table and facing towards you. Check the dough for sticking. You may need to flour the surface. Fold again, both ends to the center, then folded into a book. If the butter seems soft, chill again. Roll out again into a rectangle 20 x 12 inches, and repeat process until you have rolled out the dough 5 times or 5 turns. Chill the last "book" until very cold.

Divide the dough into halves and put half in the refrigerator. Roll the other half into a sheet ⅛ inch thick. Shape into foldup envelopes, fans or "napkins," and fill.

Place pastry on an ungreased baking sheet and let it rise in a cool place until almost doubled in bulk. Brush with the egg yolk, beaten with a little cream. Bake in a preheated 450°F. (232.2°C.) oven until golden, about 8 minutes. When cool spread with confectioners' icing. Repeat with remaining dough.

## FILLINGS FOR DANISH PASTRY

Apricot preserves and chopped nuts
Chopped cooked prunes with a dash of honey
Almond paste with chopped almonds
Strawberry jam
Prepared poppy seed fillings

*Envelopes*—Roll out the dough ⅛ inch thick and cut into 4-inch squares. Spread with 1 tablespoon of filling. Fold corners in toward the center.

ENVELOPES

*Napkins*—Roll out the dough ⅛ inch thick and cut into 3-inch squares. Place 1 teaspoon filling in the middle of the square. Overlap 2 opposite corners of the pastry to the center and seal.

NAPKINS

*Fans*—Roll out the dough ⅛ inch thick and cut into rectangles 4 x 2 inches. Place 1 teaspoon filling lengthwise down the middle. Fold over and seal the edges. Curve in each end slightly, and slash the side opposite the sealed edge 4 times with floured scissors.

FANS

# 2

# QUICK BREADS

Quick breads, those leavened with baking powder or sour milk and soda, have the advantage of easy mixing and require no rising time. They do not keep as well as yeast breads, however, but they can be frozen and reheated in foil in a preheated 375°F. (190.6°C.) oven for 15 to 20 minutes.

Coffee cakes, muffins and biscuits are best when served warm. Fruit and nut loaves, wrapped in plastic and stored in the refrigerator overnight, improve with this slight "aging" and can be cut more easily.

For all recipes requiring baking powder, use double-acting baking powder.

A recipe based on 2 cups of flour will fill a loaf pan 9 x 5 x 3 inches or 2 small loaf pans. Remove the hot bread from the pan and let it cool on a rack before wrapping.

# IRISH SODA BREAD I

Makes 1 loaf.

This bread is usually made in a round loaf with a cross cut in the top. It is especially good when toasted.

*4 Tbsp. butter (60 g)*
*½ cup sugar (100 g)*
*2 cups unbleached flour (300 g)*
*1 tsp. salt*
*1 tsp. baking soda*
*1 Tbsp. baking powder (12 g)*
*2 cups whole-wheat flour (300 g)*
*2 cups sour milk (.48 l) or buttermilk (500 g) (approximately)*

Preheat oven to 350°F. (176.7°C.). In the processor bowl fitted with the steel blade, blend the butter and sugar. Sift together the unbleached flour, salt, baking soda and baking powder. Combine with the whole-wheat flour. Put half of the flour mixture in the processor bowl and blend with on and off quick turns. Add remaining flour and blend again. With the motor running, slowly pour 1½ cups of the milk through the tube and just enough more, if needed, to make a soft loose dough. The machine may slow down. If it does, stop processing and with floured hands turn the dough out onto a floured surface; knead lightly for 1 minute.

Shape the dough into a round loaf and put in a buttered 8-inch cake pan or on a buttered baking sheet. Make a cross on top of the bread with the processor steel blade. Bake in the preheated oven for about 1 hour, or until the loaf sounds hollow when tapped. Cool on a rack.

If you like 1½ cups of raisins or dried currants (150 g) may be incorporated into the dough.

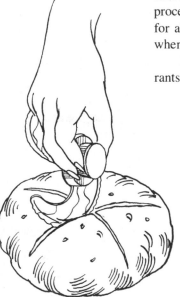

IRISH SODA BREAD
SLASHING THE TOP WITH THE STEEL BLADE

# IRISH SODA BREAD II

Makes 1 loaf.

¼ *lb. butter (1 stick)*
  *(120 g)*
*3 Tbsp. sugar (37 g)*
*1 egg*
*1¼ cups unbleached flour*
  *(187 g)*
*½ tsp. salt*
*1 tsp. baking soda*
*2½ cups whole-wheat*
  *flour (375 g)*
*1¼ cups sour milk (.30 l)*
  *or buttermilk (310 g)*
  *(approximately)*

Preheat oven to 400°F. (204.4°C.). In the processor bowl fitted with the steel blade, blend the butter and sugar. Add the egg and blend with on and off quick turns. Sift together the unbleached flour, salt and baking soda. Combine with the whole-wheat flour. Put half of the flour mixture in the processor bowl and blend with on and off quick turns. Add remaining flour and blend again. With the motor running, slowly pour 1 cup of the milk through the tube and just enough more, if needed, to make a soft loose dough. The machine may slow down. If it does, stop processing and with floured hands turn the dough out onto a floured surface; knead lightly for 1 minute. Shape the dough into a round loaf and put on a buttered baking sheet. Make a cross on top of the bread with the processor steel blade. Bake in the preheated oven for about 45 minutes, or until the loaf sounds hollow when tapped. Remove from the pan and let cool on a rack.

# FRUIT BREAD

Makes 1 loaf.

*1 cup fruit*
*6 Tbsp. butter (90 g), cut*
  *up*
*⅔ cup sugar (125 g)*
*2 eggs*
*3 Tbsp. cream (42 g)*
*2 cups flour (300 g)*
*2 tsp. baking powder*
*½ tsp. salt*
*½ cup chopped nuts*
  *(60 g) (optional)*

Preheat oven to 350°F. (176.7°C.) In the processor bowl fitted with the steel blade, chop the fruit. Set aside. Put the cut-up butter in the bowl. With the motor running, slowly add the sugar through the tube and process until creamy. Scrape down. Add the eggs, one at a time, and blend with on and off quick turns. Add the cream and chopped fruit and blend quickly. Sift together the flour, baking powder and salt and add to the bowl. Blend, turning the motor on and off 3 times, or until the flour just disappears. Fold in the nuts (chopped with the steel blade). Place the mixture in a greased loaf pan, 9 x 5 x 3 inches. Bake in the preheated oven for 50 minutes to 1 hour, or until a cake tester inserted in the center comes out clean.

## SUGGESTED FRUITS FOR FRUIT BREAD

*Applesauce*—Use 1 cup applesauce (.24 l), ¼ teaspoon ground cloves and ¼ teaspoon ground cinnamon. Substitute brown sugar for white. Omit the cream.

*Apricot-Orange*—Use 1 cup cut-up dried apricots (200 g), ¾ cup orange juice (1.5 dl) and 1 tablespoon grated orange rind. Omit the cream.

*Banana-Nut*—Use 1 cup mashed bananas (.24 l) and ½ cup chopped pecans (60 g).

*Prune*—Use 1 cup plumped drained prunes (.24 l), cut up, ¾ cup prune juice (1.5 dl) and 2 teaspoons grated lemon rind. Omit the cream.

BREAD PANS

4½ x 2½ x 2½ inches = 11 x 6.4 x 6.4 cm
7½ x 2½ x 2½ inches = 19 x 6.4 x 6.4 cm
9 x 5 x 3 inches = 23 x 13 x 7.6 cm

## MIXED FRUIT BREAD

Makes 1 loaf.

*rind of ½ lemon*
*1 cup mixed dried fruits*
   *(peaches, pears, apri-*
   *cots, prunes) (200 g)*
*6 Tbsp. butter (90 g), cut*
   *up*
*½ cup honey (160 g)*
*2 eggs*
*¾ cup sour cream (1.5 dl)*
*1 cup all-purpose flour*
   *(150 g)*
*1 tsp. baking powder*
*1 tsp. baking soda*
*½ cup whole-wheat flour*
   *(75 g)*

Preheat oven to 350°F. (176.7°C.). In the processor bowl fitted with the steel blade, chop the lemon rind and mixed dried fruits coarsely. Add the cut-up butter and the honey and blend with on and off quick turns. Add the eggs, one at a time, and blend with on and off quick turns. Quickly blend in the sour cream. Sift together the all-purpose flour, baking powder and baking soda. Add whole-wheat flour to the mixture. Put half of the flour mixture in the bowl and blend in with on and off quick turns. Add remaining flour mixture and again blend in with on and off quick turns. Spoon into a buttered loaf pan (8½ x 4½ x 2½ inches), and bake in the preheated oven for 1 hour, or until a cake tester comes out clean. Good with an orange or lemon Confectioners' Icing (see Index).

## LEMON BREAD

Makes 1 loaf.

*rind of 1½ lemons*
*1 cup granulated sugar*
   *(200 g)*
*6 Tbsp. butter (90 g), cut*
   *up*
*2 eggs*
*1½ cups flour (225 g),*
   *sifted*
*½ Tbsp. baking powder*
*½ tsp. salt*
*½ cup milk (1 dl)*
*¾ cup white raisins*
   *(50 g), floured*

Preheat oven to 350°F. (176.7°C.). In the processor bowl fitted with the steel blade, process the lemon rind and granulated sugar until the rind is chopped, about 30 seconds. Add the butter and blend until creamy. Add the eggs, one at a time, and blend with on and off quick turns after each addition. Sift together the flour, baking powder and salt. Add to the bowl and blend, turning the motor on and off 3 times, or until the flour just disappears. Pour in the milk and blend quickly. Fold the raisins into the batter. Spoon into a buttered loaf pan (8½ x 4½ x 2½ inches), and bake in the preheated oven for 1 hour.

LEMON GLAZE
½ cup confectioners'
  sugar (80 g)
½ Tbsp. warm water
1 tsp. lemon juice

Mix confectioners' sugar, water and lemon juice to make a glaze. Brush over the bread when it has cooled.

## CANDIED ORANGE BREAD

Makes 2 small loaves.

rind of 3 oranges
rind of 1 lemon
2 cups sugar (400 g)
¼ cup water (.5 dl)
2 Tbsp. butter (30 g)
1 egg
1 cup milk (.24 l)
3 cups unbleached flour
  (450 g)
4 tsp. baking powder
  (16 g)
½ tsp. salt

Preheat oven to 350°F. (176.7°C.). Cover the orange and lemon rinds with water and cook until tender. Drain. Make sugar syrup with 1 cup of the sugar and ¼ cup water. Add the citrus rinds to the syrup and cook until the syrup is almost absorbed.

In the processor bowl fitted with the steel blade, cream the butter and remaining 1 cup sugar. Add citrus rinds and process, coarsely chopping the rinds. Add the egg and blend with quick on and off turns. With the machine running add the milk through the tube. Sift the flour with the baking powder and salt, and put it in the bowl. Incorporate quickly with on and off quick turns. Place in 2 greased small loaf pans (4½ x 2½ x 2½ inches). Bake for 35 minutes, or until a cake tester comes out clean.

## GINGERBREAD

Makes 9 servings.

¼ lb. butter (1 stick)
  (120 g)
½ cup sugar (100 g)
2 eggs
½ cup dark molasses
  (160 g)

Preheat oven to 350°F. (176.7°C.). In the food processor bowl fitted with the steel blade, blend the butter and sugar until smooth. Add the eggs and molasses and blend for 3 seconds. Add the sour milk or buttermilk to which the dissolved baking soda has been added. Blend until incorporated.

½ cup sour milk *(1 dl) or*
*buttermilk, or ½ cup*
*milk plus ½ tsp. lemon*
*juice or vinegar*
*1 tsp. baking soda dis-*
*solved in 2 Tbsp. hot*
*water*
*1¾ cups flour (270 g),*
*sifted*
*½ tsp. ground cinnamon*
*1 tsp. ground ginger*
*¼ tsp. grated nutmeg*
*½ tsp. salt*

Sift the flour with the cinnamon, ginger, nutmeg and salt, and add to the mixture in the bowl. Blend, turning the machine on and off 3 times, or until the flour is just incorporated. *Do not overbeat!* Pour the batter into a greased 9-inch-square pan. Bake in the preheated oven for 40 minutes, or until a cake tester inserted in the center comes out clean.

## SPICED NUT LOAF

Makes 2 small loaves.

*1 cup shelled nuts (120 g)*
*½ lb. butter (2 sticks)*
*(227 g)*
*1½ cups brown sugar*
*(300 g)*
*1 cup molasses (240 g)*
*3 eggs, separated*
*1 tsp. baking soda, mixed*
*with 1 Tbsp. hot water*
*3 cups flour (450 g)*
*1 tsp. salt*
*1 tsp. ground cinnamon*
*1 tsp. ground cloves*
*1 cup raisins (100 g)*

Preheat oven to 350°F. (176.7°C.). Coarsely chop the nuts and set aside. In the food processor fitted with the steel blade, blend the butter and sugar until smooth. Add the molasses and blend quickly. Add the egg yolks, one at a time, and blend after each addition. Scrape down. Add the baking soda dissolved in water and blend quickly. Sift together the flour, salt and spices. Add to the mixture in the bowl and blend, turning the machine on and off 3 times, or until the flour is just incorporated. *Do not overbeat!*

Fold in by hand the floured raisins and chopped nuts. Beat the egg whites by hand until stiff but not dry, and fold them into the batter. Spoon into 2 greased small loaf pans (4½ x 2½ x 2½ inches). Bake for 1 hour. Remove from the pans and cool on a rack.

# SHORTCAKE DOUGH (BAKING POWDER BISCUITS)

Makes about 12 biscuits.

2 cups flour (300 g)
1 Tbsp. baking powder
   (12 g)
½ tsp. salt
½ tsp. cream of tartar
1 Tbsp. sugar (13 g)
¼ lb. butter (1 stick)
   (120 g), cut up
¾ cup milk (1.5 dl)
milk or melted butter, for
   glaze

Preheat oven to 450°F. (232.2°C.). Sift together the dry ingredients. In the processor bowl fitted with the steel blade, put the dry ingredients and the cut-up butter, and blend with on and off quick turns until the mixture resembles cornmeal. With the motor running, slowly pour the milk through the tube. The dough will be spongy. With floured hands turn out the dough onto a lightly floured surface and gently knead, making no more than 10 folds. Roll out the dough to ½-inch thickness. Cut with a floured biscuit cutter, being careful not to twist the cutter. Place on a lightly greased baking sheet, and glaze with milk or melted butter. Bake in the preheated oven for 10 to 12 minutes.

## LARGE SHORTCAKE

Prepare Shortcake Dough and add ½ cup (60 g) ground almonds. Divide the dough into halves and bake in 2 lightly greased 8-inch cake pans. Place sugared fruit between the layers and over them, and top with whipped cream.

## COBBLER TOPPING (DROP BISCUITS)

To make drop biscuits, follow the recipe for Shortcake Dough (Baking Powder Biscuits), but increase the milk to 1 cup (.24 l). Spoon batter over hot fruit filling. Bake at 400°F. (204.4°C.) for 30 minutes. Serve apple cobbler with Spice Sauce; peach or cherry cobbler with Wine Custard Sauce; cranberry cobbler with Banana Sauce (see Index for sauces).

# MUFFINS

The advantage of a food processor for making muffins is the ease with which solid ingredients—fruits, nuts, cheeses, herbs, etc.—may be incorporated with the liquid ingredients, sugar and shortenings. However, the processed ingredients must be stirred by hand into the dry mixture in a separate bowl to get the lumpy batter that is essential for good muffins.

## BASIC MUFFINS

Makes about 12 muffins.

*1¾ cups unbleached flour (270 g), or 2 cups cake flour*
*¾ tsp. salt*
*2 tsp. baking powder*
*¼ cup sugar (50 g)*
*4 Tbsp. butter (60 g)*
*2 eggs*
*¾ cup milk (1.5 dl)*

Preheat oven to 400°F. (204.4°C.). Sift together in a large bowl the flour, salt and baking powder.

In the processor bowl fitted with the steel blade, cream the sugar and butter for 5 seconds. Add the eggs, one at a time, and blend with 3 or 4 on and off quick turns after each addition. Add the milk and blend again with 3 or 4 quick on and off turns.

By hand stir the liquid mixture into the dry ingredients until just mixed. Spoon into greased muffin tins until two thirds full. Bake in the preheated oven for 20 to 25 minutes.

## VARIATIONS ON BASIC MUFFINS

*Blueberry*—Stir in 1 cup fresh or drained canned blueberries just before spooning batter into the tins.

*Dried Fruit—Date, Prune, Apricot*—Add ¼ pound cut-up fruit (113 g); process fruit with the sugar and butter.

*Apple*—Sift 1 teaspoon ground cinnamon and ¼ teaspoon grated mace with the flour. Add 1 cup chopped apples, chopped in the processor bowl fitted with the steel blade, just before spooning batter into the tins. Top with Streusel topping (see Index).

*Peanut Butter*—Add ½ cup peanut butter (128 g) with the milk, and blend in well.

*Cheese*—Omit the sugar. In the processor bowl fitted with the steel blade, grind coarsely ¼ pound (113 g) cut-up Cheddar cheese with 3 or 4 on and off quick turns. There should be 1 cup grated cheese. Add to the liquid ingredients and process as for basic muffins.

*Orange-Lemon*—Process the rind of ½ orange or 1 lemon with the sugar and add 1 tablespoon orange or lemon juice.

*Banana*—Purée 2 bananas with the sugar and butter.

*Nut*—Chop 1 cup shelled nuts (120 g) with the steel blade; set aside. Fold nuts into muffin mixture just before spooning batter into the tins.

*Herbs*—Omit the sugar. Blend 1 teaspoon minced fresh herbs, or ½ teaspoon dried, of your choice, 1 tablespoon snipped fresh chives and 1 small handful of fresh parsley with the butter.

## BACON-CORN MUFFINS

Makes about 12 muffins.

*1 cup unbleached flour*
  *(150 g)*
*4 tsp. baking powder*
  *(15 g)*
*½ tsp. salt*
*1 cup cornmeal (180 g)*
*4 slices of bacon*
*2 Tbsp. bacon fat*
*1 egg*
*1 cup milk (.24 l)*

Preheat oven to 425°F. (218.3°C.). Sift together the flour, baking powder and salt into a large bowl; add the cornmeal.

Sauté bacon, saving the fat. Drain the bacon on paper towels and break it into pieces. Put bacon pieces into the processor bowl fitted with the steel blade, and chop coarsely with 2 on and off quick turns. Add the bacon fat, the egg and milk, and blend with 2 or 3 on and off quick turns. Pour into the cornmeal and flour mixture. Stir until just moistened. Spoon into preheated greased muffin pans, corn-stick pans or heatproof glass custard cups. Bake in the preheated oven for 25 minutes.

## CHEESE AND HOT-TOMATO MUFFINS

Makes about 36 small muffins.

*2 cups unbleached flour*
  *(300 g)*
*1 Tbsp. baking powder*
  *(12 g)*
*½ tsp. salt*
*4 oz. sharp cheese* (113 g)
*1 cup Bloody Mary mix*
  *(.24 l)*
*1 egg*

Preheat oven to 400°F. (204.4°C.). Sift together the flour, baking powder and salt, into a large bowl. In the processor bowl fitted with the shredding disc, shred the cheese; there should be 1 cup. Add cheese to the flour.

In the processor bowl fitted with the steel blade, put the Bloody Mary mix and the egg. Blend with 2 or 3 on and off quick turns. Pour the liquid into the dry ingredients and stir quickly until just moistened. Spoon into greased miniature muffin tins, or drop by teaspoons onto a greased baking sheet. Bake in the preheated oven for 10 to 15 minutes. Excellent with salads or drinks.

# HONEY BRAN MUFFINS

Makes about 12 muffins.

*1 cup unbleached flour
(150 g)
2 tsp. baking powder
½ tsp. salt
1 cup bran* (any kind)
*(120 g)
1 cup shelled walnuts
(120 g)
2 Tbsp. shortening (30 g)
½ cup honey (160 g)
1 egg
½ cup milk (1 dl)*

Preheat oven to 425°F. (218.3°C.). Sift together the flour, baking powder and salt into a large bowl. Add the bran.

In the processor bowl fitted with the steel blade, chop the walnuts. Add the shortening, honey, egg and milk, and blend quickly with 3 on and off quick turns. Scrape down, and give the mixture one more on and off quick turn. Pour the liquid and nut mixture into the dry ingredients. Stir quickly until just moistened. Spoon into greased muffin tins until two thirds full. Bake in the preheated oven for 20 to 25 minutes.

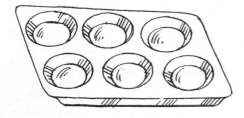

# 3

# CAKES AND TORTES

———•◦•———

A food processor is a natural for making nut tortes, fruited cakes and crumb-based cakes. The usual shortening and baking-powder cakes can also be made in the food processor, if certain precautions are taken. Emulsified shortenings and oil, when called for, may be used in place of butter. However, angel-food type cakes are not the forte of the processor.

All ingredients should be at room temperature. Sift the flour when indicated, and measure. Put the sugar, flavoring and shortening in the processor bowl, fitted with the steel blade, and process until creamy. When using citrus rinds process first with the sugar and then add the shortening and the flavoring. Add the eggs, one at a time, and process 5 seconds after each addition. Add the liquid and process for 3 seconds. Pour half of the dry ingredients over the liquid mixture in the processor bowl and blend with 2 on and off quick turns. Add the remaining dry ingredients and blend in with 2 or 3 quick turns, or until the flour just disappears.

# BASIC YELLOW CAKE

Makes 1 cake.

¼ lb. butter (1 stick)
  (120 g)
1½ cups sugar (300 g)
2 eggs
1 tsp. vanilla extract
1 cup milk (.24 l)
2½ cups cake flour
  (300 g), sifted
1 Tbsp. baking powder
  (12 g)
1 tsp. salt

Preheat oven to 350°F. (176.7°C.). In the processor bowl fitted with the steel blade, process the butter and sugar until smooth. Scrape down. Add the eggs, one at a time. Blend with on and off quick turns. Add vanilla and milk and blend. Sift together the flour, baking powder and salt and add to the mixture in the bowl. Blend by turning the machine on and off 3 times, or until the flour is just incorporated. *Do not overbeat!* Pour batter into 2 greased 8-inch cake pans, or 1 greased 9-inch square pan. Bake in the preheated oven for 30 to 35 minutes for 8-inch layers, or for 40 to 45 minutes for a 9-inch-square pan, or until a cake tester comes out clean.

# BASIC WHITE CAKE

Follow the instructions for the Yellow Cake, but substitute 4 egg whites for the 2 whole eggs.

## VARIATIONS ON BASIC YELLOW OR WHITE CAKE

*Orange*—Chop the rind of ½ orange with the sugar, then add the butter.

*Lemon*—Chop the rind of 1 lemon with the sugar, then add the butter. Substitute lemon extract for vanilla extract.

*Spice*—Sift ½ teaspoon each of ground cloves, cinnamon and ginger with the flour.

*Fruit*—Chop 1 cup drained, cooked dried apricots or prunes (.24 l) with the sugar, or fold 1 cup floured plumped raisins into the batter.

# UPSIDE-DOWN CAKE

Makes 1 large cake.

*1 recipe Yellow Cake*
*1 lb. (.453 kg) canned*
*apricots, pears,*
*peaches, pineapple*
*slices or cherries, or*
*peeled fresh apples*
*4 Tbsp. butter (60 g),*
*melted*
*½ cup brown sugar*
*(100 g)*

Make the batter for yellow cake. In the processor bowl fitted with the slicing disc, slice the fruit. Melt the butter and sugar in the bottom of a 10-inch springform pan. Arrange the sliced fruit in an attractive pattern in the pan and spoon in the cake batter. Put a piece of foil under the pan in case the pan leaks. Bake according to the recipe for yellow cake. Remove the cake from the oven and invert onto a serving plate. Do not remove the pan for 10 minutes.

# SOUR-CREAM CAKE

Makes 1 cake.

*¼ lb. butter (1 stick)*
*(120 g)*
*1½ cups sugar (300 g)*
*2 eggs*
*1 cup sour cream (.24 l)*
*1 tsp. vanilla extract*
*2 cups cake flour (240 g),*
*sifted*
*1 tsp. baking powder*
*1 tsp. baking soda*

Preheat oven to 350°F. (176.7°C.). In the container fitted with the steel blade, process the butter and sugar until smooth. Add the eggs, one at a time, blending after each addition. Add sour cream and vanilla and process with on and off quick turns. Sift together the flour, baking powder and baking soda. Add to the mixture in the container and blend, turning the machine on and off 3 times, or until the flour is just incorporated. *Do not overbeat!* Spoon into a greased and floured 8-inch tube pan. Bake in the preheated oven for 35 minutes, or until a cake tester inserted in the center comes out clean.

## VARIATIONS ON SOUR-CREAM CAKE

*Spice*—Use brown sugar instead of white and add 1 teaspoon ground cinnamon, 1 teaspoon ground allspice, ½ teaspoon ground cloves, ½ teaspoon grated nutmeg.

*Orange-Lemon*—Put the rind of 1 lemon and ½ orange in the processor bowl fitted with the steel blade. Add the sugar and process for 30 seconds. Add the butter and blend until creamy. Proceed with the recipe.

# CHOCOLATE SOUR-CREAM CAKE

Makes 1 cake.

¼ lb. butter (1 stick)
  (120 g)
2½ cups brown sugar
  (500 g)
3 eggs
1 cup sour cream (.24 l)
3 oz. unsweetened
  chocolate (85 g),
  melted
1 cup hot water (.24 l)
2¼ cups cake flour
  (270 g), sifted
2 tsp. baking soda
½ tsp. salt

Preheat oven to 350° F. (176.7°C.). In the container fitted with the steel blade, process the butter and sugar until smooth. Add the eggs, one at a time, blending after each addition. Scrape down. Add the sour cream and melted chocolate and process with on and off quick turns. Add hot water and blend. Sift together the flour, baking soda and salt. Add to the mixture in the container and blend, turning the machine on and off 3 times, or until the flour is just incorporated. *Do not overbeat!* Bake in a greased and floured 8-inch tube pan for 35 minutes, or until a cake tester comes out clean. Cool and frost.

FROSTING
¼ lb. butter (1 stick)
  (120 g)
4 oz. unsweetened
  chocolate (113 g)
1 lb. confectioners' sugar
  (.453 kg)
2 tsp. vanilla extract
milk

Melt the butter and chocolate together. In the processor bowl fitted with the steel blade, put the cooled melted chocolate-butter mixture, confectioners' sugar and vanilla. Blend thoroughly. Gradually add milk until the frosting is of spreading consistency.

CAKE PANS

8 inches = 20.3 cm     9 inches = 23 cm     10 inches = 25.4 cm
jelly-roll pan, 15 x 10 inches = 38 x 25.4 cm
12 x 8 x 2 inches = 30.5 x 20.3 x 5 cm

# MOCHA CHIFFON CAKE

Makes 1 large cake.

2½ cups cake flour
  (300 g), sifted
1 Tbsp. baking powder
  (12 g)
½ tsp. salt
1¼ cups sugar (250 g)
1 Tbsp. instant coffee
  powder
9 Tbsp. cocoa powder
  (45 g)
½ cup plus 3 Tbsp. oil
  (165 g)
5 eggs, separated
¾ cup warm water
  (1.5 dl)
1 extra egg white
½ tsp. cream of tartar

Preheat oven to 325°F. (162.8°C.). Sift the flour, baking powder, salt, 1 cup of the sugar, the powdered coffee and cocoa, and put in the processor bowl fitted with the steel blade. Add the oil and blend with 1 on and off quick turn. Add the egg yolks and blend with quick on and off turns. Add the warm water and blend quickly.

Beat the 6 egg whites and the cream of tartar with a mixer or rotary beater until stiff but not dry, adding remaining ¼ cup sugar, 1 tablespoon at a time.

Fold the egg whites into the cake batter in a separate bowl. Bake in an ungreased 10-inch tube pan for 1 hour, or until a cake tester inserted in the center comes out clean. Invert pan and cool the cake. Top with mocha whipped cream or a coffee glaze.

## VARIATIONS ON MOCHA CHIFFON CAKE

*Spice Chiffon Cake*—Omit coffee, cocoa and 3 tablespoons oil. Sift ½ teaspoon grated nutmeg, ½ teaspoon ground cloves and ½ teaspoon ground allspice with the flour.

*Orange or Lemon*—Omit coffee, cocoa and 3 tablespoons oil. Process rind of 1 lemon or ½ orange with the sugar before adding sugar to the flour.

# DEEP CHOCOLATE CAKE

Makes 1 cake.

¼ lb. butter (1 stick)
  (120 g)
2 cups sugar (400 g)
2 eggs
1 cup prepared strong hot
  coffee (.24 l)
2 cups cake flour (240 g),
  sifted
1 cup cocoa powder
  (80 g)
2 tsp. baking soda
½ tsp. salt
1 tsp. baking powder

Preheat oven to 350°F. (176.7°C.). In the processor bowl fitted with the steel blade, cream the butter and the sugar. Add the eggs, one at a time, and blend with on and off quick turns. Add coffee. Sift together the flour, powdered cocoa, baking soda, salt and baking powder, and add to the mixture in the bowl. Blend, turning the machine on and off 3 times, or until the flour is just incorporated. *Do not overbeat!* Pour the thin batter into 2 greased 8-inch cake pans. Bake for 40 minutes, or until a cake tester inserted in the center comes out clean. Frost with a butter frosting (see Index).

## GOLD CAKE

Makes 1 cake.

6 Tbsp. butter or shortening (90 g), cut up
1 cup sugar (200 g)
4 eggs
1⅔ cups cake flour
  (200 g), sifted
2 tsp. baking powder
¼ tsp. salt
½ cup milk (1 dl)

Preheat oven to 350°F. (176.7°C.). Cream the butter or shortening with the sugar in the processor bowl fitted with the steel blade. With the motor running, add the eggs and blend with 4 or 5 quick on and off turns. Sift together the flour, baking powder and salt. Divide into 2 portions. Add one portion to the egg-sugar mixture and blend with 2 quick on and off turns. Pour in ¼ cup of the milk. Blend quickly. Scrape down the sides of the bowl. Pour in remaining flour mixture and blend with 2 quick on and off turns. Scrape down. Add remaining ¼ cup milk. Blend quickly. Bake in a buttered loaf pan for 45 minutes, or until a cake tester comes out clean. Frost as desired.

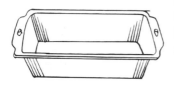

# POUND CAKE

Makes 1 cake.

*rind of 1 lemon, cut up*
*2 cups sugar (400 g)*
*½ lb. butter (2 sticks)*
*(227 g), cut up*
*5 whole eggs*
*1 tsp. vanilla extract*
*2 cups cake flour (240 g),*
*sifted*

Preheat oven to 300°F. (148.9°C.). In the processor bowl fitted with the steel blade, process the cut-up lemon rind and the sugar for 30 seconds. Scrape down the sides of the bowl. Add the cut-up butter. Cream together well for about 30 seconds. With the motor running add the eggs, one at a time, through the tube. Scrape down. Add vanilla and blend with 1 on and off turn. Pour in the sifted flour and blend, turning the machine on and off 2 times. Scrape down and turn the machine on and off once more. *Do not overbeat!* Spoon into a well-buttered 8-inch false-bottom tube pan or a loaf pan. Bake for 1½ to 1¾ hours; do not open the oven until after 1½ hours of baking. Test with a cake tester. Cool the cake, then remove from pan. Frost with citrus Confectioners' Icing (see Index), or dust with confectioners' sugar.

## VARIATIONS ON POUND CAKE

*Bourbon*—Omit lemon rind and add 2 tablespoons bourbon. Dust with confectioners' sugar.

*Brandy or Rum*—Omit lemon rind and add 2 tablespoons brandy or rum. Frost with Cream-Cheese Frosting (see Index) with rum and raisins added.

*Walnut*—Omit lemon rind and add ⅔ cup shelled walnuts (80 g), chopped in the processor bowl fitted with the steel blade and incorporated into the batter. Frost with Caramel Frosting (see Index).

# PAIN DE GÊNES

Makes 1 cake.

½ lb. blanched almonds
  (127 g)
1 cup sugar (200 g)
1⅓ cups flour (200 g)
½ Tbsp. baking powder
4 Tbsp. butter (60 g),
  softened
1 tsp. vanilla extract
½ tsp. almond extract
  (scant)
4 eggs

In the processor bowl fitted with the steel blade, chop the almonds until fine. Add ½ cup of the sugar, the flour and baking powder and blend together. Set aside. Put in the container with the steel blade the butter, remaining ½ cup sugar, and the vanilla and almond extracts. Run for 30 seconds, scraping down as necessary. Add the 4 eggs and blend until smooth, scraping down as needed. Put the almond mixture on top and with on and off quick turns blend just until the mixture disappears. Put in 2 greased and floured 8-inch cake pans. Place in a cold oven, set it at 300°F. (148.9°C.), and bake for 30 minutes. Let cool. Split the layers into halves. Frost the first layer with chocolate frosting, the second and third with a vanilla pastry cream. Cover the cake with chocolate frosting. Any combination of a creamy filling and preserves may be used between the layers (see Index for fillings and frostings).

# COCONUT CAKE

Makes 1 cake.

rind of 1 lemon
1 cup sugar (200 g)
½ lb. butter (2 sticks)
  (227 g), cut up
5 eggs, separated
1 tsp. vanilla extract
2 cups cake flour (240 g)
2½ tsp. baking powder
½ tsp. ground cinnamon
1 cup shredded coconut

Preheat oven to 350°F. (176.7°C.). In the processor bowl fitted with the steel blade, process the lemon rind with the sugar until rind is chopped, about 30 seconds. Add the cut-up butter and blend with the sugar until creamy. Add the egg yolks, one at a time, and blend with quick on and off turns after each addition. Add vanilla and blend. Sift together the flour, baking powder and cinnamon. Add the flour mixture to processor and blend with 3 on and off quick turns, or just until the flour is incorporated. *Do not overbeat!* Put mixture into a large bowl and fold in the coconut.

Beat the egg whites with a rotary beater or in a mixer until stiff but not dry. Fold into the batter. Bake in 2 buttered and floured 8-inch cake pans for 30 to 35 minutes, or until a cake tester comes out clean. Put Lemon Filling (see Index) between the layers, and frost with a white icing.

# FRESH APPLE CAKE

Makes 1 cake.

*4 large apples, cut up*
*¼ lb. butter (1 stick)*
  *(120 g)*
*¾ cup sugar (150 g)*
*2 eggs*
*1½ cups flour (225 g),*
  *sifted*
*2 tsp. baking soda*
*1 tsp. ground cinnamon*
*½ tsp. grated nutmeg*
*½ tsp. salt*
*1 cup bran flakes or bran*
  *buds (120 g)*

Preheat oven to 350°F. (176.7°C.). Coarsely chop the apples, 1 cup at a time, with the steel blade; set aside. Still with the steel blade, process the butter and sugar until smooth. Add the eggs, one at a time, and process for 5 seconds after each addition. Scrape down. Sift together the flour, baking soda, cinnamon, nutmeg and salt. Add to the mixture in the bowl and blend with 3 on and off quick turns, or until the flour is just incorporated. *Do not overbeat!* Stir the batter into the apples and bran flakes.

For a sheet cake, spoon the batter into a greased flat pan (13 x 9 x 2 inches).

For an upside-down cake, put ⅓ cup melted butter (75 g) and 3 tablespoons brown sugar (40 g) in an 8-inch springform pan. Arrange thin apple slices in an attractive pattern on the butter-sugar coating and spoon in the batter. Put a piece of foil under the pan in case the pan leaks.

Bake in the preheated oven for 45 minutes, or until a cake tester comes out clean. Cool. Serve the flat cake plain, or top with applesauce or whipped cream. For the upside-down cake, immediately invert onto a serving plate. Do not remove pan for a few minutes.

# M. B. H.'s PRESERVE CAKE

Makes 1 cake.

¼ lb. butter (1 stick)
  (120 g), cut up
1 cup sugar (200 g)
3 eggs
1 cup marmalade (200 g)
  (orange, lemon, three
  fruits, or preserves of
  your choice)
1½ cups flour (225 g)
1 tsp. ground cinnamon
½ tsp. ground cloves
½ tsp. grated nutmeg
¼ cup sour cream (56 g)
1 tsp. baking soda, dis-
  solved in 1 Tbsp. water

Preheat oven to 350°F. (176.7°C.). In the processor bowl fitted with the steel blade, blend the cut-up butter and the sugar until creamy. Add the eggs, one at a time, blending after each addition. Scrape down. Add marmalade or preserves. Blend quickly. Sift together the flour, cinnamon, cloves and nutmeg. Add to the mixture in the bowl and put in the sour cream and dissolved baking soda. Blend, turning the machine on and off 3 times, or until the flour is just incorporated. *Do not overbeat!* Butter two 8-inch cake pans and line with wax paper; butter the paper. Fill with the batter. Bake the cake for 30 minutes, or until a cake tester comes out clean. Good plain or with Browned Butter Frosting (see Index).

# ORANGE-RAISIN CAKE

Makes 1 cake.

This eighteenth-century recipe can be baked in a flat pan (13 x 9 x 2 inches), cut into squares, and served unfrosted; or it may be dressed up as described in the recipe.

1 orange
1 cup raisins (100 g)
1 cup sugar (200 g)
¼ lb. butter (1 stick)
  (120 g)
2 eggs
¾ cup sour milk (1.5 dl)
1 tsp. baking soda, dis-
  solved in 1 Tbsp. water
1 tsp. salt
1½ cups flour (225 g)

Preheat oven to 350°F. (176.7°C.). In the processor bowl fitted with the steel blade, put the pared orange rind, the fruit pulp from which the white has been removed, the raisins and sugar, and process until coarsely chopped, about 15 seconds. Add the butter and blend until creamy. Add the eggs, one at a time, and process with on and off quick turns, after each addition. Pour in the sour milk, the dissolved baking soda and the salt, and turn the machine on and off 2 or 3 times. Add the flour and blend by turning the machine on and off 3 times, or until the flour is just incorporated. *Do not overbeat!* Butter two 8-inch cake pans and line with wax paper; butter the paper. Fill with the batter. Bake the cake for 30 minutes, or until a cake tester comes out clean. Ice with vanilla Cream-Cheese Frosting or Chocolate Butter Frosting (see Index).

## YOGURT CAKE

Makes 1 large cake.

*rind of 1 lemon*
*2 cups sugar (400 g)*
*½ lb. butter (2 sticks) (227 g)*
*5 eggs, separated*
*1 cup yogurt (.24 l) (if possible, lemon flavored)*
*3 cups flour (450 g)*
*1 Tbsp. baking powder (12 g)*
*½ tsp. salt*
*confectioners' sugar*

Preheat oven to 350°F. (176.7°C.).In the processor bowl fitted with the steel blade, process the lemon rind and sugar until rind is chopped, about 30 seconds. Add the butter and blend until creamy. Add the egg yolks, one at a time, and blend with on and off quick turns after each addition. Add the yogurt and blend quickly. Place this mixture in a large bowl. Sift together the flour, baking powder and salt, and stir it thoroughly into the yogurt mixture in the bowl. Beat the egg whites with a rotary beater or mixer until stiff but not dry, and fold them in. Butter and flour a 9-inch tube pan, and spoon in the batter. Bake in the preheated oven for 1 hour, or until a cake tester comes out clean. Cool the cake in the pan for a few minutes. Place on a rack and dust with confectioners' sugar.

CAKE PANS

8 inches = 20.3 cm    9 inches = 23 cm    10 inches = 25.4 cm
jelly-roll pan, 15 x 10 inches = 38 x 25.4 cm
12 x 8 x 2 inches = 30.5 x 20.3 x 5 cm

# GERMAN FRUITCAKE

Makes 1 large cake.

Plum cake is as ubiquitous in German restaurants and homes as good *Senf* (mustard) and beer. This kind of cake is not too sweet, but it is satisfying as dessert or at a *Kaffeeklatsch*.

rind of 1 lemon
½ cup sugar (100 g)
2 Tbsp. butter (30 g)
2 eggs, separated
1 tsp. vanilla extract
juice of 1 lemon
¾ cup flour (115 g)
1 lb. (.453 kg) fresh
  plums, nectarines or
  apricots, or a mixture,
  peeled, or 1 lb. canned,
  drained
butter and sugar, for
  topping

Preheat oven to 350°F. (176.7°C.). In the processor bowl fitted with the steel blade, process the lemon rind and sugar until rind is chopped, about 30 seconds. Add the butter and blend. Add the egg yolks and blend with on and off quick turns. Scrape down. Add vanilla and lemon juice and blend quickly. Put in the flour and blend by turning the machine on and off 3 times, or until the flour is just incorporated. *Do not overbeat!* Beat the egg whites with a mixer or rotary beater until stiff but not dry. Fold the beaten egg whites into flour mixture. Pour the batter into a greased 10-inch springform pan. Arrange cut-up sections of the fruit on top of the batter in a pretty pattern. Dot all over with butter and sprinkle with sugar. Cover with foil and bake in the preheated oven for 15 minutes. Uncover and bake for 45 minutes more. Cool. Remove from pan and serve plain with heavy cream, or glaze with melted, strained apricot preserves.

CAKE PANS

8 inches = 20.3 cm     9 inches = 23 cm     10 inches = 25.4 cm
jelly-roll pan, 15 x 10 inches = 38 x 25.4 cm
12 x 8 x 2 inches = 30.5 x 20.3 x 5 cm

# ST. GREGORY'S FRUITCAKE

Makes 4 loaf cakes.

This is a fruitcake made without flour and an ideal recipe for a food processor.

*1 lb. (.453 kg) graham crackers, broken up*
*¾ lb. shelled walnuts (340 g)*
*1 lb. butter (4 sticks) (.453 kg), cut up*
*2¼ cups sugar (450 g)*
*10 eggs*
*1 Tbsp. vanilla extract*
*1 Tbsp. almond extract*
*2 lb. mixed candied peel (.9 kg)*
*1 lb. white raisins plumped in hot water or wine*
*½ cup brandy (1 dl)*
*½ cup rum (1 dl)*

Preheat oven to 275°F. (135°C.). In the processor bowl fitted with the steel blade, process the broken-up graham crackers, 1 package at a time, until fine. Place crumbs in a large bowl. Coarsely chop the walnuts and add to the graham-cracker crumbs. In the processor bowl blend ½ pound butter (2 sticks) and 1 cup sugar until creamy. With the motor running add 5 eggs, one at a time, through the tube. Add the vanilla and blend in with 1 on and off quick turn. Add the mixture to the graham crackers and nuts. Repeat the process with the remaining butter, sugar and eggs, but this time add the almond extract. Combine both mixtures in a large bowl and stir all together. Fold the raisins and candied peel into the batter. Butter 4 loaf pans, 7½ x 2½ x 2½ inches, and line with wax paper; butter the paper. Fill the pans with batter just to the top. Bake for 2½ hours. Turn the cakes out onto a rack and remove the wax paper. Return cakes to the pans and let cool. Mix together the brandy and rum and moisten each loaf with ¼ cup. Wrap cakes in foil and let them age for at least 2 weeks.

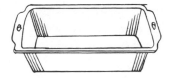

# BAKED CHEESECAKE

Makes 1 cake.

*1½ recipes Crumb Crust*
*(see Index)*
*rind of ½ orange*
*rind of 2 lemons*
*1½ cups sugar (300 g)*
*1 lb. cottage cheese*
*(.453 kg)*
*1 lb. cream cheese*
*(.453 kg)*
*4 eggs*
*3 Tbsp. cornstarch (30 g)*
*3 Tbsp. flour (30 g)*
*1 tsp. vanilla extract*
*2 cups sour cream (.48 l)*
*¼ lb. butter (1 stick)*
*(120 g), melted*

Preheat oven to 325°F. (162.8°C.) Prepare the crust with graham crackers and press into a buttered 9-inch springform pan. In the processor bowl fitted with the steel blade, process the orange and lemon rinds and the sugar until rinds are chopped, about 30 seconds. Add the cheeses and blend until smooth. Add the eggs, one at a time, processing with quick on and off turns after each addition. Put in the cornstarch, flour and vanilla and blend until smooth. Transfer the mixture to a large bowl and by hand beat in the sour cream and cooled melted butter. Spoon the mixture into the prepared crust. Bake in the preheated oven for 1¼ hours. Let the cake cool in the oven for 3 hours. Chill. This cake looks very pretty when topped with a fruit glaze or preserves, or whole fruit—strawberries, pineapple, blueberries, peaches—added before serving.

## VARIATIONS ON BAKED CHEESECAKE

*Apricot*—Chop 1 cup dried apricots (200 g) with the sugar. Omit the orange rind and use only 1 lemon rind. Flavor with 2 tablespoons (30 g) apricot brandy or rum. Drained stewed apricots may be placed on top after baking and dusted with any extra crumbs.

*Pastry Shell*—Make 1 recipe of *pâte brisée* or *pâte sucrée* (see Index). Line the springform pan with the pastry, patting it up the sides. Partially bake. Fill with the mixture and bake.

# MOCHA CHEESECAKE

Makes 1 large cake.

*1½ recipes Crumb Crust*
*(see Index)*
*1 cup sugar (200 g)*

Preheat oven to 350°F. (176.7°C.). Prepare the crust with chocolate wafers, and press the crumb mixture onto the bottom and sides of a buttered

3 eggs
1½ lb. cream cheese
(.78 kg)
6 oz. semisweet chocolate
bits (170 g), melted
2 Tbsp. cocoa powder
(10 g)
1 Tbsp. instant coffee
powder
2 Tbsp. rum (28 g)
1 tsp. vanilla extract
3 cups sour cream (.72 l)
4 Tbsp. butter (60 g),
melted
whipped cream

9-inch springform pan. In the processor bowl fitted with the steel blade, blend the sugar and the eggs. Add 1 pound of the cream cheese, cut into cubes, and blend until smooth. Transfer to a large bowl. In the processor bowl place remaining cheese, the melted chocolate, cocoa powder, coffee powder dissolved in the rum, the vanilla and sour cream. Blend until smooth. Pour in the cooled melted butter and combine with 2 or 3 on and off quick turns. Whisk the cheese mixtures together. Spoon into the prepared shell and bake in the preheated oven for 1 hour. The cake will be runny but it will become firm when it is chilled. Chill for at least 5 hours. Garnish with whipped cream.

## BLACK FOREST CHEESECAKE

Makes 1 cake.

1 recipe Crumb Crust (see
Index)
1½ lb. cream cheese
(.78 kg)
1 cup sour cream (.24 l)
1 cup sugar (200 g)
2 Tbsp. flour (20 g)
2 Tbsp. cherry brandy or
Cherry Heering (28 g)
3 eggs
1½ cups cherry pie filling
(340 g)
1 oz. semisweet chocolate
(28 g), shaved
whipped cream

Preheat oven to 350°F. (176.7°C.). Prepare the crust with chocolate wafers, and press the crumb mixture into a buttered 8-inch springform pan, on the bottom and three fourths of the way up the sides. Bake for 5 minutes. Cool. In the processor bowl fitted with the steel blade, put half of the cheese, the sour cream, half of the sugar, 1 tablespoon flour and 1 tablespoon cherry brandy or Cherry Heering. Blend until very smooth. Transfer the mixture to a large bowl. Process remaining cheese, sugar, flour and cherry brandy or Cherry Heering until very smooth. Add the eggs, one at a time, and blend with on and off quick turns. Stir into the first mixture. With a slotted spoon remove the cherries from the syrup. Reserve enough for edging and fold the rest into the cheese mixture. (Syrup is not used in this recipe.) Spoon filling into the cooled pie shell. Bake in the preheated oven for

1 hour. Turn off the oven and let the cake cool with the door open. When cool transfer to a serving plate. Make a circle of the reserved cherries around the top, 1½ inches in from the edge. Fill the center with shaved chocolate curls and pipe a rim of whipped cream around the edge. Refrigerate for at least 2 hours before serving.

## BASIC NUT TORTE

Makes 1 torte.

These light nut confections substitute ground nuts and crumbs for flour. They can be served plain or iced, and they are particularly suited to the capacities of the food processor.

*¼ lb. shelled almonds,*
 *pecans or walnuts (120 g)*
*1 slice of day-old bread*
*rind of 1 lemon*
*1 cup sugar (200 g)*
*6 eggs, separated*
*juice of 1 lemon*

Preheat oven to 350°F. (176.7°C.). In the processor bowl fitted with the steel blade, grind the nuts to make 1 cup fine crumbs; set aside. Process the torn-up slice of bread to make ½ cup bread crumbs; set aside. Process the lemon rind and sugar in the bowl until rind is grated, about 30 seconds. Add the egg yolks and blend with on and off quick turns. Scrape down. Add the lemon juice, ground nuts and bread crumbs, and blend well. Beat the egg whites with a mixer or a rotary beater until stiff but not dry. Fold them into the nut mixture, and spoon batter into an ungreased 8-inch springform pan. Bake for about 40 minutes, or until a cake tester comes out clean. Let the torte cool in the pan. Do not be concerned if the torte falls a little as it cools.

Invert torte on a serving plate. Serve plain, dusted with powdered sugar, or frost with a butter icing, or spread with custard filling, or finish with whipped cream. Sweet wafers may be used in place of bread crumbs.

# GENOA TORTE

Makes 1 torte.

½ lb. Almond Paste
  (226.8 g) (see Index)
1 cup sugar (200 g)
3 whole eggs
4 eggs, separated
⅔ cup melted butter
  (150 g)
½ cup arrowroot (80 g)
1 oz. Kirsch (28 g)

Preheat oven to 350°F. (176.7°C.). In the processor bowl fitted with the steel blade, put the almond paste, cut into bits, the sugar and the 3 whole eggs. Blend until smooth with quick on and off turns. Add the egg yolks, one at a time, Add the melted butter, arrowroot and Kirsch, and blend with on and off quick turns. Beat the egg whites with a mixer or a rotary beater until stiff but not dry and fold them into the mixture. Butter and flour an 8-inch springform pan, and line with buttered parchment or brown paper. Fill the pan with the batter. Bake in the preheated oven for 30 minutes, or until the top is spongy and the cake leaves the sides of the pan. Sprinkle cake with powdered sugar, or ice with a white icing flavored with Kirsch.

# CHOCOLATE NUT TORTE I

Makes 1 torte.

A fudgy yet rather delicate confection which may be topped with almond-flavored whipped cream.

½ cup shelled pistachios
  (80 g)
¼ cup blanched almonds
  (30 g)
5 eggs, separated
¾ cup sugar (150 g)
2 oz. unsweetened
  chocolate (56.7 g),
  melted and cooled
½ cup prepared coffee
  (1 dl)

Preheat oven to 350°F. (176.7°C.). In the processor bowl fitted with the steel blade, chop pistachios and almonds until *very* fine; set aside. Drop egg yolks into processor bowl and process for 30 seconds. With the motor running add the sugar, 2 tablespoons at a time. Pour in the cooled melted chocolate and blend quickly. Add the nut mixture and coffee and blend with 2 or 3 quick on and off turns. Scrape down if necessary. Beat the egg whites with a rotary beater or mixer until stiff but not dry. Fold into the chocolate nut mixture until no white streaks remain. Pour into a greased and floured 9-inch cake pan and bake for 1 hour. Cool. Serve with or without whipped cream or soft ice cream.

# CHOCOLATE NUT TORTE II

Makes 1 torte.

A rich chocolate dessert which may be baked in a pastry shell or by itself.

2 cups blanched almonds (240 g)
7 oz. unsweetened chocolate (198 g)
½ lb. butter (2 sticks) (227 g)
1 cup sugar (200 g)
6 eggs, separated

To bake in a pastry shell, line a 9-inch springform pan with pâte brisée. Refrigerate for 1 hour. Partially bake the pastry in a preheated 425°F. (218.3°C.) oven for 10 minutes.

Preheat oven to 350°F. (176.7°C.). In the processor bowl fitted with the steel blade, chop the almonds and chocolate until very fine. Set aside. With the steel blade, cream butter and sugar with 4 or 5 quick on and off turns. Add egg yolks, one at a time, and blend, scraping down as necessary. Put in the almond-chocolate mixture and blend together with 3 on and off turns. Beat the egg whites with a rotary beater or mixer until stiff but not dry. Fold into the chocolate-nut-egg-butter mixture until no white streaks remain. Pour into the prepared shell or into a buttered 8-inch springform pan lined with buttered wax paper. Bake for 1 hour, or until a cake tester comes out clean.

CAKE PANS

8 inches = 20.3 cm      9 inches = 23 cm      10 inches = 25.4 cm
jelly-roll pan, 15 x 10 inches = 38 x 25.4 cm
12 x 8 x 2 inches = 30.5 x 20.3 x 5 cm

# SWEDISH THOUSAND LEAVES TORTE

Makes 1 torte.

A superb Scandinavian treat

*1⅔ cups flour (250 g),*
*sifted*
*½ lb. butter (2 sticks)*
*(227 g), cut up*
*4 Tbsp. ice water*

Preheat oven to 450°F. (232.2°C.). In the processor bowl fitted with the steel blade, blend the flour and cut-up butter with on and off quick turns until the mixture resembles cornmeal. Add the ice water. If the mixture does not form a ball in 5 seconds stop the machine, add 1 more tablespoon ice water, and process just until the ball forms. Form pastry into a flat cake, wrap in wax paper, and chill for at least 1 hour.

*granulated sugar*
*1 cup applesauce or rasp-*
*berry purée (.24 l), or*
*more if needed*
*1 recipe Vanilla Cream*
*(see Index)*

Divide the dough into 6 parts. Work with 1 part at a time; the remaining portions should be kept in the refrigerator. Roll out each portion on wax paper to a very thin sheet. Using a cake pan as a guide, cut out a circle approximately 8 inches in diameter with a pastry wheel. Peel away the excess dough. Prick the circle all over with a fork or pastry pricker. Brush with ice water and lightly sprinkle with sugar. Place the circle with the wax paper underneath on a baking sheet. Bake for 8 to 10 minutes, until golden. Let cool on the wax paper. Repeat with the remaining portions of dough.

Spread layers alternately with applesauce or raspberry purée and vanilla cream. The top may be frosted with Lemon Glaze (see Index) or sifted confectioners' sugar.

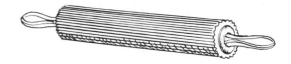

# GINGERSNAP TORTE

Makes 1 torte.

*12 oz. gingersnaps (340 g)*
*1 cup shelled pecans (120 g)*
*½ lb. butter (2 sticks) (227 g)*
*⅔ cup sugar (140 g)*
*6 eggs, separated*
*½ cup milk (.5 dl)*
*2 tsp. baking powder, dissolved in 2 Tbsp. milk*

Preheat oven to 300°F. (148.9°C.). In the processor bowl fitted with the steel blade, finely chop the gingersnaps and pecans; set aside. Cream the butter and sugar in the processor until smooth; scrape down. Add the egg yolks, one at a time, processing with quick on and off turns after each addition. Add the milk and blend again. Pour in the dissolved baking powder and blend with another on and off quick turn. Pour the mixture into the ground gingersnaps and pecans. Beat the egg whites with a rotary beater or mixer until stiff but not dry. Fold them into the gingersnap mixture. Butter a 9-inch springform pan and line the bottom with wax paper; butter the paper. Fill with the batter. Bake in the preheated oven for 1½ to 2 hours, or until a cake tester comes out clean. Serve plain or with whipped cream.

# CHESTNUT TORTE

Makes 1 torte.

*¾ cup blanched almonds (90 g)*
*1 lb. (.453 kg) fresh chestnuts in shells, or 1 can (16 oz.) chestnuts in brine, drained, or ½ lb. dried chestnuts (227 g)*
*5 eggs, separated*
*1 cup sugar (200 g)*
*2 tsp. vanilla extract*
*½ tsp. salt*
*½ Tbsp. baking powder*

Preheat oven to 350°F. (176.7°C.). In the processor bowl fitted with the steel blade, grind the almonds and set aside. Purée the cooked chestnuts with the steel blade and set aside. Beat the egg yolks in the processor; with the machine running, slowly pour the sugar through the tube. Scrape down and blend with on and off quick turns. Add the vanilla, salt, baking powder and milk, and blend. Stir the mixture into the ground almonds and puréed chestnuts.

Beat the egg whites with a rotary beater or mixer until stiff but not dry. Fold them into the al-

2 Tbsp. milk (28 g)
1 cup whipping cream
  (.24 l)
jam (optional)

mond mixture. Butter two 8-inch cake pans and line the bottoms with wax paper; butter the paper. Fill with the batter. Bake for 35 minutes, or until a cake tester comes out clean. When the torte has cooled spread the bottom layer with jam or whipped cream. Cover the top and sides with Kirsch-flavored whipped cream.

HOW TO COOK FRESH
CHESTNUTS

If fresh chestnuts are used, slit each one on the flat side. Cover with water and boil for 5 minutes. Drain and remove shells and inner skins. Again cover with water and boil for 30 minutes, or until tender. (If canned chestnuts are used do not cook them, as they are already cooked.)

HOW TO USE DRIED
CHESTNUTS

Cover dried chestnuts with a large amount of boiling water and let them soak overnight. Drain, pick off any remaining bits of inner skin, and cover with fresh water. Boil for 30 minutes, or until tender.

## CARROT TORTE

Makes 1 torte.

3 medium-size carrots  ·
  (.453 kg), peeled
rind of 1 lemon
1 cup sugar (200 g)
4 eggs, separated
juice of ½ lemon
½ cup flour (75 g)
1 tsp. baking powder
1 cup heavy cream (.24 l),
  whipped

Preheat oven to 350°F. (176.7°C.). Shred the carrots with the shredding disc; there should be 1 cup; set aside. In the processor bowl fitted with the steel blade, place the shredded carrots, lemon rind and sugar. Process until carrots and lemon rind are finely chopped. Add the egg yolks and lemon juice and blend well; scrape down. Sift the flour and baking powder and add to the bowl. Blend quickly with 2 or 3 on and off quick turns, or just until the flour is incorporated. *Do not overbeat!* Beat the egg whites with a rotary beater or mixer until stiff but not dry. Fold the carrot mixture into the egg whites. Butter two 8-inch cake pans and line the bottom with wax paper; butter the paper. Fill with the batter. Bake the cake for 30 minutes, or until a cake tester comes out clean. Fill and top with whipped cream.

# JELLY ROLL

Makes 1 roll.

rind of ½ lemon
1 cup granulated sugar
  (200 g)
1 tsp. vanilla extract, or
  ½ tsp. almond extract
4 eggs, separated
¾ cup cake flour (90 g)
1 tsp. baking powder
¼ tsp. salt
filling (see following
  suggestions)
¼ cup confectioners'
  sugar (40 g)

Preheat oven to 350°F. (176.7°C.). Generously butter a jelly-roll pan, 15 x 10 inches. Line the pan with wax paper, leaving an overhang of 2 inches at each end; butter the paper. In the processor bowl fitted with the steel blade, process the lemon rind and ¾ cup of the granulated sugar until rind is grated, about 30 seconds. Add the vanilla and the egg yolks, one at a time, and blend with on and off quick turns after each addition. Sift together the flour, baking powder and salt. Add to the processor bowl and blend in with 3 on and off quick turns, or just until the flour is incorporated. *Do not overbeat!* Beat the egg whites with a rotary beater or in a mixer and fold into the batter. Spread the mixture evenly into the prepared pan. Bake in the preheated oven for 15 to 20 minutes, until set and golden on top. Place a towel on a counter and turn out the cake onto it. Carefully strip off the wax paper and trim the crisp edges. Roll up the cake in the towel and let it cool. When ready to fill, unroll the cake, spread with the filling and roll up again. Combine confectioners' sugar and remaining ¼ cup granulated sugar, and sift on top of the roll.

## SUGGESTED FILLINGS

*Preserves*—1 cup preserves (.24 l), flavored with 1 tablespoon liqueur.

*Lemon Filling*—See Index.

*Cream*—Flavored whipped cream.

*Ice Cream*

# VARIATIONS

*Chocolate Roll*—Omit the lemon rind and sift 4 tablespoons cocoa powder with the flour.

*Spice Roll*—Sift ½ teaspoon each of ground ginger, cinnamon and allspice with the flour. Fill spice roll with whipped cream.

## BISCUIT TORTE

Makes 1 torte.

*20 vanilla wafers*
*⅔ cup shelled nuts (80 g)*
*(walnuts, pecans, al-*
*monds)*
*3 egg whites*
*1 cup sugar (200 g)*
*1 tsp. almond extract*
*½ tsp. baking powder*

Preheat oven to 350°F. (176.7°C.). In the processor bowl fitted with the steel blade, chop the vanilla wafers and nuts until very fine. Beat the egg whites with a mixer or rotary beater until stiff but not dry, adding the sugar, 1 tablespoon at a time. Add almond extract and baking powder. Fold the cracker and nut mixture into the egg whites. Spread into a buttered and floured 8-inch springform pan and bake for 30 minutes. Chill. Top with whipped cream and chopped candied gingerroot.

CAKE PANS

    8 inches = 20.3 cm      9 inches = 23 cm     10 inches = 25.4 cm
    jelly-roll pan, 15 x 10 inches = 38 x 25.4 cm
    12 x 8 x 2 inches = 30.5 x 20.3 x 5 cm

# BASIC NUT ROLL

Makes 1 roll.

½ lb. shelled nuts (226 g)
(pecans, walnuts,
toasted almonds, pis-
tachios)
7 eggs, separated
1 cup sugar (200 g)
1 tsp. baking powder
¼ tsp. almond extract
1 cup heavy cream (.24 l)
1 tsp. vanilla extract

Preheat oven to 350°F. (176.7°C.). In the processor bowl fitted with the steel blade, grind the nuts
fine to make 1½ cups; set aside. Put the egg yolks
in the bowl. With the motor running, gradually add
the sugar through the tube and blend until smooth.
Add the baking powder, almond extract and nuts.
Blend with 2 on and off quick turns. Beat the egg
whites with a mixer or a rotary beater until stiff but
not dry. Fold them into the nut mixture. Butter a
jelly-roll pan (15 x 10 inches) generously. Cover
with wax paper slightly larger than the pan so that
it can be easily peeled off later. Butter the wax
paper. Spread batter evenly in the pan. Bake in the
preheated oven for 18 to 20 minutes, or until a
cake tester comes out clean. Place a kitchen towel
on the table and turn cake out onto it. Carefully
remove the wax paper, and cut off any crisp edges
of the cake. Roll up cake in the towel and let cool.

Whip the cream and vanilla with a mixer or
rotary beater. Unroll the cake, spread with half of
the cream, and roll up again. Place on a serving
platter and frost with remaining whipped cream.

# 4

# COOKIES AND
# SMALL CAKES

———◆———

Cookies can be formed by dropping, rolling, cutting out, molding, and pressing. The processor is a whiz for mixing many kinds of cookies. In general, cookies should be quickly mixed, never overprocessed.

For hard-to-handle soft doughs, roll the dough directly on the prepared baking sheet. Cut into desired shapes, remove any scraps around the shaped cookies, and bake according to directions.

If cookies should stick to the pan, put the pan back in the hot oven for a minute or two, then remove; this usually loosens them easily.

Cookies may be iced, sandwiched with filling, or dusted with confectioners' sugar. They make an excellent finger-food dessert.

# DROP COOKIES

## DROP COOKIE DOUGH I

Makes about 48 wafers, 2¼-inch size.

¼ lb. butter (1 stick)
  (120 g), cut up
½ cup sugar (100 g)
1 egg
1 tsp. vanilla extract
1 cup flour (150 g), sifted
¼ tsp. baking soda
½ tsp. salt

Preheat oven to 375°F. (190.6°C.). In the processor bowl fitted with the steel blade, put the cut-up butter. With the motor running, add the sugar slowly through the tube. Add the egg and vanilla to sugar mixture, and blend with on and off quick turns. Sift the flour, baking soda and salt, and add to the bowl. Blend with on and off quick turns. Drop by teaspoons onto a lightly, greased cookie sheet, placing mounds 3 inches apart (they run). Bake in the preheated oven for 8 to 10 minutes. Cool cookies slightly before removing from the cookie sheet.

### SUGGESTED VARIATIONS

Add any of these to Drop Cookie Dough I.

*Chocolate Chip*—Use a scant ¼ cup white sugar and a scant ¼ cup brown sugar in place of ½ cup white sugar. Fold in 6 ounces chocolate bits (170 g).

*Citrus*—Add ½ tablespoon grated citrus rind and 1 teaspoon lemon or orange extract with the sugar. Then add the butter.

*Cinnamon-Nut*—Add 2 cups shelled nuts (240 g), chopped, and 1 teaspoon ground cinamon.

*Coffee*—Add 1 tablespoon instant coffee powder dissolved in 2 tablespoons hot water.

*Apricot Brandy*—Add 1 tablespoon brandy (14 g) with the vanilla extract.

*Rum*—Add 1 tablespoon rum (14 g) and omit the vanilla extract.

*Almond*—Add ½ cup chopped blanched almonds (60 g) and 1 teaspoon almond extract, and omit the vanilla extract.

## DROP COOKIE DOUGH II

Makes about 48 cookies, 2¼-inch size.

¼ lb. butter (1 stick)
  (120 g), cut up
3 oz. cream cheese (85 g)
½ cup confectioners'
  sugar (80 g)
1 egg
1 Tbsp. flavoring (vanilla,
  etc.)
1 cup sifted flour (scant
  150 g)

Preheat oven to 350°F. (176.7°C.). In the processor bowl fitted with the steel blade, blend the butter and cream cheese until smooth. With the motor running add the sugar slowly through the tube. Add egg and liquid flavoring and blend with on and off quick turns. Add the flour to the bowl and blend with 2 or 3 on and off quick turns, or until the flour is just incorporated. *Do not overbeat!* Drop the batter by teaspoons onto a lightly greased cookie sheet and bake in the preheated oven for 10 minutes.

## OATMEAL DROP COOKIES

Makes about 48 cookies, 2-inch size.

¼ lb. butter (1 stick)
  (120 g), cut up
1½ cups firmly packed
  brown sugar (300 g)
1 egg
¼ cup milk (.5 dl)
1½ cups flour (225 g)
½ tsp. baking soda
½ tsp. salt
¼ tsp. ground ginger
1¾ cups quick-cooking
  rolled oats (80 g)
1 cup dried currants
  (100 g)

Preheat oven to 375°F. (190.6°C.). In the processor bowl fitted with the steel blade, put the cut-up butter. With the motor running, slowly pour in the sugar through the tube; scrape down. Add the egg and milk to the sugar mixture and blend until smooth. Sift the flour, baking soda, salt and ginger. Place in the bowl and blend with on and off quick turns. Fold in the oats and currants by hand. Drop batter by spoonfuls onto a greased cookie sheet, placing the mounds 3 inches apart. Bake in a preheated oven for 20 minutes.

# BRANDY SNAPS

Makes 12 to 16 snaps.

*4 Tbsp. butter (60 g), cut up*
*¼ cup sugar (50 g)*
*2 Tbsp. corn syrup (40 g)*
*¼ tsp. ground ginger*
*1 Tbsp. brandy (15 g)*
*½ cup flour (75 g)*

Preheat oven to 350°F. (176.7°C.). In the processor bowl fitted with the steel blade, put the cut-up butter. With the motor running, slowly pour in the sugar through the tube. Add remaining ingredients and blend with on and off quick turns until smooth. Drop batter by teaspoons onto a foil-lined cookie sheet, placing mounds 2 inches apart. Bake in the preheated oven for 10 minutes.

# FLORENTINES

Makes about 24 thin cookies.

*½ cup heavy cream (1 dl)*
*½ cup sugar (100 g)*
*¼ tsp. salt*
*1¼ cups blanched almonds or hazelnuts (150 g)*
*¼ cup candied orange peel (80 g)*
*¼ cup flour (40 g)*

Preheat oven to 325°F. (162.8°C.). Heat cream, sugar and salt together. In the processor bowl fitted with the steel blade, coarsely chop the nuts and candied orange peel with on and off quick turns. Add the flour and turn the machine on and off. Stir this into the hot ingredients and cook until the mixture thickens, about 2 minutes. Drop batter by teaspoons, 2 inches apart, on a well-greased cookie sheet. Bake for 12 minutes, or until brown around the edges. Let cool slightly on the cookie sheet. Remove and let cool until crisp.

CHOCOLATE FILLING
*8 oz. semisweet chocolate (227 g), melted*
*3 Tbsp. butter (45 g)*
*1 Tbsp. Grand Marnier (15 g)*

Mix filling ingredients together. Spread the flat side of one cookie with filling and top with a second cookie. Be sure the filling is firm and cookie "sandwiches" set before serving.

# MACAROONS

Makes about 30 macaroons, 2-inch size.

*½ lb. Almond Paste (227 g) (see Index), cut up*
*¾ cup confectioners' sugar (120 g)*
*½ cup granulated sugar (100 g)*
*3 egg whites*
*1 tsp. almond extract*

In the processor bowl fitted with the steel blade, place the cut-up almond paste, the sugars, 2 egg whites and the almond extract. Blend until smooth. The dough should be soft but not runny, and it should be able to hold its shape when dropped from a spoon or piped through a pastry tube. If the dough is too stiff, beat remaining egg white until foamy and add it, a little at a time, to the batter, turning the motor on and off until the right consistency is achieved. Line a cookie sheet with parchment paper or brown paper. Drop batter by spoonfuls, or squeeze through a pastry bag with a star or round tip. Let the cookies rest, covered, for 2 hours or overnight. Brush with water. Bake in a preheated 325°F. (162.8°C.) oven for 20 to 25 minutes, or until lightly browned.

# CITRUS COOKIES

Makes about 6 dozen cookies.

*rind of ½ orange*
*1 whole lemon*
*1 cup sugar (200 g)*
*¼ lb. butter (1 stick) (120 g), cut up*
*1 egg*
*1½ cups flour (225 g)*
*½ tsp. baking powder*
*¼ tsp. baking soda*
*¼ tsp. ground ginger*

Preheat oven to 350°F. (176.7°C.). In the processor bowl fitted with the steel blade, put the orange rind, the lemon which has been seeded and cut into pieces, and the sugar. Process until well blended, about 30 seconds. Add the cut-up butter and blend until creamy; scrape down. Add the egg and blend with on and off quick turns. Sift the flour, baking powder, baking soda and ginger. Place half of the flour mixture in the container and blend very quickly with 2 or 3 off and on turns. Add remaining flour mixture and again quickly blend in. *Do not overbeat!* On a greased cookie sheet drop the batter, ½ teaspoon at a time, 2 inches apart. Bake in the preheated oven for 15 minutes, or until the edges are golden. Slip the cookies off the cookie sheet with a spatula and cool on a rack.

## CIDER APPLE COOKIES

Makes about 5 dozen cookies.

*1 cup shelled walnuts (120 g)*
*2 medium-size apples, un-peeled*
*½ lb. butter (2 sticks) (227 g), cut up*
*1⅓ cups brown sugar (280 g)*
*1 egg*
*2 cups flour (300 g)*
*½ tsp. baking soda*
*1 tsp. baking powder*
*½ tsp. salt*
*1 tsp. ground cinnamon*
*½ tsp. grated nutmeg*
*¼ cup cider or apple juice (.5 dl)*

GLAZE
*1 Tbsp. butter (15 g)*
*1½ cups confectioners' sugar (240 g)*
*pinch of salt*
*2½ Tbsp. (35 g) cider or apple juice, or ½ small apple, chopped fine*
*¼ tsp. vanilla extract*

Preheat oven to 400°F. (204.4°C.). In the processor bowl fitted with the steel blade, chop the walnuts to fine crumbs; set aside. Core the apples, cut into pieces, and chop; set aside. Blend the cut-up butter and brown sugar until creamy. Add the egg and blend well. Sift together the flour, baking soda, baking powder, salt, cinnamon and nutmeg. Add half of the flour mixture to the processor and blend in with 2 on and off quick turns. Add the cider or apple juice and blend with 2 on and off quick turns. Add remaining flour and turn the motor on and off 3 times, or just until the flour disappears. *Do not overbeat!* Fold in the walnuts and apples. Drop batter by teaspoons onto a greased baking sheet, spacing the mounds 2 inches apart. Bake in the preheated oven for 10 to 12 minutes. Place on a rack and glaze while still warm.

In the processor bowl fitted with the steel blade, blend all the glaze ingredients until smooth. Drizzle or spoon or brush on the warm cookies.

## ALMOND LACE COOKIES

Makes about 48 cookies.

*1 cup blanched almonds*
*(120 g)*
*¼ lb. butter (1 stick)*
*(120 g), cut up*
*1 cup sugar (200 g)*
*3 Tbsp. flour (30 g)*
*2 Tbsp. milk (28 g)*

Preheat oven to 350°F. (176.7°C.). In the processor bowl fitted with the steel blade, place the almonds and grind to fine crumbs; set aside. Put the cut-up butter in the container; with the motor running, slowly add the sugar through the tube. Scrape down. Add the flour, milk and ground almonds and blend for 3 to 5 seconds. Heat the mixture, stirring constantly, until warm. Cover a cookie sheet with foil, and drop the warm batter on it by teaspoons, spacing the mounds 3 inches apart. Bake in the preheated oven until golden brown, 8 to 10 minutes. Allow to cool slightly, then gently remove with a broad spatula.

## CHOCOLATE ALMOND LACE COOKIES

Add to the ingredients for Almond Lace Cookies 2 ounces (56 g) unsweetened chocolate, melted, and proceed with the recipe. Bake the cookies for *exactly 9 minutes.* Allow to cool slightly and carefully remove with a broad spatula.

## BROWN NUT COOKIES

Makes about 6 dozen cookies.

*¼ lb. shelled nuts*
*(115 g) (about 1 cup)*
*3 Tbsp. butter (45 g)*
*1 cup brown sugar*
*(200 g)*
*1 egg*
*3 Tbsp. flour (30 g)*

Preheat oven to 300°F. (148.9°C.). In the processor bowl fitted with the steel blade, chop the nuts and add remaining ingredients. Blend together with on and off quick turns. On a greased or foil-lined cookie sheet drop the dough by ½ teaspoons, spacing the mounds 3 inches apart. Bake in the preheated oven for 15 minutes. Allow to cool slightly, then gently remove with a broad spatula. If cookies stick to the pan or foil, return them to the oven for a minute or two. They should come loose.

---

# MOLDED COOKIES

## NUT COOKIES

Makes about 60 cookies.

½ lb. shelled nuts (227 g)
½ lb. sweet butter (2 sticks) (227 g), cut up
½ cup confectioners' sugar (80 g)
2 tsp. vanilla extract
2 cups flour (300 g)
½ tsp. salt
granulated sugar

Preheat oven to 350°F. (176.7°C.). In the processor bowl fitted with the steel blade, chop the nuts. Add the cut-up butter, confectioners' sugar and vanilla to the nuts. Process with on and off quick turns until well incorporated. Add the flour and salt, and blend with 2 or 3 on and off quick turns, or until the flour just disappears. Chill until the dough is easy to handle. Form 1-inch balls and place them on a greased cookie sheet. Press them flat with a fork or use a cookie stamp. Bake in the preheated oven for 25 minutes. Dust with granulated sugar while still warm. This dough can also be formed into triangles, rolls or crescents.

### SUGGESTED VARIATIONS

Add any of these to the dough for Nut Cookies before baking.

*Crystallized Fruit*—Dip cookies into slightly beaten egg white and roll in chopped crystallized fruit (gingerroot, citron).

*Extra Nutty*—Dip cookies into slightly beaten egg white and roll in chopped nuts.

*Tropical*—Roll dough balls in shredded coconut.

*Surprise*—Shape each cookie around a toasted almond or a sugared pecan.

*Tender Rounds*—Add 2 teaspoons double-acting baking powder to the flour. After baking, while still warm, glaze cookies with lemon juice and confectioners' sugar.

*Butterscotch Chews*—Grind 6 ounces butterscotch bits (170 g) with the nuts.

## RUM BALLS

Makes about 45 balls, 1-inch size.

*1½ cups shelled pecans*
  *(180 g)*
*3 cups broken-up vanilla*
  *wafers*
*1 cup confectioners' sugar*
  *(160 g)*
*3 Tbsp. white corn syrup*
  *(60 g)*
*3 Tbsp. cocoa powder*
  *(15 g)*
*½ cup rum (1 dl), or*
  *enough to bind the mix-*
  *ture*
*cocoa powder*

In the processor bowl fitted with the steel blade, grind the pecans and vanilla wafers to fine crumbs. Add the remaining ingredients except rum and blend. Add the rum a little at a time until the mixture just holds together. Form into balls and refrigerate overnight. Dust with more cocoa before serving.

Bourbon can be used instead of rum to make Bourbon Balls.

## CHOCOLATE CRESCENTS OR BALLS

Makes about 60 cookies.

*¼ lb. butter (120 g)*
  *(1 stick)*
*½ cup sugar (100 g)*
*½ cup cocoa powder*
  *(40 g)*
*1 egg*
*¼ cup water (.5 dl)*
*1 tsp. vanilla extract*
*2 cups flour (300 g)*

Preheat oven to 350°F. (176.7°C.). In the processor bowl fitted with the steel blade, blend the butter and sugar until smooth. Add the cocoa, egg, water and vanilla, and blend. Add 1 cup of the flour and mix in with 2 or 3 on and off quick turns. Add remaining flour and with on and off quick turns blend in the flour until it just disappears. *Do not overbeat!* Form dough into crescents or balls and place on a greased cookie sheet. Bake in the preheated oven for 12 to 15 minutes.

# REFRIGERATOR COOKIES

Makes about 72 cookies, 2-inch size.

½ lb. butter (2 sticks),
    (227 g), cut up
½ cup granulated sugar
    (100 g)
½ cup brown sugar
    (100 g)
2 eggs
½ Tbsp. flavoring
2¾ cups flour (410 g),
    sifted
½ tsp. baking soda
1 tsp. salt

In the processor bowl fitted with the steel blade, put the cut-up butter. With the machine running, slowly add the sugars and process until creamy. Add the eggs, one at a time, and quickly blend after each addition. Blend in the flavoring. Sift the flour, baking soda and salt and add to the butter mixture. Blend with 2 or 3 on and off quick turns, or until the flour is just incorporated. Divide the dough into halves and form each portion into a roll about 2 inches in diameter. Wrap in wax paper and chill until stiff.

When ready to bake, cut roll into thin slices. Bake on an ungreased cookie sheet in a preheated 400°F. (204.4°C.) oven for 6 to 8 minutes.

# SUGAR COOKIES

Makes about 60 cookies.

¼ lb. butter (1 stick)
    (120 g)
1 cup sugar (200 g)
1 egg
1 tsp. flavoring
2¼ cups flour plus ¼ cup
    for sifting (375 g)
2 tsp. baking powder
sugar

Preheat oven to 425°F. (218.3°C.). In the processor bowl fitted with the steel blade, cream the butter and sugar until smooth. Add the egg and flavoring and blend with on and off quick turns. Sift the flour and baking powder. Add 1⅛ cups of the flour to the butter mixture and blend with on and off quick turns just until the flour is incorporated. Add remaining flour and again blend in with quick on and off turns or just until the flour is incorporated. *Do not overbeat!* Place the dough on a floured piece of wax paper. Sift ¼ cup flour over the dough and gently work in. Cover dough with wax paper and chill.

Roll out the dough between the 2 layers of wax paper. Cut into any desired shape, sprinkle with sugar, and place on a lightly greased cookie sheet. Bake in the preheated oven for 8 to 10 minutes.

## NÜRNBERGERS

Makes about 48 cookies.

*4 oz. candied orange peel
  (113 g)*
*⅓ cup shelled nuts (40 g)*
*¾ cup brown sugar
  (150 g)*
*1 cup honey (300 g)*
*1 egg*
*2 Tbsp. orange juice
  (28 g)*
*3½ cups flour (525 g),
  sifted*
*½ tsp. baking soda*
*½ tsp. ground cinnamon*
*¼ tsp. ground cardamom*
*¼ tsp. ground cloves*
*Confectioners' Icing (see
  Index)*

In the processor bowl fitted with the steel blade, chop the orange peel and nuts to fine bits. Add the brown sugar and honey and blend. Add the egg and blend. Add the orange juice, and blend. (If the machine slows down, turn it off.) Sift together the flour, baking soda, cinnamon, cardamom and cloves. Add half of the flour mixture to the nut mixture and process with 2 or 3 quick on and off turns. Add remaining flour and again blend with 2 or 3 on and off quick turns, or just until the flour is incorporated. Turn the dough out onto floured wax paper and pat into an oval. Cover with another sheet of wax paper and refrigerate overnight. (The dough will be sticky.)

Preheat oven to 400°F. (204.4°C.). Divide the dough into 4 portions. Roll out one portion, keeping the others in the refrigerator, to a ⅛-inch-thick sheet on a well-floured board. Cut into 2½-inch rounds and place 1 inch apart on a greased cookie sheet. Bake in the preheated oven for 8 to 10 minutes. Frost with confectioners' icing.

# KOURABIETHES

Makes about 5 dozen cookies.

These famous very short Greek cookies are splendid with tea or coffee or as an extra fillip with fruit ices or sherbets. Stored in an airtight container, they seem to improve with age and may be kept for 2 or 3 weeks. The dough can also be frozen and baked when needed.

*⅓ cup blanched almonds (40 g)*
*½ cup confectioners' sugar (80 g)*
*½ lb. unsalted butter (2 sticks) (227 g)*
*2 Tbsp. brandy (28 g)*
*2 Tbsp. lemon juice (28 g)*
*2¼ cups flour (340 g)*
*½ tsp. baking powder*
*2 egg yolks*
*confectioners' sugar, for topping*

In the processor bowl fitted with the steel blade, grind the almonds to fine crumbs. Add the sugar and cut-up butter and blend until creamy. Scrape down. Add the brandy and lemon juice and blend with on and off quick turns. Sift the flour and baking powder. Add to the bowl and mix with 2 or 3 quick on and off turns. Add the egg yolks and incorporate very quickly. *Do not overbeat!* The dough is extremely soft and crumbly. Scoop it out onto wax paper and pat into a thick oval. Chill in the refrigerator overnight or in the freezer until firm.

Preheat oven to 350°F. (176.7°C.). Working with a small amount of dough at a time, keeping the remainder in the refrigerator, pinch off pieces the size of walnuts and with the palms of your hands roll into short ½-inch rolls. Form into crescents. Bake on an ungreased cookie sheet for approximately 20 minutes, or until the tips begin to color and the bottoms are light brown. Sift confectioners' sugar on a piece of wax paper and place the crescents on the sugar. Sift more confectioners' sugar over them and allow to cool. Place in a tin box and sift more confectioners' sugar over them. Cover tightly.

# KOULARAKIA

When chopped walnuts are substituted for the almonds in the preceding recipe and ½ walnut is placed on top of the crescent before baking, they change their name to *koularakia*. A little cinnamon may be sifted with the confectioners' sugar.

# UPPAKRA COOKIES

Makes about 36 cookies.

⅓ cup shelled nuts (40 g), for topping
½ lb. butter (2 sticks) (227 g), cut up
⅓ cup sugar (70 g)
1¾ cups flour (270 g)
¾ cup potato flour (120 g)

1 egg, slightly beaten
pearl sugar for topping

In the processor bowl fitted with the steel blade, chop the nuts; set aside. In the processor bowl blend the cut-up butter and sugar until creamy. Add the flours and blend with on and off quick turns or just until flours are incorporated. *Do not overbeat!* The dough will be crumbly. Pat dough together, wrap in wax paper, and chill for 30 minutes to 1 hour.

Preheat oven to 350°F. (176.7°C.). Roll out the dough directly on a buttered cookie sheet. Cut into 2-inch rounds, and remove the scraps of dough around the cut-out shapes. Fold each round over, as you would a Parker House roll, smoothing the back fold, and brush with the slightly beaten egg. Sprinkle with pearl sugar and chopped nuts. Bake in the preheated oven for 10 to 12 minutes, or until golden.

# CREAM-CHEESE COOKIES

Makes about 30 cookies.

5½ Tbsp. butter (98 g),
  cut up
3 oz. cream cheese (85 g),
  cut up
½ cup sugar (100 g)
¼ tsp. almond extract
1 cup flour (150 g)
2 tsp. baking powder
½ tsp. salt

In the processor bowl fitted with the steel blade, put the cut-up butter and cream cheese, and blend. Add the sugar and almond extract and process until smooth. Sift together the flour, baking powder and salt. Add to the cheese mixture and blend in with 3 on and off quick turns, or until the flour is just incorporated. *Do not overbeat!* Chill for 2 hours.

Preheat oven to 350°F. (176.7°C.). Form dough into small balls and place on an ungreased baking sheet. Bake in the preheated oven for 15 to 18 minutes, or until cookies are golden on the bottom. The balls may be rolled in finely chopped nuts or toasted coconut before baking.

# SHORTBREAD

½ lb. butter (2 sticks)
  (227 g), cut up
⅝ cup sugar (125 g)
2½ cups flour (375 g),
  sifted
¼ tsp. baking powder
½ tsp. salt

Preheat oven to 325°F. (162.8°C.). In the processor bowl fitted with the steel blade, put the cut-up butter. With the machine running, slowly add the sugar through the tube. Sift together the flour, baking powder and salt, and add to the butter and sugar mixture. Blend until flour is well incorporated. Chill the dough and roll out ½ inch thick. Cut into any desired shape. Prick the dough with a fork or pastry pricker. Bake on an ungreased baking sheet in the preheated oven for 20 to 25 minutes.

## LANGUES DE CHATS (Cats' Tongues)

Makes about 24 cookies.

*¼ lb. butter (1 stick)*
*(120 g)*
*½ cup sugar (100 g)*
*1 tsp. vanilla extract*
*4 egg whites*
*1 cup cake flour (120 g),*
*sifted*

Preheat oven to 425°F. (218.3°C.). In the processor bowl fitted with the steel blade, process the butter and sugar until creamy. Add the vanilla and the egg whites, one at a time, blending with on and off quick turns after each addition. Add the flour and blend in with 2 on and off quick turns, or just until the flour is incorporated. *Do not overbeat!* Place the batter in a pastry bag fitted with a small plain tube, and squeeze out portions 2 to 3 inches in length and as big around as a crayon onto a greased and floured baking sheet. Bake in the preheated oven for 6 to 8 minutes, or until the edges start to brown. Immediately remove from the baking sheet and cool on a rack.

## JANE ISAAC'S BROWNIES

Makes about 15 large brownies.

This recipe for the best brownies ever was given to us by Jane who has been making them since she was in fourth grade. (She is now in seventh grade.)

*12 oz. semisweet choco-*
*late bits (340 g)*
*½ lb. unsalted butter (2*
*sticks) (227 g)*
*1 cup sugar (200 g)*
*4 eggs*
*½ Tbsp. vanilla extract*
*1 cup cake flour (120 g)*
*1 tsp. baking powder*

Preheat oven to 375°F. (190.6°C.). Melt the chocolate bits and butter in the top part of a double boiler over hot water, and cool. In the processor bowl fitted with the steel blade, put the sugar and add the eggs, one at a time, blending after each addition. Add the vanilla and the chocolate-butter mixture and blend thoroughly. Sift together the flour and baking powder and add to the mixture in the bowl. Blend, turning the machine on and off 3 times, or until the flour is just incorporated. *Do not overbeat!* Pour the batter into a greased pan, 11¾ x 7½ x 1¾ inches. Bake in the preheated oven for exactly 20 minutes. Cool thoroughly, for several hours, before cutting.

# LEMON DELIGHTS

Makes about 18 cookies.

An old-fashioned sweet which may be baked with thick or thin layers, to be served as a dessert or as a cookie. Halve the recipe if you only want a small amount.

PASTRY BASE
½ lb. butter (2 sticks) (227 g)
½ cup confectioners' sugar (80 g)
½ tsp. salt
2 cups flour (300 g)

Preheat oven to 350°F. (176.7°C.). In the processor bowl fitted with the steel blade, blend the butter and sugar for 30 seconds. Add the salt and the flour, 1 cup at a time, blending until a soft crumbly dough forms. Pat into a rectangular pan (13½ x 9½ x 2 inches) or two 9-inch-square pans. Bake in the preheated oven for 15 to 20 minutes. Remove from the oven and let cool. Make the filling.

FILLING
rind of 1 lemon
1½ cups sugar (300 g)
4 Tbsp. flour (40 g)
1 tsp. baking powder
pinch of salt
½ cup lemon juice (1 dl)
4 eggs

In the processor bowl fitted with the steel blade, process the lemon rind and sugar for 30 seconds. Add the flour, baking powder, salt and lemon juice. Blend with on and off quick turns. Add the eggs, one at a time, and blend each time with 1 on and off quick turn. Blend for 10 seconds. Pour the filling over the pastry base and bake for 25 to 30 minutes or until set. Let cool. Glaze, if desired, with Lemon Glaze (see Index). Cut into squares. A thin layer of pastry and topping makes fragile cookies, thicker layers make a satisfying dessert.

BAKING PANS

8½ x 4½ x 2½ inches = 21.6 x 11 x 6.4 cm
11½ x 9 x 2 inches = 29 x 23 x 5 cm
13 x 9 x 2 inches = 33 x 23 x 5 cm

# PECAN MERINGUE BARS

Makes about 18 bars.

PASTRY
½ *lb. butter (2 sticks)*
*(227 g), cut up*
½ *cup confectioners'*
*sugar (80 g)*
½ *tsp. salt*
*2 cups flour (300 g)*

Preheat oven to 350°F. (176.7°C.). In the processor bowl fitted with the steel blade, blend the cut-up butter and sugar until creamy. Add salt and the flour, 1 cup at a time, blending until a soft crumbly dough forms. Pat into a rectangular pan, 13½ x 9½ x 2 inches, or two 9-inch-square pans. Bake in the preheated oven for 15 to 20 minutes. Let cool. Make the filling.

FILLING
*1 cup shelled pecans*
*(120 g)*
¾ *cup brown sugar*
*(150 g)*
¾ cup granulated sugar
*(150 g)*
*4 eggs, separated*
½ *cup milk ( 1 dl)*
*4 Tbsp. flour (40 g)*
*1 tsp. baking powder*
*2 tsp. maple flavoring*
¼ *tsp. cream of tartar*
⅔ *cup confectioners'*
*sugar (100 g)*
*1 tsp. vanilla extract*

In the processor bowl fitted with the steel blade, chop the pecans and set aside. Place the brown and granulated sugars in the bowl; with the motor running, add the egg yolks, one at a time. Add the milk and blend in. Mix together the flour and baking powder and quickly blend into the sugar-egg mixture. Add the maple flavoring and mix with on and off quick turns. Spread the filling over the pastry base. Beat the egg whites and cream of tartar with a rotary beater or mixer, adding the confectioners' sugar, 1 tablespoon at a time. Add the vanilla. Fold in the chopped pecans. Spread the meringue over the filling. Bake in the preheated 350°F. oven for 30 to 35 minutes, or until the meringue begins to brown.

# ALMOND PRESERVE BARS

Makes about 18 bars.

PASTRY
½ lb. butter (2 sticks)
   (227 g), cut up
½ cup confectioners'
   sugar (80 g)
½ tsp. salt
2 cups flour (300 g)

Preheat oven to 350°F. (176.7°C.). In the processor bowl fitted with the steel blade, blend the cut-up butter and sugar until creamy. Add the salt and the flour, 1 cup at a time, blending until a soft crumbly dough forms. Pat into a rectangular pan, 13½ x 9½ x 2 inches, or two 9-inch-square pans. Bake in the preheated oven for 15 to 20 minutes. Let cool. Make the filling.

FILLING
½ cup Almond Paste
   (150 g) (see Index)
6 oz. cream cheese
   (170 g)
2 eggs
1½ cups preserves or jam
   (.36 l)

In the processor bowl fitted with the steel blade, blend the almond paste and cream cheese. Add the eggs, one at a time, and blend in. Spread the filling over the pastry base and top with the preserves. Bake in the preheated 350°F. (176.7°C.) oven for 25 to 30 minutes.

# CHARLESTON BARS

Makes about 20 bars.

1 cup shelled nuts (120 g)
¼ lb. butter (1 stick)
   (120 g)
1 cup granulated sugar
   (200 g)
3 eggs, separated
1 tsp. vanilla extract
1½ cups flour (225 g)
1 tsp. baking powder
¼ tsp. salt
1 lb. brown sugar
   (.453 kg)
1 tsp. lemon juice

Preheat oven to 375°F. (190.6°C.). In the processor bowl fitted with the steel blade, chop the nuts; set aside. Blend the butter and granulated sugar until creamy. Add the egg yolks, vanilla and 1 egg white and process with on and off quick turns. Sift the flour, baking powder and salt together and add to the sugar-egg mixture. Blend in with on and off quick turns, or just until the flour is incorporated. With floured hands pat the dough into a buttered and floured pan, 11½ x 9 x 2 inches. In the processor bowl filled with the steel blade, cream the brown sugar, 2 egg whites and lemon juice, and spread evenly on the dough. Sprinkle the nuts on top. Bake in the preheated oven for 25 to 30 minutes. Cut into squares. Serve plain or with whipped cream.

## CRYSTALLIZED GINGER DIAGONALS

Makes about 24 bars.

*2 Tbsp. candied ginger-*
*root (30 g)*
*⅔ cup sugar (135 g)*
*⅜ lb. butter (1½ sticks)*
*(180 g)*
*1 egg*
*2 tsp. vanilla extract*
*2 cups flour (300 g)*
*½ tsp. baking powder*
*jam*

Preheat oven to 350°F. (176.7°F.). In the processor bowl fitted with the steel blade, process the candied gingerroot and the sugar until gingerroot is finely chopped. Add the butter and blend until smooth. Put in the egg and vanilla and blend with on and off quick turns; scrape down. Sift the flour and baking powder and put in the container. Blend with 3 on and off quick turns, or until the flour is just incorporated. *Do not overbeat!* Turn the dough out onto a lightly floured surface and divide into 4 parts. Form each into a roll 12 inches long and 1 inch thick. Place the rolls 4 inches apart on an ungreased baking sheet. Make a trench the length of the dough and fill with jam. Bake in the preheated oven for 15 to 20 minutes, or until golden. While still warm cut diagonally into bars and cool on a rack.

## JAM SQUARES

Makes 16 squares.

*½ cup shelled walnuts*
*(60 g)*
*¼ lb. butter (1 stick)*
*(120 g), cut up*
*½ cup sugar (100 g)*
*1 Tbsp. maple extract*
*(15 g)*
*1 egg*
*1½ cups cake flour*
*(180 g)*
*1 Tbsp. baking powder*
*(12 g)*
*1 cup jam (.24 l), approx-*
*imately*

Preheat oven to 350°F. (176.7°C.). In the processor bowl fitted with the steel blade, grind the walnuts. Add the cut-up butter and the sugar and blend until creamy; scrape down. Add the maple extract and egg and blend with on and off quick turns. Sift the flour and baking powder. Place half of the sifted flour in the container and blend very quickly with 2 or 3 on and off turns. Add remaining flour and again quickly blend in. *Do not overbeat!* Divide the dough into 2 portions. Pat one half into a greased 8-inch-square pan. Spread the surface with the jam of your choice. Carefully pat remaining dough on top. Bake in the preheated oven for 40 minutes, or until golden. Cut into squares while warm.

# 5

# DESSERT PUDDINGS

# BREAD DESSERTS

Bread puddings, often considered nursery fare, can be made into surprisingly sophisticated desserts.

## CRUMB BREAD PUDDING

Makes 8 servings.

*8 slices of white bread*
*1 cup milk (.24 l)*
*2 eggs*
*½ cup molasses (160 g)*
*1 tsp. ground cinnamon*
*1 cup white raisins*
  *(100 g)*

Preheat oven to 325°F. (162.8°C.). In the processor bowl fitted with the steel blade, grind the torn-up slices of bread, 1 cup at a time, to coarse bits; put bread bits in a buttered 6-cup baking dish or 8-inch-square baking pan. Put the milk, eggs, molasses and cinnamon in the processor bowl and blend with on and off quick turns. Scatter the raisins on top of the bread crumbs and gently stir in the custard mixture. Set the baking dish in a pan of hot water. Bake for 45 minutes, or until a cake tester inserted comes out clean. Serve with a fruit sauce (see Index).

## APPLE BREAD PUDDING

Makes 8 to 10 servings.

*½ loaf of whole-wheat*
  *bread (227 g)*
*butter*
*4 or 5 medium-size*
  *cooking apples*
*½ cup water (1 dl)*
*4 Tbsp. brown sugar*
  *(50 g)*
*½ tsp. ground cinnamon*

Preheat oven to 350° F. (176.7°C.). Remove the crusts from the bread and cut into thin slices. Butter the slices. Butter a rectangular pan, 11½ x 9 x 2 inches, or a 13-inch oval dish. Cut enough of the bread slices into halves to cover the bottom of the baking dish. Place the half-slices, buttered side up, on the bottom. Core and peel the apples and slice them with the slicing disc. Spread the apples over the bread and sprinkle the water over the fruit. Sprinkle with the brown sugar mixed with the cinnamon. Cover with another layer of buttered bread slices, buttered side up. Bake until crisp, about 1 hour. Serve with Wine Custard Sauce (see Index).

## CLAFOUTI BREAD PUDDING

Makes 8 to 10 servings.

This is an adaptation of an old French recipe, a type of cherry custard pie.

*½ loaf of white bread (227 g)*
*butter*
*2 cups drained canned dark cherries (.48 l), or pitted fresh cherries*
*½ cup sugar (100 g)*
*2 cups milk (.48 l)*
*3 whole eggs*
*2 extra egg yolks*
*1 tsp. vanilla extract, or 1 Tbsp. Kirsch*

Preheat oven to 350°F. (176.7°C.). Cut the bread into thin slices and remove the crusts. Butter each slice. Cut slices into triangles and place under the broiler for a few minutes, until golden. Cover the bottom of a buttered rectangular pan (11½ x 9 x 2 inches) with the bread triangles, toasted side up, and arrange in a square pattern. Place the drained cherries over the toast and sprinkle with ¼ cup of the sugar. In the processor bowl fitted with the steel blade, put the milk, whole eggs, egg yolks, remaining sugar, and vanilla or Kirsch; blend well. Gently spoon the egg-sugar mixture over the cherries. Place remaining toasted bread triangles neatly over the custard and with a broad spatula push them down so that they absorb the liquid. Set the dish in a pan of hot water and bake for 45 minutes, or until the custard is set.

# BREAD PUDDING WITH MERINGUE

Makes 8 to 10 servings.

½ lb. or ½ loaf of white
    bread (227 g)
3 Tbsp. butter (45 g)
rind of 1 lemon
½ cup sugar (100 g)
3 egg yolks
3 cups milk (.72 l)
½ tsp. salt
1 tsp. vanilla extract

Preheat oven to 350°F. (176.7°C.). Remove crusts from the bread and cut it into ½-inch cubes. Sauté the bread cubes in the butter until golden. Pile into a rectangular pan (11½ x 9 x 2 inches) or an oval baking dish. In the processor bowl fitted with the steel blade, process the lemon rind and sugar until rind is chopped, about 30 seconds. Add the egg yolks, milk, salt and vanilla, and blend well. Spoon the custard mixture over the bread cubes. Set the baking dish in a pan of hot water and bake for 45 minutes, or until the custard is set. Cool.

MERINGUE
3 egg whites
¼ tsp. cream of tartar
2 Tbsp. sugar (25 g)

3 to 4 Tbsp. tart jelly
    (50 g)

Beat the egg whites with the cream of tartar and sugar until you have a stiff meringue. Spread the meringue on top of the pudding. With the back of a spoon make depressions in the meringue every 2 inches. Bake the pudding in a preheated 300°F. (148.9°C.) oven for 10 minutes, or until light-golden. Spoon a dab of tart jelly into each depression. Serve warm.

# SUMMER PUDDING

Makes 8 to 10 servings.

This old-fashioned New England dessert tastes as good as it looks. Make it the day before it is to be eaten. Serve with Wine Custard Sauce (see Index) or heavy cream.

1 loaf of 2-day-old white
    bread
1 cup sugar (200 g)
½ cup water (1 dl)
4 cups berries (1 l)

Remove the crusts from the bread and cut it into thin slices. Combine the sugar and water and cook until sugar is completely dissolved and becomes syrupy. Add the fruit and simmer over low heat for 5 minutes, stirring gently. Should the fruit not be sweet enough, add a little more sugar. Line a 2-quart bowl with the slices of bread and spoon some of the fruit over it. Continue to layer the bread and the fruit, ending with bread layer. Cover with wax paper or foil. On top place a flat plate or the bottom of a false-bottom pan. Put a heavy weight on the plate. Refrigerate the pudding overnight. Turn the pudding out onto a flat dish and serve with a sauce or cream.

---

# PUMPERNICKEL BREAD DESSERTS

Desserts made with this dark bread are remarkably good. No one ever guesses the basic ingredient.

## CHOCOLATE PUMPERNICKEL TORTE

Makes 6 to 8 servings.

*3 or 4 slices of pumpernickel, crusts removed*
*rind of ½ lemon*
*¾ cup sugar (150 g)*
*3 oz. unsweetened chocolate (85 g), cut up*
*7 Tbsp. butter (110 g)*
*5 eggs, separated*
*½ cup white raisins (50 g)*

Preheat oven to 350°F. (176.7°C.). In the processor bowl fitted with the steel blade, process pieces of pumpernickel bread until fine; there should be ⅔ cup crumbs; set aside. Process the lemon rind and sugar until rind is chopped, about 30 seconds. Add the cut-up chocolate and chop until chocolate is finely ground. Put in the butter and blend well. Add the egg yolks and blend in. Place the mixture in a large bowl. Beat the egg whites with a rotary beater or a mixer until stiff but not dry. Fold the pumpernickel crumbs into the chocolate mixture. Add the raisins, then fold in the egg whites. Put into a greased and floured 8-inch springform pan. Bake for 45 minutes, or until a cake tester comes out clean when inserted in the center of the torte. The torte will fall a little as it cools. Serve plain, or frost with a butter icing, or finish with whipped cream.

## HELENE'S PUMPERNICKEL DESSERT

Makes 8 to 10 servings.

*1 lb. pumpernickel bread
(.453 kg)crusts removed
½ cup cherry jam or jelly
(80 g)
½ cup Kirsch (120 g)
2 cups heavy cream
(.48 l)
2 cans (17 oz. each) sour
cherries (.48 l)
1 cup sugar (200 g)*

Remove crusts from bread and tear slices into pieces. In the processor bowl fitted with the steel blade, put the torn-up bread, 1 cup at a time, and crumble. To the last batch add the cherry jam or jelly and the Kirsch. Blend with 3 on and off quick turns. Add to the other batches of crumbled bread and set aside. Whip the cream with a rotary beater. Place a layer of the crumbs in the bottom of a 2-quart bowl, then add a layer of drained cherries, sprinkled with part of the sugar. Spoon whipped cream over the cherries. Continue to layer, ending with whipped cream. Chill. This is particularly attractive when served in a glass bowl.

## PUMPERNICKEL PUDDING (DRUNKEN BROTHER)

Makes 4 to 6 servings.

*6 slices of pumpernickel
bread, crusts removed
rind of 4 lemons
1½ cups sugar (300 g)
½ cup blanched almonds
(60 g)
1 tsp. ground cinnamon
¼ tsp. ground cloves
6 eggs, separated
1 cup white raisins
(100 g) or cut-up
prunes (200 g)
1 cup red wine (.24 l)*

Preheat oven to 350°F. (176.7°C.). In the processor bowl fitted with the steel blade, put pieces of the pumpernickel bread and process until fine; there should be 1 cup of crumbs. Set aside in a large bowl. Process the lemon rind and ½ cup of the sugar until rind is chopped, about 30 seconds. Add the almonds, cinnamon and cloves, and process until almonds are chopped. Add the egg yolks and blend in. Fold in the crumbs and then the raisins or prunes. Put the mixture in a buttered 1-quart mold. Place the mold in a pan and add boiling water halfway up the mold. Bake for 1 hour. Invert the pudding onto a serving dish. Boil the red wine and remaining 1 cup of sugar together until the sugar is thoroughly dissolved. Spoon wine over the pudding and let it soak in. Pudding may be eaten warm or cold and is delicious with whipped cream.

# BRIOCHE STRAWBERRY CHARLOTTE

Makes 8 to 10 servings.

*1 quart strawberries (1 l)*
*½ cup sugar (100 g)*
*½ cup sherry (1 dl)*
*1 recipe Brioche dough*
*(see Index)*
*1 recipe Crème Saint-*
*Honoré (see Index)*
*1 cup heavy cream (.24 l)*
*Strawberry Glaze (see*
*Index)*

Preheat oven to 350°F. (176.7°C.). Set aside enough whole strawberries to form a ring at the base of the pudding. In the processor bowl fitted with the slicing disc, slice remaining strawberries. Place berries in a bowl and add the sugar and sherry; let the berries macerate. Make the *brioche* dough and bake it in 2 small loaf pans (4½ x 2½ x 2½ inches). Chill *brioche* until firm. Butter and sugar a 2-quart bowl or Charlotte mold. Slice the *brioche* and put a layer of slices in the mold. Drain the strawberries and save the sherry. Put a layer of strawberries on the layer of *brioche* slices. Spoon in a layer of *crème Saint-Honoré*. Add another layer of *brioche* slices. Continue layering until the mold is filled, ending with *brioche*. Spoon the sherry over the top. Chill overnight.

Turn out the pudding onto a flat serving plate. Mask pudding with whipped cream. Place the whole berries around the base of the pudding. Serve with strawberry glaze.

# 6

BASIC PASTRIES

# PÂTE À CHOUX
## (CREAM-PUFF PASTRY)

Cream puffs, éclairs, profiteroles and great dessert constructions such as *croquembouche* and Paris-Brest are based on *pâte à choux*.

*¼ lb. butter (1 stick)*
  *(120 g)*
*1 cup hot water (1 dl)*
*1 cup flour (150 g)*
*½ tsp. salt*
*1 Tbsp. sugar (13 g)*
*4 eggs*

Preheat oven to 400°F. (204.4°C.). Combine the butter and water in a heavy pan and heat until butter is melted. Mix the flour, salt and sugar. When the butter-water mixture comes to a boil, add the flour all at once and stir vigorously with a wooden spoon until the dough forms a firm ball and pulls away from the sides of the pan. Let cool.

Place the dough in the processor bowl fitted with the steel blade, and blend for 10 to 15 seconds. With the motor running, add the eggs, one at a time, through the tube. Process until dough is smooth and shiny. Shape according to the recipe you are making. Bake in the preheated oven for 10 minutes, or until puffed up. Reduce oven temperature to 350°F. and bake for 15 to 20 minutes longer, depending on the size of the puff, until golden. While puffs are still in the oven, prick each one on the side to allow steam to escape. Turn off the oven. With the oven door slightly ajar let them rest for 10 minutes, or until dry. Break open one of the puffs. If the center is moist, use a demitasse spoon to scoop out the centers through the slit in the side, or split the puffs horizontally and remove the moist portion. Fill the halves and put back together.

## TO FORM CREAM PUFFS

*Large Puffs*—1 recipe of Pâte à Choux makes 10 to 12 puffs about 3 inches in diameter. Drop the batter from a tablespoon onto a greased baking sheet, using enough to form mounds 2 inches in diameter and 1 inch high. Place mounds 2 inches apart. Or they may be formed with a pastry bag using a ¾-inch round tip.

*Small Puffs*—1 recipe of Pâte à Choux makes 38 to 40 puffs 1½ inches in diameter. Drop the batter from a spoon onto a greased baking sheet, using enough to form mounds 1 inch in diameter and 1 inch high. Place mounds 2 inches apart. Or they may be formed with a pastry bag using a ½-inch round tip.

*Filling*—Puffs may be split horizontally, filled, and put together again, or they may be filled through a hole in the shell by means of a pastry bag, using a ¼-inch tip.

## TO FORM ÉCLAIRS

With 1 recipe of Pâte à Choux you can make about 12 éclairs. Use a pastry bag with ½-inch tip, or shape batter with a spatula into fingers 4 inches long and 1 inch wide. For small éclairs make the mounds 2 inches long. For filling, use the same methods as for Cream Puffs. For the simplest icing for éclairs, mix 2 teaspoons flavoring with ½ cup confectioners' sugar. Éclairs may be frosted with Confectioners' Icing (see Index), or melted semisweet chocolate may be drizzled over them.

## PROFITEROLES

*Profiteroles* are very small puffs filled with ice cream or creamy fillings and topped with a sauce—chocolate, butterscotch, maple, etc.

## MOCK PUFF PASTE

½ lb. cold butter (227 g), cut up
1⅔ cups flour (250 g)
4 Tbsp. ice water (.5 dl)

In the processor bowl fitted with the steel blade, put the cut-up butter. Sift the flour and add to the butter. Blend with on and off quick turns until the mixture resembles cornmeal. Add the ice water and incorporate with on and off quick turns. The dough will be very soft. Place the dough on floured wax paper and flatten into a rectangle ¼ inch thick. Sprinkle with more flour and cover with another sheet of wax paper. Chill in the freezer for 30 minutes. Remove the top layer of wax paper. Fold the dough in thirds. Top again with wax paper and roll out into a rectangle ¼ inch thick. Fold the dough and repeat 2 more times, chilling for 30 minutes each time. The dough can now be formed into any desired shape—circles, crescents, shells. Bake in a preheated 500°F. (260°C.) oven for 8 to 10 minutes.

# BASIC PASTRIES
# FOR PIES AND TARTS

All these pastries are made with the steel or plastic blade.

The secret of fine pastry making is a light touch. *Never overprocess!* Just blend the dry ingredients with the shortening for 3 seconds. After adding the liquid, it is not necessary to form a real ball of dough. Just gather the mass together, pat it into a ball, flatten it, and when necessary refrigerate it.

After the dough is made, wrap it in wax paper and chill for at least 1 hour, or store it in the refrigerator overnight, or wrap and freeze. Lard and vegetable shortening crusts need not be refrigerated.

For making pastry shells of any size, roll out the dough ⅛ inch thick. Roll the dough from the center out into a circle or rectangle in one direction only, not back and forth. Roll up the dough around the rolling pin and drape gently over the pan to be filled. Ease the dough into the pan, pressing it carefully against the sides. Do not stretch it: stretched dough shrinks in baking. Or fold the dough into fourths and place the point of the dough in the center of the pan. Open the folded dough and pat into place. Trim and crimp or flute the edges. If using a flan ring or fluted pan, roll the pin across the pan to remove excess dough. For a firmer edge push the dough slightly above the rim of the pan.

## Prebaked and Partially Baked Shells

Roll out dough and fill pie pan or small tart pans. Small tarts may be also made by covering inverted muffin tins with dough. Prick dough all over.

Refrigerate for 20 minutes to 1 hour. Line dough with foil and weight with dried beans, rice or pie weights. Bake in a preheated 425°F. (218.3°C.) oven for 8 to 10 minutes. Remove beans, rice or weights and the foil, and continue baking for 4 to 5 minutes for a partially baked shell, 10 to 12 minutes for a completely baked shell.

"Waterproof" the bottom of partially baked shells with egg white, beaten with 1 tablespoon of water, or for sweet tarts with a glaze of melted, strained apricot preserves, before filling.

### One-Step Pies and Tarts

When the filling is put into unbaked pastry and crust and filling are baked together, the pie must be cooked at high heat, 400°F. (204.4°C.), on the lowest rack of the oven for 10 to 15 minutes to set the crust. Then move the pie to the center rack and finish at 350°F. (176.6°C.) for 30 minutes more or until the crust is golden and the filling cooked.

## PÂTE BRISÉE

Makes enough pastry for one 9- or 10-inch crust.

*10 Tbsp. chilled butter (150 g), cut up*
*1¾ cups all-purpose flour (270 g)*
*1 tsp. salt*
*⅓ to ½ cup ice-cold water, white wine or vermouth (.6 to 1 dl)*

In the processor bowl fitted with the steel blade, blend the cut-up butter, the flour and salt with on and off quick turns until the mixture resembles cornmeal. Add ¼ cup of the liquid and process for 3 seconds. With the motor running, add more liquid, 1 tablespoon at a time, through the tube, until a ball of dough begins to form a mass around the blade. *The instant the dough has begun to form, stop the machine.* Chill pastry for at least 1 hour. To roll out and bake, see directions on page 164.

## SWEET PÂTE BRISÉE

For Sweet Pâte Brisée, add 1 tablespoon of sugar to the Pâte Brisée recipe.

## VARIATIONS ON PÂTE BRISÉE

*Lemon*—Add the rind of ½ lemon and substitute the juice of ½ lemon for part of the ice water.

*Orange*—Add the rind of ¼ orange and for the liquid use half orange juice and half water.

*Nut*—Add ½ cup finely chopped nuts (80 g) to the flour.

*Coconut*—Add ½ cup flaked coconut (80 g) to the flour.

# PÂTE SUCRÉE

Makes enough pastry for one 9- or 10-inch crust.

*10 Tbsp. chilled butter
(150 g), cut up
1¾ cups all-purpose flour
(270 g)
2 Tbsp. sugar (25 g)
pinch of salt
1 egg yolk
enough ice water to
loosely form the dough*

In the processor bowl fitted with the steel blade, blend the cut-up butter, the flour, sugar and salt with on and off quick turns until the mixture resembles cornmeal. Add the egg yolk and blend with on and off quick turns. With the motor running, slowly dribble in ice water just until a mass of dough forms. *The instant the dough has begun to form, stop the machine.* Chill the pastry for at least 1 hour. To roll out and bake, see directions on page 164.

# BASIC PIECRUST

Makes enough pastry for two 8- or 9-inch crusts.

*⅔ cup shortening (lard or
hydrogenated vegetable
shortening) (150 g), cut
up
2 cups flour (300 g)
1 tsp. salt
¼ to ½ cup ice water (.5
to 1 dl)*

In the processor bowl fitted with the steel blade, blend the cut-up shortening, the flour and salt with on and off quick turns until the mixture resembles cornmeal. Add ¼ cup of the ice water and process for 3 seconds. With the motor running, add more ice water, 1 tablespoon at a time, through the tube, until the dough just masses around the blade. *The instant the dough has begun to form, stop the machine.* Chill the pastry for at least 1 hour. To roll out and bake, see directions on page 164.

# CREAM-CHEESE PASTRY

Makes enough pastry for one 9-inch shell or several small tarts.

A simple flaky crust good for tartlets, *empanadas* and other turn-overs, and roll-ups, as well as for piecrust. This pastry becomes soft in a warm kitchen. Use a little at a time, keeping the rest refrigerated until needed.

*¼ lb. butter (1 stick)*
*(120 g), cut up*
*3 oz. cream cheese (85 g),*
*softened*
*1 cup flour (150 g), sifted*
*¼ tsp. salt*

In the processor bowl fitted with the steel blade, blend the cut-up butter and cream cheese quickly. Add the flour and salt and process just until a soft ball of dough begins to form around the blade. Refrigerate.

# COTTAGE-CHEESE PASTRY

Makes enough pastry for one 9-inch shell or several small tarts.

A quick satisfying pastry for turnovers or *bouchées* or for filled small tea pastries.

*¼ lb. butter (1 stick)*
*(120 g), cut up*
*½ cup cottage cheese*
*(1 dl)*
*1 cup flour (150 g), or*
*more to form a*
*loose ball*

In the processor bowl fitted with the steel blade, put the cut-up butter and cottage cheese and blend well. Add 1 cup flour and process until a soft ball of dough begins to mass around the blade. It may be necessary to add more flour, ¼ cup at a time, to make a smooth pliable dough. Chill.

# SHARP CHEESE PASTRY

Makes enough pastry for two 9-inch crusts.

A natural for apple pie, interesting for vegetable quiches too.

*4 oz. sharp cheese (113 g)*
*1¾ cups flour (270 g)*
*½ tsp. salt*
*¼ lb. butter (1 stick)*
*(120 g), cut up*
*⅓ to ½ cup ice water (.6*
*to 1 dl)*

In the processor bowl fitted with the shredding disc, shred the cheese; set aside. Replace the shredding disc with the steel blade and blend the flour, salt, cut-up butter and the shredded cheese until the mixture resembles cornmeal. Add ⅓ cup ice water and process for 3 seconds. If a ball of dough does not begin to mass around the blade, turn on the motor again and dribble in just enough more ice water to help the dough begin to form a mass. *The instant the dough has begun to form, stop the machine.* Wrap the dough in wax paper and chill before using.

# CHOCOLATE PASTRY

Makes enough pastry for one 9-inch crust.

Delectable with custard fillings, particularly lime, lemon, orange or peppermint.

*1 cup flour (150 g)*
*3 Tbsp. sugar (38 g)*
*3 Tbsp. cocoa powder*
*(15 g)*
*¼ tsp. salt*
*6 Tbsp. butter (90 g), cut*
*up*
*¼ tsp. vanilla extract*
*⅓ to ½ cup ice water*
*(.6 to 1 dl)*

In the processor bowl fitted with the steel blade, blend the flour, sugar, cocoa powder, salt, cut-up butter and vanilla for 3 seconds. Add ⅓ cup ice water and process again for 3 seconds. If a ball of dough does not begin to mass around the blade, turn on the motor again and dribble in just enough more ice water to help the dough begin to form a mass. *The instant the dough has begun to form, stop the machine.* Wrap the dough in wax paper and chill before using.

## CRUMB SHELLS

Makes one 9-inch shell.

*1½ cups crumbs*
*6 Tbsp. butter (90 g)*
*¼ cup sugar (50 g)*

Preheat oven to 375°F. (190.6°C.). Make crumbs from any of the following: graham crackers, zwieback, chocolate or vanilla wafers, dried cake, gingersnaps. Use ½ cup finely ground nuts as a substitute for half of the crumbs if you like. In the processor bowl fitted with the steel blade, grind the broken-up crumb ingredients until fine. Add butter and sugar and blend well with on and off quick turns. Pat into a buttered pie tin or springform pan. Bake for 8 minutes for a crisp shell, or chill unbaked for 30 minutes before filling. Good with chiffon fillings, ice cream or custard fillings.

## NUT CRUST

Makes one 9-inch shell.

*½ lb. shelled nuts (227 g)*
*3 Tbsp. sugar (45 g)*
*2 Tbsp. butter (30 g),*
  *melted*
*½ tsp. salt*
*2 Tbsp. flour (20 g)*

Preheat oven to 375°F. (190.6°C.). Place the nuts (pecans, almonds, Brazil nuts or hazelnuts) in the processor bowl fitted with the steel blade, and chop until finely ground. Add the sugar, melted butter, salt and flour. Blend with quick on and off turns. Press the mixture against a heavily buttered pie plate. Bake in the preheated oven for 8 minutes. These shells may also be used chilled and unbaked.

## MERINGUE CRUMB SHELL

Makes two 9-inch shells.

*10 to 20 cookies, broken up*
*¼ lb. shelled nuts (113 g)*
*6 egg whites*
*¼ tsp. cream of tartar*
*2 cups superfine sugar (200 g)*
*1 tsp. flavoring extract*

Preheat oven to 275°F. (135°C.). Place broken-up cookies (graham crackers, chocolate or vanilla wafers, macaroons) and the nuts (pecans, walnuts or hazelnuts, etc.) in the processor bowl fitted with the steel blade, and chop coarsely. There should be 1 cup of nut crumbs and 1 cup of cookie crumbs. Beat the egg whites and cream of tartar with a rotary beater or in a mixer until stiff but not dry. Add the sugar gradually, 1 tablespoon at a time. Fold in the nuts, crumbs and flavoring. Spread into 2 buttered and floured 9-inch pie plates, piling meringue high around the edges. Or pile the meringue into buttered and floured 9-inch false-bottom layer pans, or into one 8-inch springform pan. Bake in the preheated oven for 1 to 1½ hours, or until the meringue begins to shrink from the sides of the pan. When using a deep springform pan, allow 20 to 30 minutes more. Fill the pies with an airy filling or ice cream. If meringue is in layers or a single cake, it may be frosted with flavored whipped cream.

# 7

# PASTRY, PIES AND TARTS

## *For Entrée and Hors d' Oeuvre*

—◆—

Pies, shallow or deep-dish, or baked in quiche form, large pastries and turnovers are as good-looking as good-tasting. They may be made as individual tarts, quiches, turnovers or pasties for fine finger food for picnics.

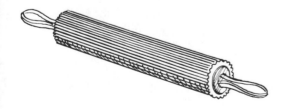

# GOUGÈRE WITH HAM FILLING

¼ lb. Swiss cheese
(113 g)
2 oz. Parmesan cheese
(56 g), cut up
Cream-Puff Pastry (see
Index)
1 tsp. dry mustard, moistened with 1 Tbsp. vin-
egar (15 g)
1 egg

In the processor bowl filled with the shredding disc, shred the Swiss cheese; set aside. With the steel blade, grate the cut-up Parmesan cheese; set aside. Prepare the cream-puff pastry, incorporating the shredded Swiss cheese and the mustard. With a tablespoon drop pieces of the dough around a buttered 9-inch pie plate or fluted porcelain quiche dish so that the dough pieces touch each other. Brush the tops with the egg beaten with 1 tablespoon water, and sprinkle with the Parmesan cheese. Bake in a preheated 425° (232.2°C.) oven for 20 minutes. Reduce heat to 300°F. (148.9°C.) and bake for 5 minutes longer, or until the puffs are golden. Prick around the top to allow steam to escape. Turn off the oven and leave the gougère inside.

HAM FILLING
½ lb. mushrooms (227 g)
2 Tbsp. butter (30 g)
1 lb. boneless cooked ham
(.453 kg)

In the processor bowl fitted with the slicing disc, slice the mushrooms. Sauté them in the butter. Cut up the ham and chop coarsely, 1 cup at a time, with the steel blade. Add to the mushrooms.

CREAM SAUCE
4 Tbsp. butter (60 g), cut
up
4 Tbsp. flour (40 g)
½ tsp. salt
¼ tsp. pepper
3 cups milk (.72 l),
scalded
2 Tbsp. Madeira or
sherry wine (28 g) (op-
tional)

In the processor bowl fitted with the steel blade, put the cut-up butter, the flour, salt and pepper. Blend with quick on and off turns until the mixture resembles cornmeal. With the motor running pour the scalded milk through the tube and process until smooth. Cook, stirring constantly, until thickened. Stir in the Madeira or sherry.

To assemble: Measure 2 cups of the cream sauce (remaining sauce can be used for another recipe). Add the ham-mushroom mixture to the sauce. Fill the gougère ring and serve.

# VARIATION

This cream-puff paste ring, flavored with cheese, is a light and very pretty dish when filled with a sauced fish, vegetable or meat. It may also be served unfilled as an hors d'oeuvre; pull pieces off to serve. Instead of making a ring of *gougère,* large individual puffs may be made and filled for an entrée, or small ones can serve for hors d'oeuvre.

# DEEP-DISH FISH PIE

Makes 6 servings.

½ recipe Basic Piecrust
  (see Index)
6 hard-cooked eggs
½ cup parsley sprigs
4 Tbsp. flour (40 g)
4 Tbsp. butter (60 g), cut
  up
½ tsp. salt
¼ tsp. pepper
1 cup milk (.24 l), scalded
1 cup clam juice (.24 l),
  scalded
1 Tbsp. lemon juice (14 g)
3 tomatoes (.453 kg),
  peeled
butter for pan
1 cup bread crumbs
3 lb. flaked cooked fish
  (1.36 kg)

Make pastry and roll out to a 10-inch square, large enough to cover the dish with extra all around. Preheat oven to 400°F. (204.4°C.). In the processor bowl fitted with the plastic blade, coarsely chop the cut-up eggs with 2 or 3 on and off quick turns; set aside. Chop the parsley with the steel blade. Add the flour, the cut-up butter, salt and pepper to the parsley, and blend. With the motor running, pour the scalded milk and clam juice through the tube and process until the mixture is smooth. Add lemon juice and blend. Cook the sauce mixture, stirring constantly, until thickened. Slice the tomatoes by hand.

Butter a 9-inch-square heatproof glass dish, and sprinkle it with bread crumbs. Put in half of the fish. Spoon on half of the chopped eggs and top with half of the tomato slices. Sprinkle with more bread crumbs. Spoon half of the cream sauce on top of the tomatoes. Repeat layering, ending with remaining tomatoes and remaining cream sauce.

Roll the sheet of pastry on top; fold the edges of the pastry under and flute just inside the edge of the pan. Cut vents in the pastry. Bake in the preheated oven for 35 minutes, or until the top is golden.

# SHRIMP TART

Makes 6 servings.

*1 baked 9-inch quiche or
pie shell, made of Pâte
Brisée (see Index)*
*1½ lb. mushrooms
(.68 kg)*
*4 Tbsp. flour (40 g)*
*4 Tbsp. butter (60 g)*
*½ tsp. salt*
*¼ tsp. pepper*
*2 cups milk (.48 l),
scalded*
*1 Tbsp. lemon juice (14 g)*
*1½ lb. cooked shrimps
(.68 kg), shelled*
*½ cup heavy cream (1 dl)*

Preheat oven to 400°F. (204.4°C.). In the processor bowl fitted with the steel blade, chop the mushrooms very fine, and press in a cloth or potato ricer, over a bowl, to remove the moisture; save the moisture for stock. In the processor bowl fitted with the steel blade, blend the flour, butter, salt and pepper with on and off quick turns. With the motor running, pour the scalded milk through the tube and process until smooth. Add the lemon juice and blend quickly. Add the sauce to the mushrooms and cook, stirring constantly, until thickened. Spread the bottom of the pastry shell with half of the mushroom sauce. Place a layer of the shrimps on top. Add remaining sauce and another layer of shrimps. Pour the heavy cream on top. Bake in the preheated oven until heated through and bubbly, 10 to 15 minutes.

# INDIAN CURRY PIE

Makes 6 servings.

*1 baked 9-inch pie shell,
made of Pâte Brisée
(see Index)*
*1 cup shelled peanuts
(150 g)*
*2 medium-size cooking
apples cored*
*1 garlic clove*
*1 medium-size onion, cut
up*
*1 Tbsp. oil (15 g)*

Preheat oven to 350°F. (176.7°C.). In the processor bowl fitted with the steel blade, coarsely chop the peanuts, and spread over the bottom of the prepared pastry shell. Chop the apples coarsely with the steel blade; set aside. Still with the steel blade, chop the garlic and cut-up onion; sauté them in the oil and 2 tablespoons of the butter until limp. Still with the steel blade, blend the flour, curry powder, salt and remaining 2 tablespoons butter with on and off quick turns. With the motor running, pour the scalded milk through the tube and

4 Tbsp. butter (60 g)
2 Tbsp. flour (20 g)
2 to 3 tsp. curry powder
½ tsp. salt
1½ cups milk (.36 l),
    scalded
1 egg
3 cups cubes of cooked
    lamb or poultry (510 g)
½ cup white raisins (50 g)
1 cup chutney (.24 l)

process until smooth. Add the egg and process with 2 on and off turns. Add the mixture to the sautéed onion and cook, stirring constantly, until thickened. Fold into the sauce the cubed meat or poultry, the raisins and the chopped apples. Spoon the curry mixture over the peanuts in the shell and top with the chutney. Bake the pie in the preheated oven until it is heated through, about 20 minutes. Serve with more chopped peanuts and shredded coconut, if desired.

## TONGUE QUICHE

Makes 8 servings.

pastry for 1-crust, 10-inch
    deep quiche or pie dish
1 lb. cooked tongue
    (.453 kg)
½ lb. Swiss cheese
    (227 g)
1 onion, cut up
2 Tbsp. butter (30 g)
1 Tbsp. flour (10 g)
1½ cups light cream
    (.36 l)
½ tsp. salt
¼ tsp. pepper
½ cup parsley sprigs
½ tsp. ground sage
4 eggs

Make pastry and roll out to a sheet large enough to line a 10-inch deep quiche or pie dish. Fit pastry into the dish and crimp edges. Preheat oven to 375°F. (190.6°C.). In the processor bowl fitted with the steel blade, coarsely chop the tongue; set aside. With the shredding disc shred the Swiss cheese; add it to the tongue. With the steel blade chop the cut-up onion; sauté onion in the butter. In the processor bowl fitted with the steel blade, put the flour, cream, salt, pepper, parsley and sage, and blend with on and off quick turns. Add the eggs, one at a time, blending after each addition. Mix the tongue, cheese and sautéed onion with the egg mixture and spoon into the pastry-lined pan. Bake in the preheated oven for 40 to 45 minutes, or until a cake tester inserted into the center comes out clean.

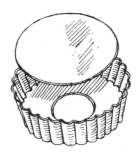

DEEP QUICHE PAN WITH REMOVABLE BOTTOM

# PROVENÇAL TOMATO QUICHE

Makes 6 servings.

*pastry for 1-crust, 9-inch pie, made of Basic Pie-crust (see Index)*
*½ lb. Gruyère cheese (227 g)*
*2 bunches of scallions*
*1 garlic clove*
*1 Tbsp. butter (15 g)*
*oil for sautéing*
*½ cup pitted black olives (110 g)*
*2 eggs*
*1 cup heavy cream (.24 l)*
*2 large tomatoes*
*½ cup flour (75 g)*
*1 tsp. salt*
*½ tsp. pepper*
*2 oz. Parmesan cheese (57 g)*
*½ cup parsley sprigs*

Preheat oven to 425°F. (218.3°C.). Make pastry and roll out to a sheet large enough to line a 9-inch pie dish. Fit pastry into the dish, line with foil and fill with weights, and bake for 10 to 15 minutes. Remove weighrs and foil and bake for 4 or 5 minutes until partially baked.

Reduce oven to 350°F. (176.7°C.). In the processor bowl fitted with the shredding disc, grate the cheese; set aside. With the steel blade, chop the scallions and garlic. Sauté scallions and garlic in the butter and 2 tablespoons of oil until limp; drain. Spread on the partially baked pastry. With the slicing blade slice the olives and add to the scallions. In the processor bowl fitted with the steel blade, put the grated cheese, the eggs and heavy cream, and blend. Cut the tomatoes by hand into ½-inch-thick slices. Mix flour with salt and pepper. Dip tomatoes into the seasoned flour and quickly sauté in oil. (Do not overcook.) Place the tomato slices on top of the scallions and olives in the pastry, and pour the egg-cheese mixture over all. Cook in the preheated oven for 30 to 35 minutes, or until a cake tester inserted in the middle comes out clean. Grate the Parmesan cheese and parsley with the steel blade, and sprinkle on top.

# CHEESE TOMATO QUICHE

Makes 6 servings.

*pastry for 1-crust 9-inch deep quiche or pie dish, made of Pâte Brisée (see Index)*
*½ lb. sharp cheese (227 g)*
*1 cup sour cream (.24 l)*
*1 tsp. salt*
*½ tsp. white pepper*
*1 tsp. dried basil*
*1 tsp. dried orégano*
*3 eggs*
*3 tomatoes (.453 kg)*
*1 can (2 oz.) flat anchovies (57 g) (optional)*

Preheat oven to 425°F. (218.3°C.). Make the pastry, roll out to a thin sheet, and line a deep 9-inch quiche or pie dish. Fill with foil and weights and put in the oven and bake for about 10 minutes. Remove weights and foil, and bake for 4 or 5 minutes longer, until partially baked.

Reduce oven to 350°F. (176.7°C.). In the processor bowl fitted with the steel blade, grate the cheese. Add the sour cream, salt, pepper, basil and orégano. Blend with on and off quick turns. Add the eggs, one at a time, and blend in with on and off quick turns after each addition. Cut the tomatoes by hand into thin slices. Pour the cheese mixture into the partially baked quiche shell and bake for 30 minutes. Remove from the oven and place drained sliced tomatoes on top. Arrange anchovy fillets on top of and around the tomatoes. Bake again for 5 more minutes.

Cherry tomatoes, cut into halves and placed cut side down, may be used in place of the tomato slices, and rolled anchovies in place of the flat ones, for a very pretty variation.

# MIXED VEGETABLE TART

Makes 6 servings.

pastry for 1-crust, 9-inch
  deep quiche or pie
  shell, made from Pâte
  Brisée (see Index)
¼ lb. Cheddar cheese
  (113 g)
4 Tbsp. flour (40 g)
4 Tbsp. butter (60 g)
½ tsp. salt
¼ tsp. pepper
2½ cups milk (.6 l),
  scalded
3 pkg. (10 oz. each) fro-
  zen mixed vegetables
  (850 g), cooked
6 strips of bacon

Preheat oven to 425°F. (218.3°C.). Make the pastry, roll out to a thin sheet, and line the 9-inch deep quiche or pie dish. Fill with foil and weights and put in the oven and bake for about 10 minutes. Remove weights and foil, and bake for 4 or 5 minutes longer, until partially baked.

Reduce oven to 350°F. (176.7°C.). In the processor bowl fitted with the steel blade, grate the cheese. Add the flour, butter, salt and pepper, and blend. With the motor running pour the scalded milk through the tube and process until smooth. Cook, stirring constantly, until sauce is thickened and cheese melted. Mix the cooked vegetables with the cream sauce and spoon into the pastry shell. Cover with the bacon. Bake in the preheated oven for 25 minutes.

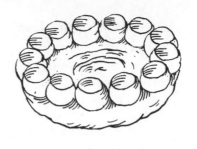

# 8

# PASTRY, PIES
# AND TARTS

## *For Dessert*

—◆—

# GÂTEAU SAINT-HONORÉ

Makes 8 servings.

A magnificent French dessert. It is far easier than it looks and sounds. It is made of *pâte brisée* and *pâte à choux,* put together with caramelized sugar, and filled with *crème Saint-Honoré*.

*1 recipe Pâte Brisée (see Index)*
*1 recipe Pâte à Choux (see Index)*
*1 recipe Crème Saint-Honoré (see Index)*
*1 recipe Caramel Syrup (see Index)*

Preheat oven to 425°F. (218.3°C.). Roll out the *pâte brisée* to a sheet ⅛ inch thick. Place a 9-inch cake tin, pot lid or flan ring on the dough for a pattern, and cut out a circle. Roll the dough onto the rolling pin and unfold onto a baking sheet. Prick all over with a fork and chill.

Make the *pâte à choux*. Fill a pastry bag fitted with a plain ½-inch tip and pipe a circle of *pâte à choux* around the edge of the *pâte brisée* base. Bake in the preheated oven for 15 minutes. Reduce heat to 350°F. (176.7°C.) and bake for 20 minutes more, or until pastry is golden. While still in the oven prick the puff pastry on the side to allow steam to escape. Turn off the oven and with the oven door slightly ajar let the shell rest for 10 minutes.

With the remaining *pâte à choux* form small puffs on a greased baking sheet. Bake in a 425°F. (218.3°C.) oven for 15 minutes. Reduce heat to 350°F. (176.7°C.) and bake for 20 minutes more, or until puffs are golden. While still in the oven prick each puff on the side to allow steam to escape. Turn off the oven and with the oven door slightly ajar let puffs rest for 10 minutes, or until

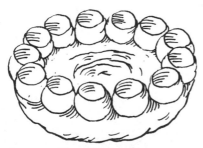

**a** the baked ring of *pâte brisée* with the filled *choux* in place

**b** the *gâteau* filled with *crème Saint-Honoré*

dry. With a demitasse spoon scoop out any moist dough through a slit in the side, or split the puffs horizontally and remove the moist dough.

Fill the small puffs with *crème Saint-Honoré;* then, holding each puff on a fork or small knife, dip it into the caramel syrup and place it, caramel side down, on well-buttered wax paper. Let the puffs cool.

To finish, "glue" the little puffs to the crown with a dab of caramel syrup. Fill the center of the *gâteau* with remaining *crème Saint-Honoré* and chill until set.

Individual *gâteaux* can also be made.

c an individual *gâteau* before filling

d an individual *gâteau* filled with *crème Saint-Honoré*

## BEIGNETS

Makes about 45 small beignets.

*1 recipe Pâte à Choux*
*(see Index)*
*fat for deep-frying*
*confectioners' sugar*

Prepare the *pâte à choux* and chill for at least 30 minutes, or until you are ready to make the *beignets. Beignets* should be cooked just before serving. Drop the dough by teaspoons into hot fat 375°F. (190.6°C.). Fry until *beignets* are puffed and golden brown, then drain on paper towels. Powder with confectioners' sugar and serve with a fruit or jam sauce (see Index) or maple syrup.

# PARIS-BREST

Makes 8 servings.

A large *pâte à choux* ring filled with *crème pâtissière* or flavored whipped cream and dusted with sugar and almonds.

*1 recipe Pâte à Choux (see Index)*
*1 egg yolk*
*2 Tbsp. cream (28 g)*
*⅓ cup toasted sliced almonds (60 g)*
*1 recipe praline-flavored Crème Pâtissière (see Index)*
*confectioners' sugar*

Preheat oven to 375°F. (190.6°C.). Trace a 9-inch circle on a floured and buttered cookie sheet, using a 9-inch cake tin, pot lid or flan ring as a pattern. With a pastry bag fitted with a ½-inch plain tip, pipe a circle of *pâte à choux* dough, 2 inches wide and ¾ inch high, around the traced circle. Then pipe another ring inside the first and a third ring on top of the others. Brush with the egg yolk mixed with the cream. Do not allow the egg glaze to drip on the pan as it may prevent the dough rising. Sprinkle dough with sliced almonds. Bake in the preheated oven for 50 minutes, or until the ring is well puffed and golden. Without removing the circle from the oven make 4 or 5 small slits in the pastry to let steam escape. Reduce oven temperature to 325°F. (162.8°C.) and bake for 15 minutes longer, or until the pastry is dry.

Slice the circle horizontally and remove any moist dough. Let pastry cool. Fill the lower half with flavored whipped cream or *crème pâtissière* flavored with praline powder. Replace top and dust with confectioners' sugar. Serve cold.

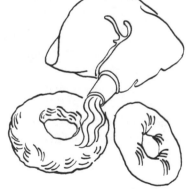

# CROQUEMBOUCHE

Makes about 25 servings.

This famous French confection is nothing more than small puffs (*profiteroles*) fitted with one of the flavored cream fillings or whipped cream and put together in a pyramid with caramel syrup.

*2 recipes Pâte à Choux*
*(see Index)*
*2 recipes Whipped Cream*
*(see Index)*
*2 recipes Caramel Syrup*
*(see Index)*
*confectioners' sugar*

CROQUEMBOUCHE

Make 80 small *profiteroles* by piping 1-inch rounds, using a small plain tip in the pastry bag, or drop by ½ teaspoons onto a greased baking sheet. Bake in a preheated 400°F. (204.4°C.) oven for 10 minutes. Reduce oven temperature to 350°F. (176.7°C.) and continue to bake for 20 to 25 minutes, until pastry is puffed and golden. While still in the oven prick each puff on the side to allow steam to escape. Turn off the oven and with the oven door slightly ajar let puffs rest for 10 minutes, or until dry. With a demitasse spoon scoop out any moist dough through a slit in the side, or split the puffs horizontally and remove the moist dough.

Using a pastry bag with a small plain tip fill the puffs from the bottom with any cream filling. Make 2 recipes of caramel syrup, one batch at a time. Place the syrup over hot water to keep it from hardening. Lightly oil a 10-inch serving plate. Holding the puffs with a fork, dip them, one at a time, into the syrup, and on the serving plate make a single layer of puffs, 9 inches in diameter. Continue to pile up the caramel-coated puffs, each time making a layer of smaller circumference, until you have formed a pyramid with a single puff on top. Sift confectioners' sugar over the top, or serve with whipped cream.

Another way of building up a *croquembouche* is to use the oiled "innards" of a 10-inch false-bottom tube pan; be sure the tube is well oiled. Remove the support when the puffs are cold. To serve *croquembouche*, pull it apart with 2 forks, separating a few puffs for each serving.

## SWEDISH PUFF-PASTE SWEET

Makes about 16 pastries.

*1 recipe for Mock Puff*
*    Paste (see Index)*
*1 egg white, beaten*
*sugar*
*jam*

Quickly roll out the mock puff-paste dough to a sheet approximately ¼ inch thick. Cut into an even number of 2½-inch circles. Brush half of the circles with lightly beaten egg white. Cut out a small circle of dough from the remaining rounds, using a very small cutter or the metal cap of a liquor bottle. (These little pieces of dough can be rolled out to make more circles, or they can be brushed with sugar or jam and baked for tiny treats.) Sprinkle the tops with granulated sugar. Place the big cut-out rounds on top of the matching solid circles. Fill the center with jam. Place on a cookie sheet and chill for 10 minutes. Bake in a preheated 500°F. (260°C.) oven for 8 to 10 minutes.

If needed, fill with more jam when cool.

## OLD-FASHIONED APPLE PIE

Makes 6 servings.

*1 recipe Basic Piecrust*
*    (see Index)*
*6 large cooking apples,*
*    about 3 lb., peeled and*
*    cored*
*¾ cup sugar (150 g)*
*2 tsp. ground cinnamon*
*½ tsp. grated nutmeg*
*3 Tbsp. cream (45 g)*
*sugar*

Preheat oven to 350°F. (176.7°C.). Prepare the piecrust dough and divide into halves. Roll out 1 portion and fit it into a 9-inch pie plate. Prick the bottom. In the processor bowl fitted with the slicing disc, slice the apples, pressing down on the pusher firmly to get as thick slices as possible. Pile slices high in the dough-lined pan. Mix together the sugar, cinnamon and nutmeg, and sprinkle over the apples. Gently stir the sugar mixture into the apples. Roll out remaining dough and place on top of the apples. Crimp the edges, brush the crust with cream, and sprinkle with more sugar. To allow steam to escape, prick the piecrust in several places. Bake in the preheated oven for 1 hour, or until the crust is golden.

## APPLE TART I

Makes 6 servings.

If you do not have a deep quiche pan or flan rings, false-bottom cake pans work very well. For any apple tart use cooking apples—greenings, Granny Smith, Golden Delicious.

*pastry for 1-crust 9-inch deep quiche or tart*
*6 large cooking apples about 3 lb, peeled and cored*
*3 Tbsp. sugar (38 g)*
*2 Tbsp. butter (30 g)*
*3 oz. apple jelly (85 g)*
*1 Tbsp. applejack or Calvados (15 g)*

Preheat oven to 400°F. (204.4°C.). Fit pastry into the quiche or tart pan. In the processor bowl fitted with the steel blade, put half of the peeled and cored apples and coarsely chop. Place chopped apples in the pastry-lined pan. Slice remaining apples with the slicing disc, pressing down on the pusher firmly to get as thick slices as possible. Fan out part of the slices in an overlapping pattern around the edge of the pan. Mound remaining apples into a rosette in the center. Sprinkle with the sugar and dot with the butter. Bake in the preheated oven for 1 hour and 15 minutes, or until nicely browned. When cool, glaze the top with the apple jelly melted with applejack or Calvados. Serve at room temperature.

## APPLE TART II

Makes 6 servings.

*pastry for 1-crust 9-inch tart, made of Pâte Sucrée (see Index)*
*6 to 7 cooking apples, 3 lb., peeled and cored*

Preheat oven to 425°F. (218.3°C.). Fit pastry into the tart pan, fill with foil and weights, and bake in the preheated oven for 10 minutes. Remove foil and weights and bake for 4 or 5 minutes longer, until partially baked. Cool.

3 Tbsp. butter (45 g)
rind of ½ lemon
½ cup sugar (100 g)
¼ tsp. ground cinnamon
¾ cup white wine (1.5 dl)
sugar and butter for top-
    ping

Reduce oven heat to 400°F. In the processor bowl fitted with the steel blade, put half of the cut-up apples, 1 cup at a time, and coarsely chop. Melt the butter in a skillet and add the chopped apples. With the steel blade, chop the lemon rind with the sugar and cinnamon for about 30 seconds. Add to the apples along with the wine. Cook and stir constantly until soft. Purée in the processor bowl fitted with the steel blade, and pour into the partially baked pastry. With the slicing disc, slice remaining peeled and cored apples. Arrange the apple slices in a pretty pattern on top of puréed apples. Sprinkle with sugar, and dot with butter. Bake in the preheated oven for 30 to 35 minutes. If the top becomes too brown, cover with foil.

## APPLE TART III

Makes 8 servings.

pastry for 1-crust 10-inch
    tart, made of Pâte Bri-
    sée (see Index)
1 cup shelled walnuts
    (120 g)
6 cooking apples, 3 lb.
¾ cup flour (120 g)
¾ cup sugar (150 g)
¼ tsp. grated nutmeg
¼ lb. butter (1 stick),
    (120 g), cut up

Preheat oven to 450°F. (232°C.). Make the pastry, roll out to a thin sheet, and line a 10-inch tart pan. Flute or crimp the edges. Fill with foil and weights and put in the oven. Reduce heat to 375°F. (190.6°C.), and bake for about 10 minutes. Remove weights and foil and bake for 4 or 5 minutes longer, until partially baked.

In the processor bowl fitted with the steel blade, coarsely chop the walnuts; set aside. Peel and core the apples and coarsely chop. Arrange the apples in the partially baked pastry and spread the chopped walnuts on top. Blend together the flour, sugar, nutmeg and cut-up butter. Sprinkle this mixture on top of the walnuts. Bake in the preheated oven for 40 minutes, or until the apples are tender.

# APPLE TART IV

Makes 4 to 6 servings.

*1 recipe Pâte Sucrée (see Index)*
*5 Tbsp. sugar (63 g)*
*¼ cup Almond Paste (75 g) (see Index)*
*1 cup Crème Pâtissière (see Index)*
*4 medium-size apples*
*3 eggs*
*1 cup half and half (.24 l)*
*1 Tbsp. flour (10 g)*
*1 tsp. vanilla extract*

Preheat oven to 375°F. (190.6°C.). Line an 8-inch quiche pan or false-bottom 8-inch layer-cake pan with *pâte sucrée*. Sprinkle the bottom with 3 tablespoons of the sugar. In the processor bowl fitted with the steel blade, blend the almond paste and the *crème pâtissière* (pastry cream). Spread this on the pastry. Peel and core the apples and slice with the slicing disc. Lay the apple slices in a pattern on the pastry cream. Bake in the preheated oven for 20 minutes. Let cool.

In the processor bowl fitted with the steel blade, mix the eggs, half and half, remaining 2 tablespoons sugar, the flour and vanilla. Pour mixture over the tart. Bake for 25 to 30 minutes more, or until a cake tester comes out clean.

# PECAN PIE

Makes 8 servings.

*pastry for 1-crust 8-inch pie*
*1 cup shelled pecans (120 g)*
*½ cup sugar (100 g)*
*2 eggs*
*½ tsp. salt*
*½ cup light corn syrup (160 g)*
*1 tsp. vanilla extract*
*2 Tbsp. butter (30 g), melted*
*12 pecan halves*

Make the pastry, gently fit it into an 8-inch pie pan, and crimp or flute edges. Set aside.

In the processor bowl fitted with the steel blade, coarsely chop the pecans; set aside. With the steel blade, blend together the sugar, eggs, salt, corn syrup, vanilla and melted butter. Add the chopped pecans. Pour the mixture into the pastry-lined pan. Bake in a preheated 425°F. (218.3°C.) oven for 15 minutes. Reduce heat to 350°F. (176.7°C.) and bake for 25 to 30 minutes longer, or until top is lightly browned. Arrange the pecan halves on the top.

# CRANBERRY ORANGE APPLE PIE

Makes 6 servings.

A very good substitute for the usual holiday pies.

*Basic Piecrust for 2-crust
9-inch pie (see Index)*
*2 cups whole cranberries
(.48 l)*
*1 whole orange, cut up
and seeded*
*2 cups brown sugar
(200 g)*
*¼ tsp. grated nutmeg*
*¼ cup Port wine (.5 dl)*
*5 cooking apples, peeled
and cored*
*2 Tbsp. butter (30 g), or
more*
*cream*
*granulated sugar*

Make piecrust and roll out 2 rounds to fit a 9-inch pan. Gently place the bottom pastry in the pan. Preheat oven to 375°F. (190.6°C.). In the processor bowl fitted with the steel blade, chop coarsely the cranberries and orange with brown sugar and nutmeg. Add the Port wine and blend; set aside. Slice the peeled and cored apples with the slicing disc. Put a layer of apples in the pastry-lined pan. Dot with part of the butter. Spoon a layer of the cranberry-orange mixture over the apples. Cover with more apples, dot with more butter, and continue making layers, using up all the fruit. Cover with the top pastry. Crimp or flute the edges. Cut vents in the crust. Brush pastry with cream and sprinkle with granulated sugar. Bake in the preheated oven for 50 to 60 minutes.

# SPICED GREEN TOMATO PIE

Makes 6 servings.

*Basic Piecrust for 2-crust
9-inch pie (see Index)*
*2 to 3 lb. green tomatoes
(.9 to 1.36 kg), peeled*
*1 cup white raisins
(100 g), plumped*
*5 Tbsp. flour (50 g)*
*1½ cups brown sugar
(300 g)*
*¼ tsp. grated mace*
*½ tsp. ground cinnamon*
*1 tsp. salt*

Make piecrust and roll out 2 rounds to fit a 9-inch pan. Gently place the bottom pastry in the pan.

Preheat oven to 375°F. (190.6°C.). Place tomatoes in boiling water for about 3 minutes. Run cold water over them and slip off the skins. In the processor bowl fitted with the slicing disc, slice the tomatoes; there should be 5 cups of slices. Put slices in a large bowl and add the raisins. Mix the flour, brown sugar, spices and salt. Toss gently with the tomatoes. Sprinkle the lemon juice over them, and turn the mixture into the bottom pastry. Cover with the top pastry, and crimp or flute the

2 Tbsp. lemon juice
    (28 g)
1 egg white, for glaze

edges. Cut vents in the crust and glaze with egg white mixed with 1 tablespoon water. Bake in the preheated oven for 50 to 60 minutes.

## FRUIT CREAM TARTS

Eye-appealing and mouth-watering tarts are easily made with Pâte Brisée, Crème Pâtissière (pastry cream), Jelly Sauce or other glaze, and fresh or cooked fruits.

Berries and bananas are generally used uncooked. Other fruits benefit from poaching in a syrup of two parts water to one part sugar. Do not overcook the fruits, and drain them well before arranging the pieces on the pastry cream base.

Tough-skinned fruits, such as apples, pears and peaches, should be peeled before poaching. They may be cut into slices or halves depending on their size. Plums, apricots and nectarines need not always be peeled; they are often halved for such tarts, but they can be cut into slices or wedges if they are large. Dried fruits should be stewed until just soft.

Preheat oven to 450°F. (232°C.). Make Pâte Brisée (see Index), roll out to a thin sheet, and line a tart pan. Fill with foil and weights and put in the oven. Reduce heat to 375°F. (190.6°C.) and bake for about 10 minutes. Remove weights and foil, and bake for 12 minutes longer, until fully cooked. Cool the shell.

Glaze the pastry with melted currant jelly or with strained melted apricot preserves. Spoon Crème Pâtissière (see Index) into the shell, half-filling it. Place cooked or fresh fruits on top. Glaze the fruit with Jelly Sauce or Strawberry Glaze (see Index for these), or use more strained melted preserves.

Small tarts can be made in the same way, but the small pastry shells will be baked in less time, about 5 minutes after removing weights and foil.

# APRICOT COTTAGE CHEESE QUICHE

Makes 6 to 8 servings.

*pastry for 8- or 9-inch
   quiche, partially baked*
¼ *cup shelled nuts (30 g)*
½ *lb. dried apricots
   (227 g)*
½ *cup apricot preserves
   (1 dl)*
½ *cup light cream (1 dl)*
*3 eggs*
*2 cups cottage cheese
   (.48 l)*
⅔ *cup sugar (125 g)*
*1 Tbsp. lemon juice (14 g)*
¼ *tsp. salt*
*1 Tbsp. flour (10 g)*
*2 Tbsp. apricot brandy
   (28 g) (optional)*

Preheat oven to 350°F. (176.7°C.). In the processor bowl fitted with the steel blade, chop the nuts with on and off quick turns; set aside.

Simmer dried apricots in water until just soft. Melt apricot preserves and strain for glaze.

In the processor bowl fitted with the steel blade, put the drained cooked apricots, 1 cup at a time, and coarsely chop; set aside. Put the remaining ingredients except pastry, nuts and glaze in the bowl fitted with the steel blade, and blend until smooth. Add chopped apricots and blend very quickly with 2 on and off turns.

Brush the bottom of the partially baked pastry with the apricot glaze, and pour in the filling mixture. Sprinkle with the nuts. Bake in the preheated oven for 35 to 40 minutes, or until a cake tester comes out clean. Cool before serving.

# FRUIT VELVET TART

Makes 8 servings.

*pastry for 1-crust 9-inch
   deep quiche or pie,
   partially baked*
*rind of 1 lemon*
*1 cup sugar (200 g)*
*1 lb. cooked fresh or
   canned fruit (.453 kg)*
*2 Tbsp. butter (30 g)*
*3 Tbsp. lemon juice (43 g)*
½ *tsp. salt*
*4 eggs*

Preheat oven to 450°F. (232°C.). In the processor bowl fitted with the steel blade, chop the lemon rind with the sugar for about 30 seconds. Add cooked or canned fruit and purée; there should be 1 cup of purée. Add the butter, lemon juice and salt. Blend with on and off quick turns. Add the eggs, one at a time, and blend with on and off quick turns. Pour the mixture into the partially baked pastry and bake in the preheated oven for 10 minutes. Reduce heat to 350°F. (176.7°C.) and bake for 15 minutes longer, or until a cake tester comes out clean. Cool on a rack.

# FRANGIPANE TART

Makes 8 servings.

*pastry for 1-crust deep
  8-inch quiche or 9-inch
  pie*
*¾ cup Almond Paste
  (225 g) (see Index)*
*¾ cup sugar (150 g)*
*¼ lb. butter (1 stick)
  (120 g), cut up*
*1 egg yolk*
*2 whole eggs*
*½ cup sifted cake flour
  (60 g)*

Preheat oven to 425°F. (218.3°C.). Make the pastry of your choice, roll it out, and gently fit it into a deep 8-inch quiche pan or a 9-inch pie pan. Fill with foil and weights, and bake in the preheated oven for 8 to 10 minutes. Remove weights and foil and bake for 4 or 5 minutes longer, until partially baked. Cool.

In the processor bowl fitted with the steel blade, put the almond paste, sugar and cut-up butter, and blend with on and off quick turns. Add the egg yolk and blend. Put in the 2 whole eggs and blend well. Add the cake flour and process with 2 or 3 on and off quick turns, or just until the flour is incorporated. Pour the mixture into the partially baked pastry shell. Bake in the preheated oven for 10 minutes. Reduce temperature to 400°F. (204.4°C.) and bake for 20 minutes more, or until golden brown and a tester comes out clean.

## VARIATIONS ON FRANGIPANE TART

*Pear*—Spread ½ recipe Frangipane Cream (preceding recipe) on the bottom of a partially baked shell. Cover the cream with 1 cup cake crumbs. Sprinkle with Kirsch. Halve 10 canned pears and drain. Arrange halves over the cake crumbs in a pretty pattern. Bake in a preheated 425°F. (218.3°C.) oven for 10 minutes. Reduce temperature to 400°F. (204.4°C.) and continue to bake for 20 to 25 minutes, until filling is set and piecrust is golden. Coat with currant jelly which has been melted with 1 tablespoon water. Chill.

*Apricot*—Substitute canned apricot halves for the pears, and glaze with apricot glaze.

*Bing Cherry*—Substitute canned Bing cherries or frozen dark cherries, thawed and drained, for the pears. Glaze with melted wine jelly.

## PEAR TART

Makes 6 to 8 servings.

*pastry for 1-crust 9-inch tart, made of Cottage-Cheese Pastry (see Index)*
*6 pears*
*3 Tbsp. plus 1 cup sugar (243 g)*
*½ tsp. ground ginger*
*4 Tbsp. butter (60 g)*
*½ cup water (1 dl)*

Preheat oven to 400°F. (204.4°C.). Make the pastry, roll it out, and gently fit it into a 9-inch tart pan. Fill with foil and weights and bake for 10 minutes. Remove weights and foil and continue to bake for 4 or 5 minutes, until partially baked. Cool.

Reduce oven heat to 350°F. (176.7°C.). Peel, halve, and core the pears. Poach them in water mixed with 3 tablespoons sugar and the ground ginger, until just tender. In the processor bowl fitted with the steel blade, chop 4 pear halves coarsely. Spread on the partially baked pastry. Place remaining pear halves, cut side down and narrow ends to the middle, on the chopped pears. Caramelize 2 tablespoons of the butter with ½ cup sugar in a small pan. In another pan dissolve remaining 2 tablespoons butter and ½ cup sugar in the ½ cup water. Add to the caramelized mixture. Cook until syrupy. Spoon over the pears. Bake the tart in the preheated oven for 25 minutes. Let cool to allow the syrup to thicken.

## BURNELLE'S PREACHER PIE (CUSTARD PIE)

Makes 6 to 8 servings.

*½ recipe Basic Piecrust (see Index)*
*4 eggs*
*½ cup sugar (100 g)*
*¼ tsp. salt*
*¼ tsp. grated nutmeg*
*1 tsp. vanilla extract*
*3 cups milk (.72 l)*

Make the pastry and fit it into a 9-inch pie pan. In the processor bowl fitted with the steel blade, put the eggs, sugar, salt, nutmeg and vanilla; blend. With the motor running, slowly pour the milk through the tube. Add the plum jam and blend quickly. Pour the mixture into the unbaked pastry. Bake in a 450°F. (232°C.) oven for 10 minutes. Reduce heat to 300°F. (149°C.) and bake for 45 to

*1 cup damson plum jam (.24 l)*

50 minutes, or until a knife inserted halfway between the edge and the middle comes out clean.

## VARIATIONS

*Chocolate*—Omit plum jam and substitute 2 ounces unsweetened chocolate (56.7 g), melted.

*Coconut*—Omit plum jam and add ½ cup grated coconut to the custard mixture. Sprinkle the top with coconut.

*Banana*—Top with sliced bananas.

## ORANGE PUMPKIN PIE

Makes 6 to 8 servings.

*Basic Piecrust for 1-crust 9-inch pie (see Index)*
*rind of ½ orange*
*rind of ½ lemon*
*1½ cups brown sugar (300 g)*
*3 Tbsp. butter (45 g)*
*4 eggs*
*2½ cups puréed pumpkin (.6 l)*
*¼ tsp. ground cinnamon*
*¼ tsp. ground cloves*
*¼ tsp. ground ginger*
*2 Tbsp. brandy (28 g)*
*1 cup evaporated milk (.24 l)*

Make the pastry, roll it out, and gently fit it into a 9-inch pie pan.

Preheat oven to 425°F. (218.3°C.). In the processor bowl fitted with the steel blade, process the orange and lemon rinds and brown sugar until the rind is chopped, about 30 seconds. Add the butter and blend until creamy. Add the eggs, one at a time, and quickly blend with on and off quick turns, after each addition. Put in the pumpkin and spices and blend well. Add the brandy and evaporated milk and mix together with on and off quick turns. Pour the mixture into the pastry-lined pan. Bake in the lower third of the preheated oven for 30 minutes. Reduce heat to 375°F. (190.6°C.) and bake the pie in the upper half of the oven for 15 minutes more. A cake tester when inserted in the center should come out clean. Serve plain or with Fruited Hard Sauce (see Index).

## LEMON CHEESE PIE

Makes 6 to 8 servings.

*1 baked 9-inch pie or
  quiche shell*
*rind of 1 lemon*
*½ cup sugar (100 g)*
*½ lb. cream cheese
  (227 g), cut up*
*2 eggs*
*¼ cup lemon juice
  (.5 dl)*

Preheat oven to 350°F. (176.7°C.). In the processor bowl fitted with the steel blade, process the lemon rind and sugar until rind is chopped, about 30 seconds. Add the cut-up cream cheese and blend until creamy. Add the eggs, one at a time, and blend after each addition. Put in the lemon juice and mix well. Spoon the mixture into the baked pastry shell, and bake for 20 minutes, or until just firm.

## LEMON TART

Makes 6 to 8 servings.

*1 recipe Pâte Brisée (see
  Index)*
*2 recipes Lemon Filling
  (see Index)*
*1 cup heavy cream (.24 l)*
*seedless grapes or sliced
  strawberries*

Preheat oven to 450°F. (232°C.). Make the pastry, roll it out, and line a fluted deep quiche pan or a 9-inch layer-cake pan 1½ inches deep. Fill with foil and weights, and put in the oven. Reduce heat to 375°F. (190.6°C.) and bake for about 10 minutes. Remove weights and foil and bake for 12 minutes longer, until fully baked. Cool.

Prepare the lemon filling and cool. Whip the cream with a rotary beater or in a mixer and fold it into the lemon filling. Put the mixture in the shell and cover the top with halved seedless grapes or sliced strawberries.

## CHOCOLATE ORANGE TART

Makes 6 to 8 servings.

*1 partially baked*
*9-inch pie shell*
*rind of ½ orange*
*¾ cup sugar (150 g)*
*4 Tbsp. butter (60 g)*
*3 eggs*
*1 Tbsp. Triple Sec or rum*
*(15 g)*
*12 oz. chocolate bits*
*(340 g), melted*
*¼ cup flour (40 g)*
*whipped cream*
*chocolate curls*

In the processor bowl fitted with the steel blade, process the orange rind and sugar until rind is chopped, about 30 seconds. Add the butter, and blend with on and off quick turns. Add the eggs, one at a time, and blend quickly after each addition. Add the Triple Sec or rum and melted chocolate bits and blend. Add the flour and mix it in with 2 on and off quick turns. Put the mixture in the partially baked pie shell and bake in a preheated 375°F. (190.6°C.) oven for 25 minutes. Top with whipped cream and chocolate curls.

## CREAMY CHOCOLATE PIE

Makes 8 servings.

*½ recipe Meringue*
*Crumb Shell (see Index)*
*½ lb. butter (2 sticks)*
*(227 g)*
*1½ cups sugar (300 g)*
*4 oz. unsweetened choco-*
*late (113 g), melted and*
*cooled*
*1 tsp. vanilla extract*
*6 eggs*
*whipped cream (optional)*

Prepare the meringue crumb shell, spread it in a 9-inch cake pan, and bake it in a preheated 275°F. (135°C.) oven for 1 to 1½ hours. Let the shell cool.

In the processor bowl fitted with the steel blade, cream the butter and sugar until smooth. Add the cooled melted chocolate and the vanilla and blend until very smooth, about 30 seconds. Add the eggs, one at a time, and blend. Pour the mixture into the prepared meringue shell and chill for at least 1 hour. Top with whipped cream if desired.

# STRAWBERRY GLAZED PIE

Makes 6 servings.

pastry for 9-inch deep
  quiche or pie pan, or
  for 6 small tart pans
Strawberry Glaze (recipe
  follows)
3 oz. cream cheese (85 g)
1 Tbsp. butter (15 g)
1 Tbsp. cream (14 g)
2 tsp. Kirsch, Triple Sec
  or Curaçao
3 cups whole fresh straw-
  berries

Make pastry, roll it out, and fit it into a deep 9-inch quiche or pie pan, or 6 small tart pans. Fill pans with foil and weights and bake in a preheated 425°F. (218.3°C.) oven for 10 to 12 minutes. Remove weights and foil and continue to bake for 12 minutes longer, until fully baked. Cool the shell.

Make the strawberry glaze.

In the processor bowl fitted with the steel blade, blend the cream cheese, butter, cream and liqueur until creamy. Spread this mixture over the bottom of the baked shell. Arrange the whole strawberries on top, and spoon the cooled strawberry glaze over all. Chill well before serving.

STRAWBERRY GLAZE
3 cups fresh strawberries
⅔ cup sugar (135 g)
1 Tbsp. arrowroot (10 g),
  or 3 Tbsp. cornstarch
  (30 g)
½ cup water (1 dl)
2 tsp. lemon juice

In the processor bowl fitted with the steel blade, purée the strawberries with the sugar. Add arrowroot or cornstarch dissolved in the ½ cup water, and the lemon juice. Cook over medium heat, stirring constantly, until the mixture boils. Continue cooking over low heat for 2 minutes. Strain through a fine sieve or tammy. Cool.

## VARIATION

Rhubarb—Substitute 5 cups of cut-up rhubarb, cooked in the top part of a double boiler (do not add any water) until just tender. Add ¾ cup sugar (150 g) and gently stir in. Spoon over the cheese filling and glaze with the cooked strawberry purée. Chill well.

# 9

# FILLINGS, FROSTINGS, SYRUPS AND SAUCES

—◆◆—

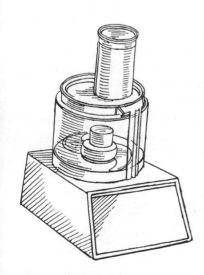

## WHIPPED CREAM

1 cup heavy cream (.24 l) makes 2 cups whipped cream. To sweeten, fold in 1 to 3 tablespoons sugar (13 to 39 g).

## VARIATIONS
## FOR WHIPPED CREAM

*Cocoa*—Add 2 tablespoons dark cocoa powder (10 g) to 1 cup whipped cream, and blend quickly.

*Liqueur*—Just before the cream reaches the proper consistency add 3 tablespoons rum, Cognac or any liqueur (45 g) for each cup of whipped cream.

*Praline*—Add ½ cup Praline Powder (60 g) (see Index) for each cup of whipped cream and blend quickly.

*Coffee*—Dissolve 2 teaspoons instant coffee powder in 2 tablespoons Crème de Cacao (30 g) for each cup of whipped cream.

*Fruit*—Purée ⅓ cup raspberries or strawberries in the processor bowl fitted with the steel blade, and fold into 1 cup whipped cream.

## CRÈME PÂTISSIÈRE (Pastry Cream)

*5 egg yolks*
*1 cup sugar (200 g)*
*¾ cup flour (235 g), sifted*
*2 cups scalded milk (.48 l)*
*1 Tbsp. butter (15 g)*
*½ Tbsp. vanilla extract*
*2 Tbsp. flavoring (30 g)*

In the processor bowl fitted with the steel blade, blend the egg yolks and sugar until pale yellow; scrape down. Add the flour and blend with on and off quick turns. With the motor running, pour the scalded milk in a thin stream through the tube. Place the mixture in the top part of a double boiler over boiling water and cook, beating all the while, until thick and smooth. Finish with the butter and flavorings. For a light filling fold in 1 cup whipped cream.

## VARIATIONS FOR CRÈME PÂTISSIÈRE

*Chocolate*—Add 2 ounces melted unsweetened chocolate (56.7 g) or 6 tablespoons cocoa powder (30 g) to the scalded milk.

*Mocha*—Add 2 teaspoons instant coffee powder to the scalded milk along with

2 ounces melted unsweetened chocolate (56.7 g) or 6 tablespoons cocoa powder (30 g).

*Coffee*—Add 1 tablespoon instant coffee powder to the scalded milk.

*Liqueur*—Add 1 tablespoon Kirsch, apricot brandy, Triple Sec or Grand Marnier (15 g) to each cup of Crème Pâtissière.

*Praline*—Add 1½ tablespoons Praline Powder (see Index) to 1 cup Crème Pâtissière.

*Lemon*—Chop the rind of 1 lemon with the sugar and substitue 1 teaspoon lemon extract for the vanilla.

## VANILLA CREAM

*1 Tbsp. potato flour (10 g), or 2 Tbsp. wheat flour (20 g)*
*2 Tbsp. sugar (25 g)*
*2 Tbsp. butter (30 g)*
*2 egg yolks*
*1 cup medium cream (.24 l)*
*1 tsp. vanilla extract*

In the processor bowl fitted with the steel blade, put all ingredients except vanilla. Blend until smooth. Cook in a double boiler, stirring constantly, until thick and smooth. Beat in the vanilla and allow the cream to cool.

The flavor of vanilla cream can be modified following any of the variations suggested for Crème Pâtissière (pastry cream).

## CRÈME SAINT-HONORÉ

*½ cup cold water (1 dl)*
*1 envelope unflavored gelatin (7 g)*
*1½ cups Crème Pâtissière (see Index), hot*
*6 egg whites*
*¼ tsp. cream of tartar*
*⅓ cup sugar (75 g)*
*½ Tbsp. vanilla extract or other flavoring*
*1 cup chopped nuts, cake bits, candied fruits (optional)*

Pour the cold water into the processor bowl fitted with the steel blade. Sprinkle gelatin over the water and soak for 10 minutes. Add the hot *crème pâtissière* and blend briefly to dissolve the gelatin. Beat egg whites and the cream of tartar with a rotary beater or mixer until stiff but not dry; as you beat, gradually add the sugar and flavoring. Fold the meringue into the cooled *crème* mixture. Fold in the nuts, cake bits or candied fruits, if using them.

## LEMON FILLING

*rind and juice of 1 large lemon*
*1 cup sugar (200 g)*
*3 eggs*

In the food processor fitted with the steel blade, process the lemon rind and sugar until the rind is chopped, about 30 seconds. Add the lemon juice and eggs and blend thoroughly. Place the mixture in the top part of a double boiler, over boiling water, and cook, beating all the while, until thick and smooth.

## ORANGE FILLING

*rind of 1 orange*
*¾ cup sugar (150 g)*
*2 egg yolks*
*⅓ cup orange juice (75 g)*
*1 Tbsp. lemon juice (14 g)*
*¼ cup flour (40 g)*

In the food processor fitted with the steel blade, process the orange rind and sugar until rind is chopped, about 30 seconds. Add the egg yolks, one at a time, and quickly blend after each addition. Add the orange juice and lemon juice and blend. Add the flour and blend with on and off quick turns. Place the mixture in the top part of a double boiler, over boiling water, and cook, beating all the while, until thick and smooth.

## RICOTTA FILLING

This is a good filling for cream puffs, éclairs and pies.

*2 Tbsp. candied orange peel (40 g)*
*2 oz. semisweet chocolate (56.7 g), cut into 4 pieces*
*1 lb. ricotta cheese (.453 kg)*
*1 cup sugar (200 g)*
*2 Tbsp. crème de cacao (30 g)*
*¼ tsp. almond extract*

In the processor bowl fitted with the steel blade, chop the orange peel and chocolate; set aside. In the bowl put the cheese, sugar, crème de cacao and almond extract, and blend until smooth. Fold all together.

## FRENCH FILLING

Good for tortes and cakes

½ cup Almond Paste
  (150 g) (see Index)
2 egg yolks
1½ cups confectioners'
  sugar (240 g)
2 Tbsp. prepared black
  coffee or liqueur of
  your choice
¼ cup cream (.5 dl)

In the processor bowl fitted with the steel blade, put all the ingredients and blend well. This filling is not cooked.

## ALMOND PASTE

2 cups blanched almonds
  (240 g)
1½ cups confectioners'
  sugar (240 g), sifted
2 egg whites
2 tsp. almond extract

Preheat oven to 300°F. (148.9°C.). Bake the almonds until dry but not brown. In the processor bowl fitted with the steel blade, grind the almonds until pulverized. Mix in sugar, egg whites and almond extract until a paste is formed. Form the paste into a ball, wrap in wax paper, and let it age in an airtight container for at least 4 days.

## PRALINE POWDER

1 cup blanched almonds
  (120 g)
1 cup sugar (200 g)
2 Tbsp. water
⅛ tsp. cream of tartar
1 tsp. vanilla extract

Preheat oven to 300°F. (148.9°C.). Bake the almonds until dry but not brown. Boil sugar, water and cream of tartar, shaking the pan in a rotary motion to prevent burning. Cook until the syrup becomes light brown. Add dried almonds and vanilla, and pour onto a large oiled baking sheet. Cool. When praline becomes hard, break it into small pieces. Process the pieces with the steel blade, until all is pulverized.

# TOPPINGS

Streusel toppings are popular for coffee cakes, simple cakes and sometimes pies. They are applied before baking.

## STREUSEL I

⅔ cup flour (100 g)
⅔ cup sugar (150 g)
6 Tbsp. butter (90 g)

In the processor bowl fitted with the steel blade, blend all the ingredients together. The mixture will be crumbly. Sprinkle over the cake and bake according to the recipe.

## STREUSEL II

½ cup shelled nuts (60 g)
½ cup brown sugar
  (100 g)
2 Tbsp. flour (20 g)
2 tsp. ground cinnamon
2 Tbsp. butter (30 g)

In the processor bowl fitted with the steel blade, coarsely chop the nuts. Add remaining ingredients and blend with on and off quick turns. The mixture will be crumbly. Sprinkle over the cake and bake according to the recipe.

# FROSTINGS AND ICINGS

Uncooked icings can be made in the processor with no effort to give perfectly smooth results. However, some of these made with confectioners' sugar may have a slightly raw taste. To overcome this, let them sit over hot water for 10 to 15 minutes. Then cool before spreading. A very few drops of liquid can alter the consistency of frosting. Add the liquid cautiously.

## CONFECTIONERS' ICING

½ cup confectioners'
  sugar (80 g)
¼ tsp. vanilla extract
milk

In the processor bowl fitted with the steel blade, blend the sugar, vanilla and 2 teaspoons of milk. It may be necessary to dribble in a little more milk to give the icing spreading consistency.

# ROYAL ICING

*1 lb. confectioners' sugar (.453 kg)*
*1 Tbsp. lemon juice (14 g)*
*2 or 3 egg whites*

In the processor bowl fitted with the steel blade, blend the sugar, lemon juice and 2 egg whites. If icing seems too stiff, gradually blend in a little more egg white, which has been beaten until foamy, until you achieve the right consistency for smooth spreading. If icing is too thin, add more sugar.

# BUTTER FROSTING

*3 cups confectioners' sugar (480 g)*
*5 Tbsp. butter (75 g)*
*1 egg yolk*
*½ Tbsp. flavoring*
*cream*

Blend first 4 ingredients in the processor bowl with the steel blade. Add just enough cream to give the frosting the right consistency for spreading. If too thin, add more sugar. Makes enough for a 9-inch cake.

## SUGGESTED VARIATIONS

Add any of these to Butter Frosting.

*Chocolate*—Melt 3 ounces unsweetened chocolate (85 g), and blend.

*Mocha*—Make chocolate frosting, but substitute prepared strong black coffee for the cream.

*Citrus*—Do not use vanilla for flavoring. Substitute citrus juice for the cream, and add 1 tablespoon grated rind.

*Coffee*—Enrich with 1 tablespoon instant coffee powder dissolved in 2 tablespoons rum or brandy (30 g). Omit the cream.

*Wine*—Substitute wine for vanilla flavoring and cream.

*Cocoa*—Use 4 tablespoons cocoa powder (20 g) mixed with 3 tablespoons hot water in place of the cream.

# FRUIT FROSTING

½ cup fruit pulp
2 cups confectioners'
sugar (320 g)
2 Tbsp. butter (30 g)
1 Tbsp. lemon juice (24 g)

In the processor bowl fitted with the steel blade, purée the fruit (bananas, cooked peaches, apricots, prunes, drained crushed pineapple). Add remaining ingredients and blend until smooth. If too thin, gradually add more sugar.

# CREAM-CHEESE FROSTING

½ lb. cream cheese
(227 g)
2 cups confectioners'
sugar (320 g)
½ Tbsp. flavoring
cream

In the processor bowl fitted with the steel blade, blend first 3 ingredients, adding cream if necessary to thin it. This is very good when it is flavored with rum and has raisins folded into it.

# CHOCOLATE FROSTING

2 oz. unsweetened chocolate (56.7 g)
2 Tbsp. butter (30 g)
2 cups confectioners'
sugar (320 g)
¼ tsp. salt
¼ cup prepared coffee,
hot

Melt the chocolate with the butter and cool. In the processor bowl fitted with the steel blade, blend the sugar, salt and chocolate-butter mixture. Add just enough of the hot coffee to give the frosting spreading consistency.

# ORANGE-LEMON FROSTING

rind of 1 lemon
rind of ½ orange
3 cups confectioners'
sugar (480 g)
2 Tbsp. butter (30 g)
¼ cup mixed lemon and
orange juice (.5 dl)

Put citrus rinds and sugar in the processor bowl fitted with the steel blade, and let machine run until rinds are grated, about 30 seconds. Add butter and blend. Add just enough lemon and orange juice to give the frosting spreading consistency.

## MOCHA FROSTING

*3 Tbsp. butter (45 g)*
*¼ cup cocoa powder*
*(20 g)*
*1 tsp. instant coffee*
*powder*
*1 tsp. vanilla extract*
*¼ tsp. salt*
*2½ cups confectioners'*
*sugar (400 g)*
*3 to 4 Tbsp. hot milk*
*(.5 dl)*

In the processor bowl fitted with the steel blade, put all the ingredients except milk, and blend well. Add just enough of the milk to give the frosting spreading consistency.

## BROWNED BUTTER FROSTING

Good for nut or spice cakes

*¼ lb. butter (1 stick)*
*(120 g)*
*3½ to 4 cups confec-*
*tioners' sugar (560 to*
*640 g)*
*¼ cup milk or cream*
*(.5 dl)*
*1 tsp. vanilla extract*

Brown the butter over low heat for 3 to 5 minutes; don't let it burn. In the processor bowl fitted with the steel blade, put the sugar and add the browned butter, milk or cream, and vanilla. Blend. If too thin, add more sugar; if too thick, add more cream until frosting is of spreading consistency.

## JAM FROSTING

Many different kinds of thick jam or marmalade can be used to make this rich frosting.

*2 Tbsp. butter (30 g)*
*3 cups confectioners'*
*sugar (480 g)*
*2 Tbsp. jam or mar-*
*malade (40 g)*
*1 to 4 Tbsp. cream*

With the steel blade process the butter, sugar and jam. Add just enough cream to give the frosting spreading consistency.

# SPICE FROSTING

Good on gingerbread, spice or apple cakes

*4 Tbsp. butter (60 g)*
*¼ tsp. ground cinnamon*
*or grated mace or nut-*
*meg*
*2 cups confectioners'*
*sugar (320 g)*
*1 to 4 Tbsp. cream*

In the processor bowl fitted with the steel blade, put the butter, spice and sugar. Blend well. Add just enough cream to give the frosting spreading consistency.

# BROILED NUT FROSTING

This quick frosting is spread on a warm sheet cake and broiled for 2 to 3 minutes.

*½ cup shelled nuts (60 g)*
*6 Tbsp. butter (90 g)*
*1 cup packed brown sugar*
*(200 g)*
*1 to 4 Tbsp. evaporated*
*milk*

Coarsely chop the nuts with the steel blade; set aside. Cream the butter and sugar and add just enough of the evaporated milk to give the frosting spreading consistency. Stir in the nuts.

# VERY ORANGE FROSTING

*rind of ½ orange, cut up*
*4 cups confectioners'*
*sugar (640 g)*
*4 Tbsp. butter (60 g)*
*½ tsp. salt*
*1 egg yolk*
*2 to 3 Tbsp. frozen con-*
*centrated orange juice*
*(30 to 45 g), thawed.*

In the processor bowl fitted with the steel blade, put the cut-up orange rind and 1 cup of the sugar; blend for 30 seconds. Add the butter, salt and egg yolk. Blend and scrape down. Add remaining sugar and blend with quick on and off turns. Add just enough of the thawed orange juice to give the frosting spreading consistency.

## CARAMEL FROSTING

2 cups brown sugar
   (400 g)
6 Tbsp. sour cream (90 g)
2 Tbsp. butter (30 g)

Put the ingredients in the processor bowl fitted with the steel blade, and blend well. Cook over low heat until frosting comes to a boil. Beat with a whisk until cool. If frosting is too thick, add more sour cream but do not reheat.

## BUTTER RUM FROSTING

½ lb. butter (2 sticks)
   (227 g)
1 lb. confectioners' sugar
   (.453 kg)
¼ cup rum (60 g) (ap-
   proximately)

With the steel blade process the butter and sugar until smooth. Add just enough of the rum to give the frosting spreading consistency.

## CARAMEL SYRUP

1 cup sugar (200 g)
⅓ cup water
¼ tsp. cream of tartar

Cook the sugar, water and cream of tartar over medium heat without stirring until the sugar turns to golden brown. Cool syrup for 1 minute and place over hot water to keep from hardening.

## ORANGE SYRUP

rind of 1 orange
½ cup sugar (100 g)
⅓ cup Triple Sec (75 g)
¼ cup orange juice (.5 dl)

In the processor bowl fitted with the steel blade, chop the orange rind with the sugar for about 30 seconds. Add the Triple Sec and orange juice and blend. Cook until the sugar dissolves.

## JELLY SAUCE

Use equal parts of either raspberry or strawberry jelly and currant jelly, blended together and heated until smooth.

# BANANA SAUCE

2 bananas, peeled
1 orange, peeled and
  seeded
1 medium-size apple,
  peeled, cored and cut up
½ cup sugar (100 g)
2 tsp. cornstarch dis-
  solved in 3 Tbsp. water
1 cup hot water (.24 l)

In the processor bowl fitted with the steel blade, purée the bananas, the orange and the apple. Add the sugar, dissolved cornstarch and 1 cup hot water, and blend with on and off quick turns. Cook over hot water, stirring constantly, until thickened.

# ROYAL SAUCE

Fine for dressing up plain cakes and fruit

rind of 1 lemon
½ cup sugar (100 g)
½ cup currant jelly
  (150 g)
1 Tbsp. brandy (25 g)
1 Tbsp. cornstarch (10 g),
  dissolved in 3 Tbsp.
  water

In the processor bowl fitted with the steel blade, process lemon rind and sugar until rind is grated, about 30 seconds. Combine grated rind and sugar, the jelly, brandy and dissolved cornstarch. Cook over hot water, stirring constantly, until thickened. If sauce seems too thick after it has cooled, add hot water, 1 tablespoon at a time, until the desired consistency is reached.

# FRUITED HARD SAUCE

1 cup peaches, strawber-
  ries, or apricots, or a
  mixture, cut up
4 Tbsp. butter (60 g), cut
  up
1 cup confectioners' sugar
  (160 g)
1 tsp. fruit liqueur
  (Kirsch, Triple Sec,
  Grand Marnier)

In the processor bowl fitted with the steel blade, purée the fruit, there should be ½ cup; set aside. Put the cut-up butter, sugar and liqueur in the bowl and blend. Add the fruit purée, a little at a time, until the desired consistency is reached. Chill for at least 2 hours.

## SPICE SAUCE

½ Tbsp. butter
½ cup sugar (100 g)
1 Tbsp. cream (15 g)
1 Tbsp. flour (10 g)
¼ tsp. ground ginger
¼ tsp. ground cinnamon
½ cup Madeira or Port
  wine (1 dl)

In the processor bowl fitted with the steel blade, blend the butter and sugar until smooth. Add remaining ingredients and blend well. Cook over hot water, stirring constantly, until thickened.

## WINE CUSTARD SAUCE

3 Tbsp. butter (45 g)
½ cup sugar (100 g)
3 egg yolks
½ cup hot water (1 dl)
2 Tbsp. sherry or rum
  (30 g)

In the processor bowl fitted with the steel blade, cream the butter and sugar until smooth. Add the egg yolks and blend with on and off quick turns. With the machine running, add the hot water through the tube. Cook over hot water until thickened, stirring constantly. Add sherry or rum after cooking.

# INDEX

Almond(s)
  Biscuit Torte, 131
  Cookies (drop), 134
  Florentines (drop cookies), 136
  Lace Cookies (drop), 139
  Lace Cookies, Chocolate (drop), 139
  Marmalade-Nut filling for Roll-Ups, 30
  Nut Crust, 109
  Nutmeat White Bread, 28
  Nut Roll, Basic, 132
  Nut Torte, Basic, 124
  Nut Torte, Chocolate, II, 126
  Pain de Gênes (cake), 116
  Paste, 201
  (and) Preserve Bars, 150
Anadama Bread, 45
Apple
  Bread Pudding, 154
  Fresh Apple Cake, 117
  Muffins, 106
  (and) Nut Whole-Wheat Bread, 32
  Pie, Old-Fashioned, 184
  Tart, I, 185; II, 185; III, 186; IV, 187
Applesauce Fruit Bread, 100
Apricot
  Cheesecake, 122
  Cottage-Cheese Quiche, 190
  Frangipane Tart, 191
  Muffins, 106
  (and)-Orange Fruit Bread, 100
Apricot Brandy Cookies (drop), 134

Bacon-Cheese Bread, baked in a flat pan, 28
Bacon-Corn Muffins, 107
Bagels (Rapidmix©), 71
Baking Pans, 19-20; sizes, chart, 148

Banana
  Custard Pie, 193
  Muffins, 106
  (and)-Nut Fruit Bread, 100
  Sauce, 208
Beefy Toasting Bread, 54
Beignets, 181
Biscuits
  Baking Powder (Shortcake Dough), 104
  Drop (Cobbler Topping), 104
  Shortcake, Large, 104
Biscuit Torte, 131
Black Forest Cheesecake, 123
Blueberry Muffins, 106
Bourbon Balls, *see* Rum Balls, 141
Bourbon Pound Cake, 115
Brandy Pound Cake, 115
Brandy Snaps (drop cookies), 136
Brazil nuts, Nut Crust, 169
Bread Desserts, 154-159
Bread Pans, sizes, chart, 46, 100
Bread Pudding with Meringue, 156
Breads—Quick, 97-108; *see also* Biscuits;
      Muffins
  Applesauce, 100
  Apricot-Orange, 100
  Banana-Nut, 100
  Candied Orange, 102
  Fruit, 100
  Fruit, Mixed, 101
  Gingerbread, 102
  Irish Soda Bread, I, 98; II, 99
  Lemon, 101
  Nut Loaf, Spiced, 103
  Prune, 100
  storing, 97
Bread Sticks, 67
Breads—Yeast, 17-96; *see also* Breads
      —Yeast, Small; Breads—Yeast,
      Sweet; Breads—Yeast, Sweet,
      Small
  Anadama, 45
  Apple-Nut Whole-Wheat, 32
  Bacon-Cheese, baked in a flat pan, 28
  baking, 25
  Beefy Toasting, 54

Breakfast Cereal, 40-43
Brioche Crust, 74
Cardamom Toasting, 54
Casserole Batter, 63
Cheese, 51
Cheese Whole-Wheat, 32
Cornmeal (Rapidmix©), 49
Cottage-Cheese Herb, 58; Variations, 59
Cracked Wheat White, 28
Currant White, 28
Dark and White Braid, 32
finish for crusts, 24-25
first rising, 22
Garlic Toasting, 54
Granola, 42
Honey Oatmeal, 47
instructions for making, 21
kneading by hand, 22
kneading in the processor, 21-22
Limpa, 39
Maltex, 41
Maple Whole-Wheat, 32
Maypo, 40
Mediterranean (French-Type), I, 54; II,
      57
Monkey Bread, 29
Niçoise, baked in a flat pan, 29
Nutmeat White, 28
Onion White, 28
Pie Pan Bread, 62
Pita, 64
Pizza Bread, baked in a flat pan, 29
Potato, 50
Pumpernickel, I, 36; II, 38
punching down, 23
Raisin White, 28
Roll-Up White, 29; Fillings, 30
Rye, 33
Rye, Sour-Cream, 35
Saffron Toasting, 54
second rising, 24
shaping, 24
Sour-Cream Rye, 35
Sour Milk and Herbs White, 28
Spiral Loaf, 32
storing, 25

Tall Bread Made in a Coffee Can, I, 60; II, 61
Temperatures, chart, 27, 34, 38, 43
Three-Grain, 44
Toasting, Basic, 53; Variations, 54
Two-Tone, 22
Wheat Germ, 48
Wheat-Germ Whole-Wheat, 32
White, baked in a flat pan, 28
White, Basic, 26; Additions, 28; Variations, 28-29
Whole Wheat, 31; Variations, 32
Breads—Yeast, Small
Bagels (Rapidmix©), 71
Bread Sticks, 67
Brioche, 73
Cloverleaf Rolls, 75
Crescent Rolls, 75
English Muffins, 69
English Muffins, Whole-Wheat, 70
Fantans, 75
Parker House Rolls, 75
Pretzels, 68
Soft Rolls, 74
Tulip Rolls, 76
Water Rolls, 66
Bread—Yeast, Sweet
Bubble Loaf, 81
Cardamom, 81
Cinnamon Roll-Up, 78
Citrus Loaf, 78
Coffee Ring, 78
Easter Bread, 85
Fruited Sweet Loaf, 78
Kulich, 81
Orange Kuchen, 88
Portuguese, 83
Saffron, 81
Sally Lunn, 89
Savarin, 87
Sour-Cream Sweet Dough, 82
Swedish Cardamom Coffee Bread, 84
Sweet Dough, Basic, 77; Variations, 78
Breads—Yeast, Sweet, Small
Croissants, 91
Danish Pastry, 94; Fillings, 95

Envelopes (Danish Pastry), 95
Fans (Danish Pastry), 96
Hot Cross Buns (Rapidmix©), 90
Kolache, 80
Napkins (Danish Pastry), 95
Pinwheels, 79
Sticky Buns, 80
Brioche, 73
Brioche Crust, 74
Brioche Strawberry Charlotte, 159
Brownies, Jane Isaac's, 147
Bubble Loaf (sweet), 81
Burnell's Preacher Pie (Custard Pie), 192; Variations, 193
Butter
Browned Butter Frosting, 205
Frosting, 203; Variations, 203
Rum Frosting, 207
Butterscotch Chews (molded cookies), 140


Cake, *see also* Cheesecake; Cookies and Small Cakes; Fruitcake; Torte
Apple, Fresh, 117
Bourbon Pound, 115
Brandy Pound, 115
Chocolate, Deep, 114
Chocolate Roll, 131
Chocolate Sour-Cream, 112
Coconut, 116
Fruit Yellow or White, 110
Gold, 114
Jelly Roll, 130; Fillings, 130; Variations, 131
Lemon Chiffon, 113
Lemon Yellow or White, 110
Mocha Chiffon, 113; Variations, 113
Nut Roll, Basic, 132
Orange Chiffon, 113
Orange-Lemon Sour-Cream, 112
Orange-Raisin, 118
Orange Yellow or White, 110
Pain de Gênes, 116
Pans, sizes, chart, 119, 120, 126, 131
Pound, 115; Variations, 115

Cake (*Continued*)
  Preserve, M. B. H.'s, 118
  Rum Pound, 115
  Sour-Cream, 111; Variations, 111
  Spice Chiffon, 113
  Spice Roll, 131
  Spice Sour-Cream, 111
  Spice Yellow or White, 110
  Upside-Down, 111
  Walnut Pound, 115
  White, Basic, 110; Variations, 110
  Yellow, Basic, 110; Variations, 110
  Yogurt, 119
Cakes and Tortes, 109-132
Candied Orange Bread, 102
Caramel Frosting, 207
Caramel Syrup, 207
Cardamom
  Bread (sweet), 81
  Coffee Bread, Swedish, 84
  Toasting Bread, 54
Carrot torte, 129
Casserole Batter Bread, 63
Cats' Tongues (Langues de Chats) (pressed
    cookies), 147
Charleston Bars, 150
Cheese
  Bread, 51
  Cottage Cheese
    Apricot Quiche, 190
    Herb Bread, 58; Variations, 59
    Pastry, 167
  Cream Cheese
    Cookies (molded), 146
    Frosting, 204
    Lemon Cheese Pie, 194
    Pastry, 167
  Gougère, 172; Variation, 173
  hard, to grind, 8
  and Hot-Tomato Muffins, 107
  Muffins, 106
  Ricotta Filling, 200
  Sharp Cheese Pastry, 168
  to chill for grating, 10
  (and) Tomato Quiche, 177
  Whole-Wheat Bread, 32

Cheesecake
  Apricot, 122
  Baked, 122; Variations, 122
  Black Forest, 123
  Mocha, 122
  in Pastry, 122
Cherry
  Bing Cherry Frangipane Tart, 191
  Clafouti Bread Pudding, 155
  Helene's Pumpernickel Dessert, 158
Chestnut(s)
  Dried, How to Use, 129
  Fresh, How to Cook, 129
  Torte, 128
Chocolate
  Almond Lace Cookies (drop), 139
  Butter Frosting, 203
  Cake, Deep, 114
  Chip Cookies (drop), 134
  Crescents or Balls (molded cookies), 141
  Custard Pie, 193
  Filling (for Florentines), 136
  Frosting, 204
  Frosting (for Chocolate Sour-Cream
      Cake), 112
  Nut Torte, I, 125; II, 126
  (and) Orange Tart, 195
  Pastry, 168
  Pastry Cream, 198
  Pie, Creamy, 195
  Pumpernickel Torte, 157
  Roll, 131
  Sour-Cream Cake, 112
  to grate, 10
Cider Apple Cookies (drop), 138
Cinnamon-Nut Cookies (drop), 134
Cinnamon Roll-Up (sweet), 78
Citrus
  Butter Frosting, 203
  Cookies (drop, with ginger), 137
  Cookies (drop, with vanilla), 134
  Loaf, 78
  rinds, to grind, 8
Clafouti Bread Pudding, 155
Cloverleaf Rolls, 75
Cobbler Topping (Drop Biscuits), 104

Cocoa Butter Frosting, 203
Cocoa Whipped Cream, 198
Coconut
  Cake, 116
  Custard Pie, 193
  Pâte Brisée, 166
Coffee
  Butter Frosting, 203
  Cookies (drop), 134
  Pastry Cream, 199
  Whipped Cream, 198
Coffee Can Bread, I, 60; II, 61
Coffee Ring, 78
Confectioners' Icing, 202
Cookies and Small Cakes, 133-151
  Almond Cookies (drop), 134
  Almond Lace Cookies (drop), 139
  Almond Preserve Bars, 150
  Apricot Brandy Cookies (drop), 134
  Bourbon Balls, *see* Rum Balls, 141
  Brandy Snaps (drop), 136
  Brownies, Jane Isaac's, 147
  Brown Nut Cookies (drop), 139
  Butterscotch Chews (molded), 140
  Charleston Bars, 150
  Chocolate Almond Lace Cookies (drop), 139
  Chocolate Chip Cookies (drop), 134
  Chocolate Crescents or Balls (molded), 141
  Cider Apple Cookies (drop), 138
  Cinnamon-Nut Cookies (drop), 134
  Citrus Cookies (drop, with ginger), 137
  Citrus Cookies (drop, with vanilla), 134
  Coffee Cookies (drop), 134
  Cream-Cheese Cookies (molded), 146
  Crystallized Fruit Cookies (molded), 140
  Crystallized Ginger Diagonals, 151
  Drop Cookie Dough I, 134; Variations, 134
  Drop Cookie Dough II, 135
  Drop Cookies, 134-139
  Extra Nutty Cookies (molded), 140
  Florentines (drop), 136
  Jam Squares, 151
  Koularakia (rolled), 144
  Kourabiethes (rolled), 144
  Langues de Chats (Cats' Tongues) (pressed), 147
  Lemon Delights (filled), 148
  Macaroons (drop), 137
  Molded Cookies, 140-141
  Nürnbergers (rolled), 143
  Nut Cookies (molded), 140; Variations, 140
  Oatmeal Drop Cookies, 135
  Pecan Meringue Bars, 149
  Refrigerator Cookies, 142
  Rum Balls (molded), 141
  Rum Cookies (drop), 134
  Shortbread (rolled), 146
  Sugar Cookies (rolled), 142
  Surprise Cookies (molded), 140
  Tender Rounds (molded), 140
  Tropical Cookies (molded), 140
  Uppakra Cookies (rolled), 145
Cornmeal Bread (Rapidmix©), 49
Cracked Wheat White Bread, 28
Cranberry Orange Apple Pie, 188
Cream-Puff Pastry (Pâte à Choux), 162
Cream Puffs, To Form, 162
Cream Sauce, 172
Cream, Whipped, 198; Variations, 198
Crème Pâtissière (Pastry Cream), 198; Variations, 198
Crème Saint-Honoré, 199
Crescent Rolls, 75
Croissants, 91
Croquembouche, 183
Crumb Bread Pudding, 154
Crumb Shells, 169
Currant White Bread, 28
Custard Pie (Burnell's Preacher Pie), 192; Variations, 193

Danish Pastry, 94; Fillings, 95
Dark and White Braid, 32
Date Muffins, 106
Drunken Brother (Pumpernickel Pudding), 158

Easter Bread, 85
Eclairs, To Form, 163
Egg whites, to whip, 10
Eggs in yeast breads, 19
English Muffins, 69
English Muffins, Whole-Wheat, 70
Envelopes (Danish Pastry), 95

Fans (Danish Pastry), 96
Fantans (Soft Rolls), 75
Feed tube, to pack for slicing and shred-
      ding, 10
Filling, Ham, for Gougère, 172
Fillings—Dessert, 198-201
   Almond Paste, 201
   Almond Preserve Filling (for Almond
      Preserve Bars), 150
   Chocolate Filling (for Florentines), 136
   Chocolate Pastry Cream, 198
   Cocoa Whipped Cream, 198
   Coffee Pastry Cream, 199
   Coffee Whipped Cream, 198
   Cream, Whipped, 198; Variations, 198
   Crème Pâtissière (Pastry Cream), 198;
      Variations, 198
   Crème Saint-Honoré, 199
   for Danish Pastry, 95
   French Filling, 201
   Fruit Whipped Cream, 198
   Honey Nut Filling (for Kolache), 80
   for Jelly Roll, 130
   Lemon Filling, 200
   Lemon Filling (for Lemon Delights), 148
   Lemon Pastry Cream, 199
   Liqueur Pastry Cream, 199
   Liqueur Whipped Cream, 198
   Mocha Pastry Cream, 198
   Orange Filling, 200
   Pecan Filling (for Pecan Meringue Bars),
      149
   Praline Pastry Cream, 199
   Praline Powder, 201
   Praline Whipped Cream, 198
   Prune Filling (for Kolache), 80

   Ricotta Filling, 200
   Vanilla Cream, 199
Fish Pie, Deep-Dish, 173
Florentines (drop cookies), 136
Flour
   graham, 18
   measuring, 21
   rye, 18
   specialty, 19
   white, hard wheat, unbleached, 18
   whole-wheat, 18
Frangipane Tart, 191; Variations, 191
French Filling, 201
Frostings, Icings, Glazes, 202-207
   Browned Butter Frosting, 205
   Butter Frosting, 203; Variations, 203
   Butter Rum Frosting, 207
   Caramel Frosting, 207
   Chocolate Butter Frosting, 203
   Chocolate Frosting, 204
   Chocolate Frosting (for Chocolate
      Sour-Cream Cake), 112
   Citrus Butter Frosting, 203
   Cocoa Butter Frosting, 203
   Coffee Butter Frosting, 203
   Confectioners' Icing, 202
   Cream-Cheese Frosting, 204
   Fruit Frosting, 204
   Glaze for Cider Apple Cookies, 138
   Jam Frosting, 205
   Lemon Glaze, 102
   Mocha Butter Frosting, 203
   Mocha Frosting, 205
   Nut Frosting, Broiled, 206
   Orange-Lemon Frosting, 204
   Royal Icing, 203
   Spice Frosting, 206
   Strawberry Glaze, 196
   Streusel, I, 202; II, 202
   Very Orange Frosting, 206
   Wine Butter Frosting, 203
Fruit(s)
   Bread, 100
   Bread, Mixed Fruit, 100
   Cream Tarts, 189
   Crystallized Fruit Cookies (molded), 140

Dried Fruit Muffins, 106
Frosting, 204
Fruited Hard Sauce, 208
Fruited Sweet Loaf, 78
in yeast breads, 19
Velvet Tart, 190
Whipped Cream, 198
Yellow or White Cake, 110
*see also* names of fruits
Fruitcake, German, 120
Fruitcake, St. Gregory's, 121

Garlic Toasting Bread, 54
Gâteau Saint-Honoré, 180
Genoa Torte, 125
German Fruitcake, 120
Gingerbread, 102
Ginger, Crystallized Ginger Diagonals, 151
Gingersnap Torte, 128
Gluten, 18
Gold Cake, 114
Gougère with Ham Filling, 172
Gougère Variation, 173
Granola Bread, 42

Ham Filling for Gougère, 172
Hazelnuts
   Florentines (drop cookies), 136
   Meringue Crumb Shell, 170
   Nut Crust, 169
Helene's Pumpernickel Dessert, 158
Herb Muffins, 106
Honey
   Bran Muffins, 108
   Nut Filling for Kolache, 80
   Oatmeal Bread, 47
Hot Cross Buns (Rapidmix©), 90

Icings, *see* Frostings, Icings, Glazes
Indian Curry Pie, 174

Irish Soda Bread, I, 98; II, 99
Isaac, Jane, Brownies, 147

Jam Frosting, 205
Jam Squares, 151
Jelly Roll, 130; Fillings, 130; Variations, 131
Jelly Sauce, 207

Kolache, 80
Koularakia (rolled cookies), 145
Kourabiethes (rolled cookies), 144
Kulich, 81

Langues de Chats (Cats' Tongues) (pressed cookies), 147
Lemon
   Bread, 101
   Cheese Pie, 194
   Chiffon Cake, 113
   Delights (filled cookies), 148
   Filling, 200
   Filling (for Lemon Delights), 148
   Glaze, 102
   Muffins, 106
   Pastry Cream, 199
   Pâte Brisée, 166
   Tart, 194
   Yellow or White Cake, 110
Limpa Bread, 39
Liqueur Pastry Cream, 199
Liqueur Whipped Cream, 198
Liquids for yeast breads, 19

Macaroons (drop cookies), 137
Machine, 8
   overheating, 8
   to remove mixtures from the bowl, 9

Maltex Bread, 41
Maple Whole-Wheat Bread, 32
Maypo Bread, 40
Meats, to freeze for slicing, 10
Meats, to grind, 8
Mediterranean Bread (French-Type), I, 54;
    II, 57
Meringue, 156
Meringue Crumb Shell, 170
Metric System, 13-15
  Capacity, 13
  Mass and Weight, 13
  Pan sizes, 14; *see also* charts for Baking
    Pans; Bread Pans; Cake Pans
  Temperatures, 14-15; *see also* chart for
    Temperatures for Yeast
Mocha
  Butter Frosting, 203
  Cheesecake, 122
  Chiffon Cake, 113; Variations, 113
  Frosting, 205
  Pastry Cream, 198
Mock Puff Paste, 163
Monkey Bread, 29
Muffins, 105-108
  Apple, 106
  Bacon-Corn, 107
  Banana, 106
  Basic, 105; Variations, 106
  Blueberry, 106
  Cheese, 106
  Cheese and Hot-Tomato, 107
  Dried Fruit (Date, Prune, Apricot), 106
  Herb, 106
  Honey Bran, 108
  Lemon, 106
  Nut, 106
  Orange, 106
  Peanut Butter, 106

Napkins (Danish Pastry), 95
Niçoise Bread, baked in a flat pan, 29
Nürnbergers (rolled cookies), 143
Nut(s)
  Charleston Bars, 150

Cinnamon Nut Cookies (drop), 134
Cookies (molded), 140; Variations, 140
Cookies, Brown (drop), 139
Crust, 169
Extra Nutty Cookies (molded), 140
Frosting, Boiled, 206
in yeast breads, 19
Loaf, Spiced, 103
Muffins, 106
Nutmeat White Bread, 28
Pâte Brisée, 166
Roll, Basic, 132
Torte, Basic, 124
Torte, Chocolate, I, 125; II, 126
*see also* names of nuts

Oatmeal Drop Cookies, 135
Omnichef, 7
Onion Bread, baked in a flat pan, 29
Onion White Bread, 28
Orange
  Candied Orange Bread, 102
  Chiffon Cake, 113
  Filling, 200
  Kuchen, 88
  Muffins, 106
  Pâte Brisée, 166
  Pumpkin Pie, 193
  Raisin Cake, 118
  Syrup, 207
  Very Orange Frosting, 206
  Yellow or White Cake, 110
Orange-Lemon
  Frosting, 204
  Sour-Cream Cake, 112

Pain de Gênes, 116
Pan Sizes, metric conversions, 14; *see also*
    charts for Baking Pans; Bread Pans;
    Cake Pans
Paris-Brest, 182
Parker House Rolls, 75

Pastry—Basic, 161-170
  Chocolate Pastry, 168
  Coconut Pâte Brisée, 166
  Cottage-Cheese Pastry, 167
  Cream-Cheese Pastry, 167
  Cream-Puff Pastry (Pâte à Choux), 162
  Cream Puffs, To Form, 162
  Crumb Shells, 169
  Eclairs, To Form, 163
  Lemon Pâte Brisée, 166
  Meringue Crumb Shell, 170
  Mock Puff Paste, 163
  Nut Crust, 169
  Nut Pâte Brisée, 166
  One-Step Pies and Tarts, 165
  Orange Pâte Brisée, 166
  Pâte Brisée, 165; Variations, 166
  Pâte Brisée, Sweet, 165
  Pâte Sucrée, 166
  Piecrust, Basic, 166
  for Pies and Tarts, 164-170
  Prebaked and Partially Baked Shells, 164
  Profiteroles, To Form, 163
  Sharp Cheese Pastry, 168
Pastry—Dessert
  Beignets, 181
  Croquembouche, 183
  Gâteau Saint-Honoré, 180
  Paris-Brest, 182
  Puff-Paste Sweet, Swedish, 184
Pastry—Entrée or Hors d'Oeuvre
  Gougère with Ham Filling, 172
  Gougère Variation, 173
Pastry Cream (Crème Pâtissière), 198; Variations, 198
Pâte
  Brisée, 165; Variations, 166
  Brisée, Sweet, 165
  à Choux (Cream-Puff Pastry), 162
  Sucrée, 166
Peanut Butter Muffins, 106
Pear Frangipane Tart, 191
Pear Tart, 192
Pecan(s)
  Biscuit Torte, 131
  Filling (for Pecan Meringue Bars), 149

Gingersnap Torte, 128
Marmalade-Nut filling for Roll-Ups, 30
Meringue Bars, 149
Meringue Crumb Shell, 170
Nut Crust, 169
Nutmeat White Bread, 28
Nut Roll, Basic, 132
Nut Torte, Basic, 124
Pie, 187
Rum Balls, 141
Pie Pan Bread, 62
Pies and Tarts—Dessert
  Apple Pie, Old-Fashioned, 184
  Apple Tart, I, 185; II, 185; III, 186; IV, 187
  Apricot Cottage-Cheese Quiche, 190
  Apricot Frangipane Tart, 191
  Banana Custard Pie, 193
  Bing Cherry Frangipane Tart, 191
  Chocolate Custard Pie, 193
  Chocolate Orange Tart, 195
  Chocolate Pie, Creamy, 195
  Coconut Custard Pie, 193
  Cranberry Orange Apple Pie, 188
  crusts, *see* Pastry—Basic
  Custard Pie (Burnell's Preacher Pie), 192; Variations, 193
  Frangipane Tart, 191; Variations, 191
  Fruit Cream Tarts, 189
  Fruit Velvet Tart, 190
  Green Tomato Pie, Spiced, 188
  Lemon Cheese Pie, 194
  Lemon Tart, 194
  Orange Pumpkin Pie, 193
  Pear Frangipane Tart, 191
  Pear Tart, 192
  Pecan Pie, 187
  Rhubarb Strawberry Glazed Pie, 196
  Strawberry Glazed Pie, 196; Variation, 196
Pies and Tarts—Entrée and Hors d'Oeuvre
  Cheese Tomato Quiche, 177
  crusts, *see* Pastry—Basic
  Fish Pie, Deep-Dish, 173
  Indian Curry Pie, 174
  Mixed Vegetable Tart, 178

Pies and Tarts (*Continued*)
  Provençal Tomato Quiche, 176
  Shrimp Tart, 174
  Tongue Quiche, 175
Pinwheels, 79
Pistachios, Nut Roll, Basic, 132
Pita Bread, 64
Pizza Bread, baked in a flat pan, 29
Plastic blade, 9
Portuguese Bread, 83
Potato Bread, 50
Pound Cake, 115; Variations, 115
Praline
  Pastry Cream, 199
  Powder, 201
  Whipped Cream, 198
Preserve Cake, M. B. H.'s, 118
Pretzels, 68
Profiteroles, To Form, 163
Provençal Tomato Quiche, 176
Prune
  Filling for Kolache, 80
  Fruit Bread, 100
  Muffins, 106
Pudding—Dessert, 153-159
  Apple Bread, 154
  Bread, with Meringue, 156
  Brioche Strawberry Charlotte, 159
  Clafouti Bread, 155
  Crumb Bread, 154
  Pumpernickel (Drunken Brother), 158
  Pumpernickel Dessert, Helene's, 158
  Summer, 156
Pumpernickel
  Bread, I, 36; II, 38
  Bread Desserts, 157-158
  Pudding (Drunken Brother), 158
Pumpkin, Orange Pumpkin Pie, 193


Quiche
  Apricot Cottage-Cheese, 190
  Cheese Tomato, 177
  Tomato, Provençal, 176
  Tongue, 175

Raisin White Bread, 28
Refrigerator Cookies, 142
Rhubarb Strawberry Glazed Pie, 196
Roll-Up Sweet Bread, Cinnamon, 78
Roll-Up White Bread, 29
  Cinnamon, Sugar and White Raisin
    filling, 30
  Duxelles filling, 30
  Green Goddess filling, 30
  Marmalade-Nut filling, 30
Royal Icing, 203
Royal Sauce, 208
Rum
  Balls (molded cookies), 141
  Cookies (drop), 134
  Pound Cake, 115
Rye Bread, 33
Rye Bread, Sour-Cream, 35


Saffron Bread (sweet), 81
Saffron Toasting Bread, 54
St. Gregory's Fruitcake, 121
Sally Lunn, 89
Salt for yeast breads, 19
Sauce—Dessert
  Banana, 208
  Hard Sauce, Fruited, 208
  Jelly, 207
  Royal, 208
  Spice, 209
  Wine Custard, 209
Sauce—Entrée
  Cream, 172
Savarin, 87
Shortbread, 146
Shortcake Dough (Baking Powder Bis-
    cuits), 104
Shortcake, Large, 104
Shortening for yeast breads, 19
Shredding disc, 10
Shrimp Tart, 174
Slicing disc, 10
Soft Rolls, 74
Sour Cream
  Cake, 111; Variations, 111

Chocolate Cake, 112
Rye Bread, 35
Sweet Dough, 82
Sour Milk and Herbs White Bread, 28
Spice, Spiced
Chiffon Cake, 113
Frosting, 206
Green Tomato Pie, 188
Nut Loaf, 103
Roll, 131
Sauce, 209
Sour-Cream Cake, 111
Yellow or White Cake, 110
Spiral Loaf, 32
Steel blade, 8
Sticky Buns, 80
Strawberry
Brioche Strawberry Charlotte, 159
Glaze, 196
Glazed Pie, 196; Variation, 196
Streusel, I, 202; II, 202
Sugar Cookies (rolled), 142
Sugary mixtures, to process, 9
Summer Pudding, 156
Surprise Cookies (molded), 140
Swedish Cardamom Coffee Bread, 84
Swedish Puff-Paste Sweet, 184
Swedish Thousand Leaves Torte, 127
Sweet Dough, Basic, 77; Variations, 78
Sweeteners for yeast breads, 19
Syrup
Caramel, 207
Orange, 207
for Savarin, 87

Tarts, *see* Pies and Tarts—Dessert; Pies and Tarts—Entrée and Hors d'Oeuvre
Temperatures, metric conversions, 14-15; *see also* chart for Temperatures for Yeast
Temperatures for Yeast, chart, 27, 34, 38, 43
Tender Rounds (molded cookies), 140

Three-Grain Bread, 44
Toasting Bread, Basic, 53; Variations, 54
Tomato
Cheese Tomato Quiche, 177
Green Tomato Pie, Spiced, 188
Quiche, Provençal, 176
Tongue Quiche, 175
Torte
Biscuit, 131
Carrot, 129
Chestnut, 128
Chocolate Nut, I, 125; II, 126
Chocolate Pumpernickel, 157
Genoa, 125
Gingersnap, 128
Nut, Basic, 124
Thousand Leaves, Swedish, 127
Tropical Cookies (molded), 140
Tulip Rolls, 76
Two-Tone Breads, 32

Uppakra Cookies (rolled), 145
Upside-Down Cake, 111
Utensils for bread and pastry making, list, 11-12

Vanilla Cream, 199
Vegetable Tart, Mixed, 178

Walnut(s)
Apple Nut Whole-Wheat Bread, 32
Apple Tart III, 186
Biscuit Torte, 131
Cider Apple Cookies, 138
Jam Squares, 151
Marmalade-Nut filling for Roll-Ups, 30
Meringue Crumb Shell, 170
Nutmeat White Bread, 28
Nut Roll, Basic, 132

Walnut(s) (*Continued*)
  Nut Torte, Basic, 124
  Pound Cake, 115
Water Rolls, 66
Wheat Germ Bread, 48
Wheat Germ Whole-Wheat Bread, 32
White Bread, Basic, 26; Baked in a Flat
    Pan, 28
White Cake, Basic, 110; Variations, 110
Whole-Wheat Bread, 31; Variations, 32
Whole-Wheat English Muffins, 70

Wine Butter Frosting, 203
Wine Custard Sauce, 209

Yeast, 18
  proofing the yeast, 20
  Rapidmix© method, 20
Yellow Cake, Basic, 110; Variations, 110
Yogurt Cake, 119